Practice and Learn

Sixth Grade

Editor
Walter Kelly, M.A.

Editorial Manager
Karen J. Goldfluss, M.S. Ed.

Editor in Chief
Sharon Coan, M.S. Ed.

Illustrator
Howard Chaney

Cover Artist
Chris Macabitas
Jeff Sutherland

Art Coordinator
Denice Adorno

Creative Director
Elayne Roberts

Imaging
James Edward Grace
Ralph Olmedo, Jr.

Product Manager
Phil Garcia

Publishers
Rachelle Cracchiolo, M.S. Ed.
Mary Dupuy Smith, M.S. Ed.

Authors

Sheila Greenberg and *Betty Weiss*

Teacher Created Materials, Inc.

6421 Industry Way

Westminster, CA 92683

www.teachercreated.com

©1999 Teacher Created Materials, Inc.

Made in U.S.A.

W9-CYG-569

Table of Contents

Introduction

To Teachers and Parents

The wealth of knowledge a person gains throughout his or her lifetime is impossible to measure, and it will certainly vary from person to person. However, regardless of the scope of knowledge, the foundation for all learning remains a constant. All that we know and think throughout our lifetimes is based upon fundamentals, and these fundamentals are the basic skills from which all learning develops.

Within this book are hundreds of pages designed to teach and reinforce the skills that are mandatory for successful completion of sixth-grade curricular standards. The Table of Contents (page 2) clearly delineates the basic content areas.

Skills are reinforced in these content areas:

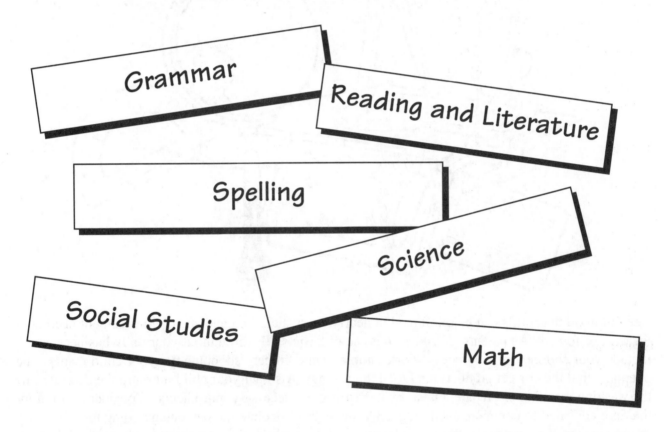

Grammar

Reading and Literature

Spelling

Science

Social Studies

Math

The work sheets and activities in this book are ideal for both home and classroom use. Research shows us that skill mastery comes with exposure and drill. To be internalized, concepts must be reviewed until they become second nature. Parents may foster the classroom experience by exposing their children to the necessary skills whenever possible, and teachers will find that these pages perfectly complement their classroom needs.

Introduction *(cont.)*

In addition to this resource, there are a variety of hands-on materials that will prove vital when reinforcing basic skills. These include math function flash cards, measuring spoons and cups, balance scales and weights, Celsius and Fahrenheit thermometers, a stopwatch, a steel tape measure, a metric ruler and conversion chart, a globe, maps, mechanic's wrenches, a geometry compass, a directional compass, magnets, protractor, a magnifying glass, microscope, charts, graphs, and musical instruments. Be aware that any hands-on device, from a library card to a computer, may be used to promote and reinforce learning. Hands-on experience, in short, promotes learning of all types and levels of complexity.

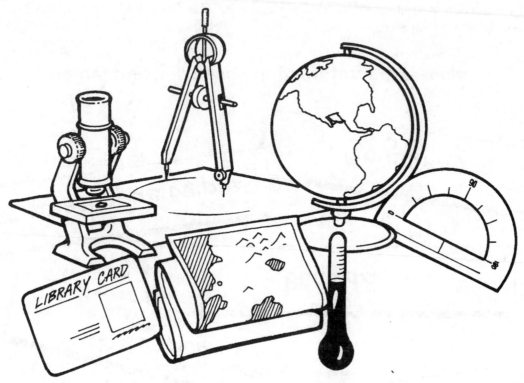

Keep in mind that skills can be reinforced in nearly every situation, and such reinforcement need not be invasive or forced. As parents, consider your use of basic skills throughout your daily business, and include your children in the process. For example, while grocery shopping, let your child manage the coupons, find the correct products, and total the savings. Also, let your child measure the detergent for the washing machine or prepare a meal by measuring the necessary ingredients. Consider as a family the time allocated to commercials during a TV show and calculate the percentage going to advertisement. Do some comparison budgeting with your child, including costs of his or her clothing and school expenses.

There are, likewise, countless ways that teachers can reinforce skills throughout the school day. Seek ways to incorporate what you are teaching into the daily lives and routines of your students. Perhaps you could vary roll call by assigning numbers to each student and then posing math problems with those numbers as the answers. The children will answer "present" when they calculate the problems and realize their numbers are the answers. Or assign countries to student names and call out the capital cities for the same results.

Since basic skills are used every day in untold ways, make the practice of them part of your children's or students' routines. Such work done now will benefit them in countless ways throughout their lives.

Flight

At the turn of the century, very few believed that flight was possible in a heavier-than-air machine. Two of the few who did believe were Wilbur and Orville Wright. Wilbur Wright was born in 1867 in Indiana, and Orville was born four years later in Ohio. As children the two were fascinated by mechanics and even earned small amounts of money by selling homemade mechanical toys. Both went to school, but neither received a high school diploma. When they grew up, Orville built a printing press and started a printing business, developing a weekly newspaper which Wilbur edited. Next, they tried their hands at renting and selling bicycles, and finally they began to manufacture the bikes themselves.

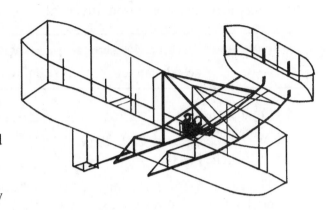

In 1886 the brothers read about the death of a pioneer glider named Otto Lilienthal, and his work sparked their interest. They started to read everything available on aeronautics and soon became as expert on the subject as any pioneer could be. The Wrights then contacted the National Weather Bureau to determine the best place to carry out their experiments with flight. The Bureau advised them to try a narrow strip of sandy land called Kill Devil Hill near Kittyhawk, North Carolina. In 1900, they tested a glider that could hold a person, and in 1901 they tried again with a larger glider. Neither glider could lift as they had hoped, although they did achieve some success in controlling balance.

The Wright brothers felt confident that flight was possible; therefore, they theorized that previous data concerning air pressure on curved surfaces must be inaccurate. They built their own wind tunnel and over 200 model wings in order to make their own pressure tables. Their tables became the first reliable ones ever made.

In 1902 they tried a third glider, using their new information. It vastly exceeded the success of all previous gliders, with some glides exceeding 600 feet (184 meters). This led the brothers to plan and build a power airplane. In 1903, at a cost just under one thousand dollars, the plane was complete. Its wings measured 40.5 feet (12 meters), and it weighed 750 pounds (340 kilograms) with the pilot. In September of 1903, they arrived in Kittyhawk, but a series of bad storms and defects delayed them. However, on December 17, 1903, they achieved flight.

Over the next few years, their experiments produced even longer and better flights. On October 5, 1905, their plane flew for 24.2 miles (39 kilometers) in just over 38 minutes. In 1908, they closed a contract with the United States Department of War for the first military airplane ever made.

The brothers went on to exhibit flight in France and the United States as well as to teach others to be pilots. Eventually, the inevitable happened: on September 17, 1890, Orville and his passenger, Lieutenant Thomas E. Selfridge, crashed due to a malfunction. Orville recovered, but Selfridge died. However, the work of the brothers continued until Wilbur died of typhoid fever in 1912. Orville carried on alone until his death in 1948. Today they are remembered as the fathers of modern flight.

Flight (cont.)

Vocabulary

Directions: Use the words from the word bank to complete the sentences correctly.

Word Bank
• aerodynamic　　　• confident　　　• exceeded　　　• glider

1. Phyllis was _____ that she could finish all her school work in time to go to the party.

2. We watched as the _____ flew above us across the open field.

3. The car was built for racing, so the engineers chose an _____ design to cut back on wind resistance.

4. The amount of money that was raised for charity _____ our expectations.

Comprehension

Directions: Answer the following questions in complete sentences.

1. Why did most people believe that flight was not possible?

   _____

2. Name three accomplishments Orville Wright achieved prior to 1886.

   _____

   _____

   _____

3. Name three businesses in which both brothers were involved.

   _____

   _____

   _____

4. Why was their interest in flight sparked in 1886?

   _____

5. Where and when was their first glider tested?

   _____

6. Why did the Wright brothers build a wind tunnel?

Flight *(cont.)*

7. Using the information presented in the story "Flight," choose an accomplishment achieved by the Wright brothers for each year and record it in the proper space on the chart below.

Year	Accomplishments
1900	
1901	
1902	
1903	
1905	
1908	

Choices
A. A contract to build the first military airplanes is signed with the U.S. Department of War.
B. A second glider is successfully flown.
C. A 24.2-mile flight is achieved by an airplane.
D. A glider that holds a person is built and tried.
E. The first power airplane is introduced.
F. A glide exceeding 600 feet is made.

The Unsinkable Titanic

In April of 1912, approximately 2,200 passengers and crew members boarded the *Titanic*, a new luxury liner ready for its maiden voyage. The *Titanic* had the best of everything, and only the elite could afford passage. Some even paid more than $4,000 for the trip, while many of the crew did not even earn $1,000 in a year. The ship's promoters claimed that their vessel was unsinkable, primarily because its hull had 16 watertight compartments. Even if two compartments flooded, the ship would still float. Everyone had complete confidence in the boat.

A number of famous people were on board, including millionaire John Jacob Astor and his wife, as well as Isidor and Ida Straus, the wealthy department store owners. In general, the passengers had complete confidence in the ship because the best design and latest technology was at their fingertips.

Late on the night of April 14, the *Titanic* was sailing in the North Atlantic Ocean on its trip from Southampton, England, to New York City. The ship was traveling at a speed of 21 knots (nautical miles per hour), which was nearly top speed. Since there was danger of icebergs in the area, the ship's speed was far too fast. At 11:40 P.M., the *Titanic* rubbed alongside an iceberg for approximately ten seconds. That was enough. The hull of the ship was made of a type of steel that became brittle in the icy waters of the North Atlantic. Several small cracks appeared instantly, and seams were unriveted. Water started to pour inside, weakening the hull still further.

Six distress signals were sent out immediately. Another passenger ship, the *California*, was just 20 minutes away at the time; however, its radio operator was not on duty, so no one there heard the *Titanic*'s signal. Another ship, the *Carpathia*, was approximately four hours away, and it responded to the signal. However, when the *Carpathia* arrived at 4:00 A.M., it was too late for many of the passengers. The *Titanic* had long since sunk. Just after 2:00 A.M., water had flooded through the hull to the ship's bow, causing the entire vessel to split in two.

At first, the passengers aboard the ship were calm, expecting to reach lifeboats with ease and then be rescued by other ships. They did not know that the *Titanic's* lifeboats only had room for approximately 1,200 people, far fewer than the number of people on board. When the passengers and crew saw how dire the situation was, many stepped aside for younger passengers to board lifeboats safely. Among these heroes were the Astors and Strauses. Captain Edward J. Smith went down with his ship. In all, 705 people survived the wreck, most of them women and children. The remaining 1,517 died in the icy waters of the North Atlantic Ocean.

When the ship was first endangered, the band on board began to play a ragtime melody to encourage the passengers. As time passed and the situation grew grim, they continued to play, but this time it was an old English hymn calling for mercy and compassion from God.

In 1985, a team of scientists found the wreckage of the *Titanic* 12,500 feet (3,800 meters) beneath the sea. Although people had previously thought that a large gash was immediately ripped in the boat because of the iceberg, the scientists were able to prove that the steel composition of the hull was truly the fatal flaw as was the speed at which the boat was traveling.

◆   ◆   ◆   ◆   ◆   ◆   ◆   ◆

The Unsinkable Titanic *(cont.)*

Vocabulary

Directions: Match the word in Column A with the correct definition in Column B.

Column A	Column B
_____ 1. elite	A. facing trouble
_____ 2. knots	B. came apart
_____ 3. unriveted	C. wealthy
_____ 4. dire	D. rip
_____ 5. endangered	E. the speed of a ship
_____ 6. gash	F. serious

Comprehension

Directions: Answer the following questions in complete sentences.

1. When was the voyage of the *Titanic,* and why was it such an exciting event?

   _____

2. How did the Titanic come to be known as a ship that could not sink?

   _____

3. Name two famous couples on the *Titanic.*

   _____

   _____

4. What were the planned departure and arrival points of the *Titanic*?

   _____

5. What problem did they face with the lifeboats?

   _____

The Unsinkable Titanic *(cont.)*

Directions: Fill in the cause or the effect on the chart below. The first one has been done for you.

Cause	Effect
1. The *Titanic* was traveling at a speed of 21 knots.	1. The collision couldn't be avoided.
2. The ship rubbed against an iceberg for ten seconds.	2.
3.	3. He couldn't hear the *Titanic's* distress signal.
4. The *Carpathia* was four hours away.	4.
5. The vessel split in half.	5.
6. The band played ragtime music.	6.
7. The *Titanic* sank.	7.
8.	8. 1,517 passengers died.

Directions: Use the following chart to help you write a summary of the events aboard the *Titanic*.

Time	Event
11:40 P.M.	The ship rubs against an iceberg.
2:00 A.M.	The vessel splits in two.
4:00 A.M.	The *Carpathia* arrives.

Coming to America

Immigration was not new to the 1920s, but the complexion for the situation changed dramatically in the early part of the twentieth century. From its earliest years the United States of America had an open door policy toward immigrants, placing few restrictions on the number of people entering this country. It was not until 1882 that the first law was passed banning people from a specific country. The Chinese Exclusion Act forbade Chinese laborers because it was feared that they would work for lower pay. In 1907 a "gentleman's agreement" between the United States and Japan barred Japanese immigrants.

In the early 1900s there were two groups who sought to have the doors closed to certain ethnic members. American laborers feared that they would lose their jobs to new immigrants who were willing to work for lower wages. A second group believed that the newcomers were inferior. Still, it was not until 1917 that restrictions were in place, preventing 33 different categories of people from obtaining entry to the United States.

Immigration in the 1920s changed in another important way. Prior to 1880 newcomers originated mostly from countries in northern and western Europe. When the immigration population shifted to southern and eastern European countries, some Americans became alarmed at the customs and languages. World War I produced a temporary halt to the problem as very few people came to America during that period. Once the war ended, the wave of immigrants rose steadily, with over 600,000 people arriving in 1921. With the passage of a new law that same year, immigration was limited by a quota system. The National Origins Act of 1924 established severe quotas from southern and eastern European countries. For example, 100,000 Italians had arrived in one year in the early 1900s, but the new quota limited Italy to 5,082 people per year; Greece was allowed only 307 people per year, while Russia was permitted 2,784 per year. Not until the 1960s, when Lyndon Johnson became president, did those quota laws change.

Coming to America *(cont.)*

Directions: Complete each sentence correctly by choosing one of the words in the word bank.

Word Bank		
• immigrants	• gentleman's agreement	• ban
• quota	• restriction	• excluded

1. Even though Mr. Reed had no contract showing that he agreed to buy the horse from Mr. Eagan, they shook hands with each other, knowing they had reached a _____ .

2. The colonists in Boston agreed to _____ the purchase of tea from the British.

3. _____ coming from all countries saw the Statue of Liberty as their ship came into New York Harbor.

4. The merchant had a _____ on the amount of merchandise he could sell at one time.

5. When Tom was sick, he knew that he would be _____ from the class picnic and confined to bed.

6. The _____ stated that a person under 18 cannot drive in some states.

Directions: Answer the following questions in complete sentences.

1. What law was passed in 1882, and why was it enacted?

_____

2. Name two reasons new immigrants were prevented from entering the United States.

_____

_____

3. From which areas were immigrants arriving prior to the 1880s and after the 1920s?

_____

_____

4. What did the National Origin Act of 1924 seek to do?

_____

Coming to America *(cont.)*

5. Organize the countries according to their quotas of immigrants from greatest to least. Next to each country list their quota of immigrants. Research to see if you can find quotas for some countries not mentioned on page 11.

Country	Quota

Prefixes

Prefixes are added to the beginnings of many words. They change the meanings of the base words. Circle the prefixes of each word and then use them in a sentence of your own.

im—not   **in**—not   **pre**—before   **re**—again   **ex**—not

1. exclude _____

2. inferior _____

3. prevent _____

4. restrict _____

5. immigrant _____

6. incomplete _____

Farmers and the Dust Bowl

Farmers did not share in the prosperity of World War I, and things were worse after the recession of 1921. Federal support for agriculture ended, and many farmers who had expanded their production to meet wartime needs lost their land and stock. For those who survived, low crop prices meant low income. In the 1930s wheat prices dropped to below what it cost to grow the crop. Rather than sell at such prices, some farmers destroyed their own crops. A series of natural disasters made matters even worse and led to the greatest westward migration that the United States has ever seen.

Americans had long disregarded the warnings of conservationists. Farmers had misused the land, depleting fertile soil and then moving on to farm new land. In the Great Plains, farmers plowed up natural grasses to plant wheat. Agriculturalists who advised the use of contour plowing to prevent erosion and planting trees as windbreakers were ignored. When a seven-year drought struck, beginning in 1931, winds blew the topsoil into thick, dark clouds of dust that sometimes lasted for several days. To protect themselves from the dust storms, farmers hung damp sheets over the windows of their homes. Still, dust poured through the cracks of the farmhouse walls, leaving dust in their food, hair, eyes, mouths, and pockets. For many, there was nothing left to do but leave their farms and head west.

Over three million people eventually migrated from the Great Plains region to California, where there was the promise of jobs. In most cases, that was all it was—a promise. Conditions in California proved little better than the farms they had left. While there was not much dust to contend with, there were not nearly enough jobs. Californians resented these new people and labeled them "Okies," a synonym for dumb and lazy. Hatred against them was so great that some farmers destroyed their surplus food rather than share it with the starving Okie families.

Finally, the government stepped in and created some labor camps in the San Joaquin Valley, which provided relief and education for the migrants. Much was written about these people and their struggles. John Steinbeck's novel *The Grapes of Wrath* described conditions among the Okies in California. Dorothea Lange photographed and documented their misery, while Woody Guthrie sang songs about their predicament. It was a dark time in American history in more ways than one.

◆   ◆   ◆   ◆   ◆   ◆   ◆   ◆

Farmers and the Dust Bowl *(cont.)*

Directions: Use the words in the word bank to complete the sentences.

Word Bank
• prosper   • agriculture   • conserve   • resent

1. Farmers study _____ so they can learn the best methods of growing crops.

2. John said, "I _____ the fact that you accepted the invitation to the party without asking me first."

3. We decided that we would _____ our food supply by eating only small amounts.

4. The students of the graduating class voted Tim the one most likely to achieve success and _____ in business.

Life worsened for the farmers after World War I. Match the effect that each of the following causes had on the farmers and agriculture.

Cause	Effect
_____ 1. End of federal support for agriculture	A. Westward migration begins.
_____ 2. Low crop prices	B. The topsoil of the land is blown away as clouds.
_____ 3. Natural disasters	C. Farmers lose their land and stock.
_____ 4. Farmers misuse of land	D. The soil is depleted.
_____ 5. Seven-year drought	E. Dust is found in food, hair, eyes, mouths, and pockets.

Directions: On the back of this page, answer the questions in full sentences.

1. Name two ways in which the farmers misused the land.

2. What is the meaning of the label *Okie,* and who are Okies?

3. How did the people in California show their resentment of the three million migrants?

4. What did the government do to help the migrant workers?

5. How did the following people make others aware of the problems and conditions faced by the Okies?

   A. John Steinbeck   B. Dorothea Lange   C. Woody Guthrie

Three First Ladies

During the 1970s there were three first ladies: Pat Nixon, Betty Ford, and Rosalyn Carter. Each had a distinctive personality and brought a different flair to the White House. Read the short biographies that follow and complete the activities on page17.

Pat Nixon: When Pat Nixon became first lady, she was the mother of two teenage daughters, Tricia and Julie. Continuing in the tradition of Jackie Kennedy, Mrs. Nixon proceeded with the renovation of the White House to make it a museum of American heritage. In addition, she supported the cause of volunteerism and urged Americans to get involved with their communities. Her greatest political success was as a goodwill ambassador on trips to Africa. Pat Nixon died in 1993 and is buried beside her husband in Yorba Linda, California, at the Richard Nixon Library and Birthplace.

Betty Ford: Betty Ford is most remembered for her candor about her personal life. When she spoke publicly about her battle with breast cancer, she raised public awareness of the disease and served as an inspiration to others who faced cancer. As first lady, Betty Ford also supported the Equal Rights Amendment and valued both the traditional role of women and the role of women in the workplace. After leaving the White House, Mrs. Ford publicly described her struggle with addiction to alcohol and pain medication, and she founded the Betty Ford Clinic for substance abuse in Rancho Mirage, California.

Rosalyn Carter: When Jimmy Carter was president, his wife Rosalyn served as his most trusted advisor and represented him officially during a trip to Central and South American countries. She sometimes sat in on cabinet meetings where she quietly took notes. These acts aroused much criticism, but there were also those who admired her. Rosalyn's own agenda included supporting mental health reform, actively supporting legislation to reform Social Security, and urging approval of the Equal Rights Amendment. A woman of action, Rosalyn believed firmly in the necessity of women pursuing careers outside the home.

Three First Ladies (cont.)

Directions: Each of the women in the article accomplished many things while her husband was the president of the United States. Under each heading, list four things each woman accomplished.

I. **Pat Nixon**

A. _____

B. _____

C. _____

D. _____

II. **Betty Ford**

A. _____

B. _____

C. _____

D. _____

III. **Rosalyn Carter**

A. _____

B. _____

C. _____

D. _____

Directions: Use the information in your outline to help you answer the questions.

1. Which woman wanted to carry on the tradition set by a former first lady? _____

2. Which woman received great criticism for being involved in White House meetings? _____

3. Name one cause that each woman championed while her husband was in office.

   A. Pat Nixon _____

   B. Betty Ford _____

   C. Rosalyn Carter _____

The Technological Home and Office

The average American home of the eighties differed quite a bit from the same home in the seventies, and technology was the reason. Suddenly it seemed there were new technologies to handle a variety of tasks. Answering machines took phone messages, videocassette recorders (VCRs) taped television shows when people were not home to watch them, cable television broadened the spectrum of television viewing options, compact discs (CDs) enhanced sound for the listener of recorded music, and personal computers rapidly became an exciting new source of entertainment and productivity. Perhaps most significant and influential in the technologic advances of the decade were the VCR and the personal computer.

◆

VCRs: VCRs brought about a revolution in the entertainment industry. Previously, people's choice of films was limited to what could be seen in theaters or the occasional few movies screened on network television. Children of the middle decades can recall special television events when popular movies such as *The Wizard of Oz* were broadcast annually. With the advent of VCRs, people could buy or rent videotapes of movies and watch them whenever they chose. They could also record any movie or show from television to watch at their leisure. Some even began watching a show on one channel while taping one on another. With the dawn of the VCR came a new line of stores that sold and rented videos. This became one of the fastest growing industries of the 1980s.

Initially developed in the late fifties and early sixties, VCR technology grew from the need of television studios for a reliable method of recording programs for viewing in different time zones, or for repeat usage. These early systems were far too complex and expensive for home use, however. In 1975 Sony corporation introduced its Betamax, based on the system used by stations and networks. Matsushita Electrical Industrial Corporation quickly released a competing system called Video Home System, or VHS. When the VHS system was adopted by the leading American television manufacturer, popularity of the Betamax waned. The VCR industry boomed throughout the eighties.

PCs: The personal computer also took off in popularity through the decade. Although in 1979 only 325,000 Americans had personal computers in their homes, by 1984 the number of owners had climbed to fifteen million.

The first home computers were used primarily for entertainment with such games as Space Invaders and Pac Man. Advances in microchip technology and the availability of affordable peripherals like modems and user-friendly software led to growing awareness of the computer's usefulness, particularly to students. By 1985, students had become the largest users of personal computers.

While the price of both VCRs and personal computers has dropped over time, VCRs are usually more affordable for the average family, while personal computers, still relatively expensive, are often out of reach. However, most schools have computers so that students are exposed to them before entering into the business world where they are a necessity.

The Technological Home and Office *(cont.)*

Directions: Column one contains the abbreviation of an invention of the 1980s. Write the full name for that invention in column two. In column three list the major achievement or contribution it made.

Invention	Full name	Contribution
VCR		
CD		
PC		

Directions: Answer the questions in complete sentences.

1. Name three ways that VCRs changed the entertainment industry.

   A. _____

   B. _____

   C. _____

   D. _____

2. How were VCRs first used?

   _____

3. Name the role each company played in popularizing the VCR.

   A. Sony Corporation _____

   _____

   B. Matsushita Electrical Industrial Corporation _____

   _____

4. What scientific advances contributed to the popularity of PC home use?

   _____

The Technological Home and Office *(cont.)*

Directions: The Venn diagram below compares the VCR to the personal computer by showing how each is different and alike. Insert the information in the correct area of the diagram.

Information
1. It is more affordable.
2. It is expensive.
3. Its prices became lower.
4. It advanced because of microchip technology.
5. It is used by schools.
6. It uses a modem and software.
7. It helped form a new line of business.
8. It was the fastest growing industry in the 1980s.
9. It was used in the entertainment industry.
10. It is used for home entertainment.

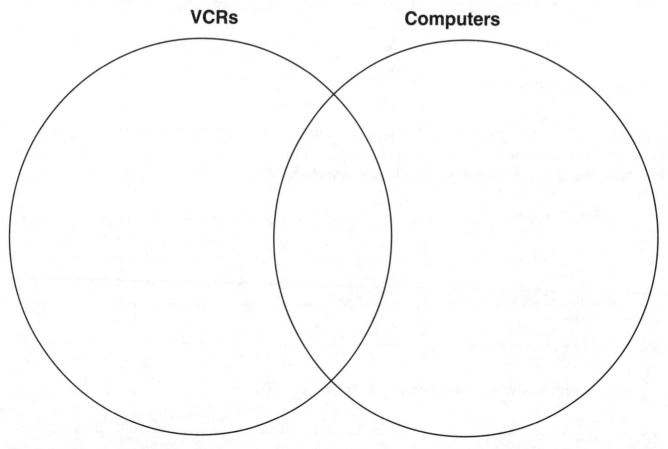

VCRs   **Computers**

Norman Rockwell

For 47 years Norman Rockwell painted covers for the *Saturday Evening Post.* His inviting paintings provided an intimate glimpse into the everyday lives of Americans during the first half of the century and have come to be regarded as classic Americana.

Norman Rockwell was born on February 2, 1894, in New York. When he was nine, the family moved to Mamaroneck. To gain acceptance, the resourceful Rockwell drew pictures to entertain his classmates. He left high school to study at the National Academy of Design and earned money by drawing greeting cards. At age 16, he studied at the Art Students League and began illustrating books and magazines. By the time he was 18, Rockwell was the art director for *Boys' Life* magazine.

Rockwell achieved fame after the five illustrations he sold to the editor of *Saturday Evening Post* were used as covers on the magazine. In all, Norman Rockwell provided 318 covers for the *Post* through his 47-year association with them.

When World War I broke out, Rockwell tried to enlist in the navy, but he was rejected for being underweight. Undeterred, he ate a diet of bananas and donuts until he gained the necessary ten pounds. After acceptance into the service, Rockwell was assigned to the navy yard in Charleston, South Carolina, where he painted for the navy. He also continued to work for the *Saturday Evening Post* and other magazines. After the war, he returned to New York, where he built a studio for himself. By that time he was enjoying both fame and fortune from his paintings.

The process used by Norman Rockwell to create a painting was long and detailed. First, he sketched the scene. Next, he made individual drawings of each element in the scene. Full-size charcoal drawings were the next step, followed by color sketches. Only then was he ready to begin actual painting.

In the late 1930s Rockwell moved to Arlington, Virginia. Fire destroyed his studio in 1943, along with many of his drawings and paintings. Although he was saddened by the loss, Rockwell began painting more directly from life rather than relying on a model. Although he ceased working for the *Saturday Evening Post* in 1963, he continued to work for other magazines. His latter years were spent traveling to foreign countries. Norman Rockwell died in 1978.

◆   ◆   ◆   ◆   ◆   ◆   ◆   ◆

Norman Rockwell *(cont.)*

Directions: The following events of Norman Rockwell's life are not in the correct order. Sequence them by number to show which happened first and last.

A. _____   His studio was destroyed by fire.

B. _____   He drew greeting cards.

C. _____   He moved to Mamaroneck.

D. _____   He illustrated books and magazines.

E. _____   He traveled to foreign countries.

F. _____   He drew for the *Saturday Evening Post*.

G. _____   He started drawing pictures to entertain people.

H. _____   He served in the navy.

I. _____   He became the art director for *Boy's Life Magazine*.

J. _____   He moved to New York and built an art studio.

Directions: Norman Rockwell followed a particular procedure when painting. Using the steps listed below, put them in the outline in correct order.

Steps

- He made full-size charcoal drawings.
- He sketched a picture.
- He painted the picture.
- He made individual drawings of each element in each scene.
- He made color sketches.

A. _____

B. _____

C. _____

D. _____

E. _____

Directions: Using the correctly ordered outline, write a paragraph explaining the steps that Norman Rockwell used to produce a finished painting. Be sure to include transition words such as *first, next, then, after, before,* and *finally* to make the paragraph flow smoothly.

An Extraordinary Bus Ride

She has been called the mother of the civil rights movement, but Rosa McCauley Parks does not consider herself to be extraordinary. Born on February 4, 1915, in Tuskegee, Alabama, McCauley had a normal childhood. She grew up on a farm and attended an all-black school in her neighborhood. Her high school education was cut short by her mother's death, but she finished her schooling after her marriage to Raymond Parks. In 1943 she joined the NAACP (National Association for the Advancement of Colored People) and worked with the Voters' League, registering African Americans to vote. Then came the fateful day.

Rosa McCauley Parks

The bus ride on December 1, 1955, began as usual. After completing her job as a seamstress for a Montgomery department store, Parks boarded the bus to go home. As was required, she took a seat in the back of the bus. When all the seats filled up, Parks was asked to vacate hers for a white man who was just getting on the bus. (At that time in Montgomery the law required blacks to sit at the back of the bus and to give up their seats for white people when all other seats were filled.) On this day, however, Parks refused to move. The bus driver stopped the bus and called for policemen who whisked her away to jail. NAACP leader Edgar Daniel Nixon posted her bail and determined that Rosa Parks would be the last African American arrested for such an action.

Along with other black leaders, including Dr. Martin Luther King, Jr., Nixon declared a one-day boycott of all city buses. Leaflets announcing the boycott were distributed throughout the city, and on the appointed day the results were dramatic. Not one African American rode on any buses there. Because it was such a success, the boycott was extended indefinitely.

For their actions blacks were harassed on the street, hundreds of their leaders were arrested, and many lost their jobs. Still, the boycott continued with African Americans turning to alternative methods of transportation, including walking, carpooling, riding bicycles, and even riding mules. The boycott ended when, after 381 days, the U.S. Supreme Court ruled in favor of Rosa Parks and declared Alabama bus segregation laws unconstitutional. It had cost the bus company $750,000 in lost revenues, but the gains in human dignity were priceless.

◆   ◆   ◆   ◆   ◆   ◆   ◆   ◆

An Extraordinary Bus Ride *(cont.)*

Directions: Choose the word that best completes each sentence.

1. John's mother felt that her grandmother's vase was _____ and could never be replaced.

    a. clay   b. new   c. priceless

2. The colonists decided to protest the tax on tea by _____ its purchase.

    a. delaying   b. boycotting   c. revolting

3. The new laws, having no time limit, will go on _____ unless a change is enacted.

    a. indefinitely   b. limited   c. repeal

4. When the fire broke out, the people had to _____ the burning building.

    a. support   b. vacate   c. uphold

5. The boys' and girls' locker rooms are _____ .

    a. revamped   b. abandoned   c. segregated

6. We had to plan an _____ activity in case it rained and our picnic was canceled.

    a. alternative   b. cooperative   c. coordinating

Directions: Complete each sentence by adding correct information.

1. Rosa Parks is called the _____ .

2. Rosa was born and educated in _____ .

3. She joined the _____ and worked with the _____ .

4. Rosa worked as a _____ in a department store.

5. Refusing to _____ caused her to be arrested.

6. _____ and _____ declared a boycott of city buses.

7. Three results of the boycott were

    A. _____

    B. _____

    C. _____

An Extraordinary Bus Ride *(cont.)*

8. Four alternative methods of transportation used during the boycott were the following:

_____

_____

_____

_____

9. The boycott lasted _____ days.

10. The United States Supreme Court ruled Alabama bus segregation laws were _____ .

Directions: Write a paragraph explaining how you as a bystander would have felt while watching the events unfold as Rosa Parks was told to give up her seat on the bus.

_____

_____

_____

_____

_____

_____

_____

_____

_____

_____

The Black Pearl

Pelé, born Edson Arantes do Nascimento, was only 17 when he played in his first World Cup of soccer in 1958. Some 60,000 people had jammed into the 50,000-seat arena in hopes that they would see Sweden win its first world title. The Swedish coach thought his team could win if they scored first. Brazil had a tendency to become disorganized when they trailed in a game. What happened at that game, however, stunned everyone—the spectators, coaches, and players. Pelé inspired his teammates with his enthusiastic and energetic pace. It was his magnificent moves on the field, though, that really wowed the crowd. He displayed such control of his body and such athleticism that even the Swedish fans began to chant his name. After their win, the Brazilian team returned home as national heroes, and Pelé was nicknamed "The Black Pearl."

Pelé

Pelé was born on October 23, 1940, in a small town in Minas Gerais state. His father, a soccer player, was pleased with his firstborn and predicted that the boy would grow up to become a great soccer player. As a young child Pelé ran and played with the other students in his neighborhood. They had to use grapefruits or socks filled with rags because there was not enough money for a real soccer ball. Bored with school, he quit in the fourth grade and became a cobbler's apprentice. His free time was spent playing soccer. When he was 12, he was chosen to play in a junior league where he learned the strategies and tactics of professional soccer. By the time he was 14, he was invited to join a professional team. It meant leaving home and moving to Santos near Brazil's largest city, São Paulo. Often he would be homesick, but he kept busy attending school between games and practicing with the team. Soon, people began coming out to the games just to watch this remarkable new player. Then, at age 17 he found himself on the Brazilian World Cup team.

Before the team left for Stockholm, Pelé injured his knee. He was fearful that it would not heal correctly and he would be unable to continue his professional career. Though in pain, he put on an unforgettable performance at the World Cup and led his team to victory. He went on to play until he retired from the Santos team in 1974. For three years after that, he played for a team in the newly formed North American Soccer League.

Pelé remains a public figure in his native Brazil. He starred in some movies and recorded a hit song. His future plans may include something in the political arena. Whatever his goal, he remains the most popular soccer player in the history of the game.

◆   ◆   ◆   ◆   ◆   ◆   ◆   ◆

The Black Pearl *(cont.)*

Directions: Some of the following sentences are true, and some are false. Place a check mark before each sentence that is true. If a sentence is false, change it to make it correct.

_____   1. Pelé played World Cup soccer when he was 17 years of age.

_____   2. People thought Brazil would win first place at the competition.

_____   3. Pelé was able to exhibit great control, and the Brazilian fans chanted his name.

_____   4. The Swedish team named him "The Black Pearl."

_____   5. Pelé's family could not afford to buy him a soccer ball with which to practice.

_____   6. He quit school in the fourth grade.

_____   7. He was 12 years old when he joined a professional soccer team.

_____   8. He suffered an injury to his head but still played in the World Cup.

Directions: Facts are pieces of information that can be proven. People's opinions reflect their personal thoughts and cannot be verified. Label each sentence as a fact or an opinion.

_____   1.   Pelé was the best player to ever live.

_____   2. He played for the North American Soccer League for three years.

_____   3. He was very popular with all the people in Brazil.

_____   4. Pelé recorded a hit song and appeared in movies.

_____   5. He will take on a government job.

_____   6. His real name is Edson Arantes do Nascimento.

Henry Ingersoll Bowditch

Henry Ingersoll Bowditch was born on August 9, 1808, in Salem, Massachusetts. His father was a famous mathematician named Nathaniel Bowditch, and his mother was Mary. Bowditch went to private school when he was young. When his family moved to Boston in 1823, he attended Public Latin School. Bowditch went on to study at Harvard College where he graduated in 1828. He was not sure what he wanted to do with his life, so he decided to enter Harvard Medical School. In 1832, Bowditch graduated with a degree in medicine. During his internship at Massachusetts General Hospital, Bowditch discovered that he really enjoyed the field of medicine.

Bowditch traveled to Europe in order to study medicine in France. While in Paris, he had the opportunity to work with some of the finest French physicians. They taught him to make close observations and use inductive reasoning. They inspired him to be deeply committed to the study of medicine. After spending a year in France, Bowditch went to study medicine in England. However, he did not feel that the English were as advanced in the field of medicine as the French. As a result, he returned to France for one more year of study.

In 1834, Bowditch went home to Boston where he started a medical practice. He was extremely opposed to slavery and joined the work of the abolitionists. He helped many slaves escape to the North and spoke out against fugitive slave laws. In 1861, the Civil War was being fought, and Bowditch volunteered to be a doctor for Union soldiers who were fighting in Virginia. He worked hard to convince the Senate to institute an army ambulance corps so that wounded soldiers could be taken off the battlefield.

Bowditch also struggled to improve public health in the 1860s by making people more aware of how tuberculosis was being spread. He helped to create many health boards that were used to monitor public health. He personally served on many of these boards. In 1879, he became the president of the American Medical Association. Until his death on January 14, 1892, Bowditch spoke out about many public health issues and encouraged women to pursue careers in medicine.

Henry Ingersoll Bowditch *(cont.)*

Directions: Use information that you found in "Henry Ingersoll Bowditch" to complete this outline.

I. Early Life

   A. Date of birth   _____

   B. Place of birth   _____

II. Education (schools attended)

   A. _____

   B. _____

   C. _____

   D. _____

III. Places of study

   A. _____

   B. _____

   C. _____

IV. Employment

   A. Pre-Civil War

      1. _____

      2. _____

   B. Civil War Era

      1. _____

      2. _____

V. Accomplishments

   A. _____

   B. _____

   C. _____

   D. _____

   E. _____

   F. _____

Evaluation: What do you think was Henry Ingersoll Bowditch's greatest accomplishment? Give at least two reasons to support your answer.

"The Road Not Taken"

Two roads diverged in a yellow wood,
And sorry I could not travel both
And be one traveler, long I stood
And looked down one as far as I could
To where it bent in the undergrowth;

Then took the other, as just as fair,
And having perhaps the better claim,
Because it was grassy and wanted wear;
Though as for that, the passing there
Had worn them really about the same,

And both that morning equally lay
In leaves no step had trodden black.
Oh, I kept the first for another day!
Yet knowing how way leads on to way,
I doubted if I should ever come back.

I shall be telling this with a sigh
Somewhere ages and ages hence:
Two roads diverged in a wood, and I—
I took the one less traveled by,
And that has made all the difference.

—Robert Frost

"The Road Not Taken" *(cont.)*

Directions: Using the poem "The Road Not Taken," answer the questions in complete sentences.

1. How many stanzas does this poem contain?_____

2. How many lines does each stanza contain? _____

In each of the four stanzas, Frost uses end-line rhyme.

> *Example:*   **Stanza 1,**
> *Line 1* ends with *wood.*
> This rhymes with line 3, which ends with *stood* and line 4, which ends with *could.*
> *Line 2* ends with *both.*
> This rhymes with line 5, which ends with under*growth.*

Directions: Read each stanza and list the final word in each line. Check to see if this pattern is repeated.

Stanza #2

Line 1 ends with _____ .

This rhymes with line _____ , which ends with _____ and line _____ , which ends with _____ .

Line 2 ends with _____ .

This rhymes with line _____ , which ends with _____ .

Stanza #3

Line 1 ends with _____ .

This rhymes with line _____ , which ends with _____ and line _____ , which ends with _____ .

Line 2 ends with _____ .

This rhymes with line _____ , which ends with _____ .

Stanza #4

Line 1 ends with _____ .

This rhymes with line _____ , which ends with _____ and line _____ , which ends with _____ .

Line 2 ends with _____ .

This rhymes with line _____ , which ends with _____ .

"The Road Not Taken" *(cont.)*

In all stanzas of "The Road Not Taken," Frost rhymes the ending word in line one with the ending word in line _____ and line _____ . In addition, he rhymes the ending word in line 2 with the ending word in line _____ .

Frost also uses rhythm. This is achieved by using the same number of accented syllables in each line.

1. How many syllables per line are used most often?_____

2. What is the setting of this poem? _____

3. Who is the main character in the poem?_____

4. What problem does the character face? _____

   _____

   _____

   _____

   _____

5. What does the character decide to do? _____

   _____

   _____

   _____

   _____

6. How does the character feel about his decision? _____

   _____

   _____

   _____

   _____

"The Road Not Taken" *(cont.)*

1. In the last stanza of the poem, the traveler chooses the road that fewer people traveled. Why is this a courageous decision?

_____

_____

_____

2. Besides courage, what other characteristics are possessed by this traveler? List three of them below.

_____

_____

_____

3. Why do you think most travelers chose the well-worn path rather than the one "less traveled by"?

_____

_____

_____

4. What lessons about life do you think Robert Frost wants the reader to learn?

_____

_____

_____

Activity: What important decision have you recently made? Write a paragraph about how that decision "has made all the difference" in your life.

_____

_____

_____

_____

_____

"The Courage That My Mother Had"

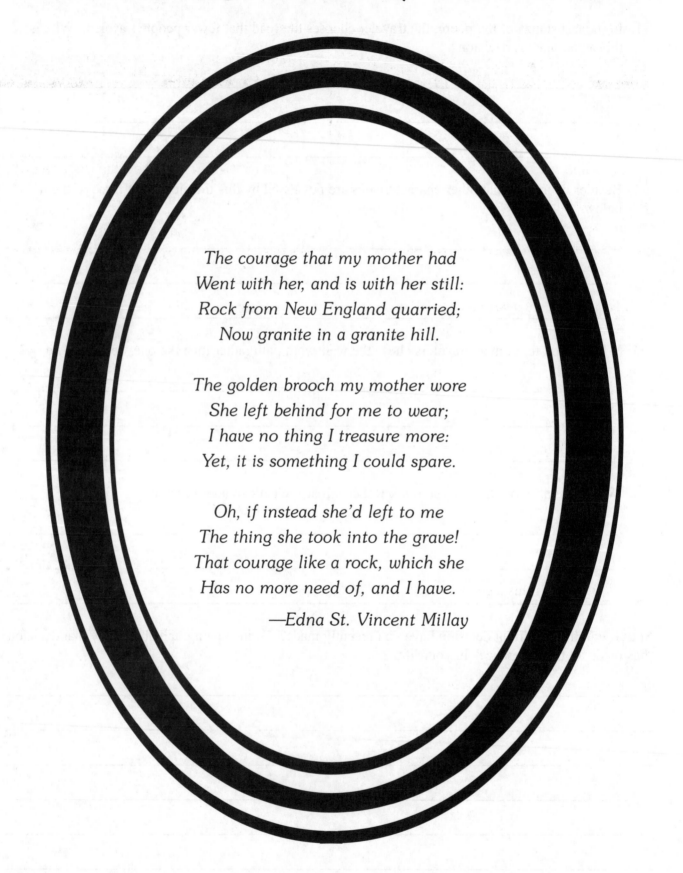

The courage that my mother had
Went with her, and is with her still:
Rock from New England quarried;
Now granite in a granite hill.

The golden brooch my mother wore
She left behind for me to wear;
I have no thing I treasure more:
Yet, it is something I could spare.

Oh, if instead she'd left to me
The thing she took into the grave!
That courage like a rock, which she
Has no more need of, and I have.

　　　　—Edna St. Vincent Millay

"The Courage That My Mother Had" *(cont.)*

Directions: Match the words in column one with the correct definitions in column two.

Column One	Column Two
1. granite	A. a type of rock or stone
2. quarried	B. bravery
3. brooch	C. to receive from a previous generation
4. courage	D. a decorative pin
5. inherit	E. to dig or blast stone

A *metaphor* is a comparison of two things without the use of the words *like* or *as*.

    Example: The cloud is fluffy white cotton candy.

A *simile* is a comparison of two things using the words *like* or *as*.

    Example: The cloud is like fluffy white candy.

Directions: Answer these questions in complete sentences.

1. In stanza one, the poet compares her mother to a *rock*.

    A. Is this a *simile* or a *metaphor*? How do you know?

    _____

    B. Why is this a good choice?

    _____

2. In stanza three, Edna St. Vincent Millay again compares her mother to a rock. Is this a metaphor or a simile, and how do you know?

    _____

3. Who is the storyteller or speaker?

    _____

"The Courage That My Mother Had" *(cont.)*

4. What does the author inherit from her mother?

_____

5. How does she feel about this object?

_____

_____

6. What does the speaker mean by the line "Yet, it is something I could spare"?

_____

_____

7. What does the speaker wish she had inherited from her mother and why?

_____

_____

8. What qualities do you feel your parents have passed down to you? Explain in the space below.

_____

_____

_____

_____

_____

_____

_____

_____

Introduction to Literature Units

A good book can touch our lives like a good friend. Within its pages are words and characters that can inspire us to achieve our highest ideals. We can turn to it for companionship, recreation, comfort, and guidance. It also gives us a cherished story to hold in our hearts forever.

In this Reading and Literature section, great care has been taken to select two books that are sure to become good friends! Those books are *Tuck Everlasting* by Natalie Babbitt and *The Cay* by Theodore Taylor. In addition, short reading passages have been chosen to stimulate the minds of our children, to enrich their lives by acquainting them with new people, places, and things, and to develop precious reading comprehension and literary skills.

Parents and children who use this unit will find the easy-to-follow materials provide an array of skills precisely designed to follow curriculum standards.

Teachers who use this unit will find the following features to supplement their own valuable ideas.

- Short passages focused on vocabulary development, reading comprehension skills, and literary skill development.
- Two novel units include the following elements:

    Brief Summaries

    Biographical Sketches and Pictures of the Authors

    Vocabulary Lists and Vocabulary Practice

    Chapters grouped for study, with each section including

    - comprehension checks
    - cross-curriculum connections
    - literary activities

    Unit Tests

    Answer Key

We are confident that these units will be a valuable resource, and we hope that as you use our ideas, the children will increase the circle of "friends" that they can have in books or any reading selections!

Tuck Everlasting
by
Natalie Babbitt

Table of Contents

About the Author

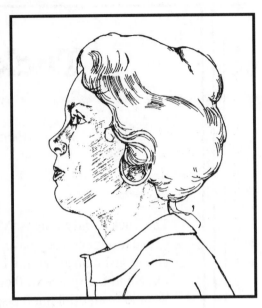

Natalie Babbitt was born in Dayton, Ohio, on July 28, 1932, to Ralph Zane and Genevieve Moore. She attended Laurel School for Girls in Cleveland and went on to Smith College in Northhampton, Massachusetts, receiving her Bachelor of Arts degree in 1954. In that same year she married Samuel F. Babbitt, who was the vice president of Brown University. They have two sons and a daughter.

Babbitt began her career as an illustrator for one of her husband's books. Because her husband soon could not find the time to continue writing, she decided to write and illustrate her own stories. Her success as a writer is evident in the many awards and honors she has received.

- *The Search for Delicious* was the *New York Times* Best Book of 1969 for children ages 9–12.

- *Kneeknock Rise* was an American Library Association (ALA) Notable Book for 1970, a John Newbery Honor Book for 1971, and on the *Horn Book* honors list.

- *Goody Hall* was named a Children's Spring Book Festival Honor Book by *Book World* in 1971, a Children's Book Council Showcase title in 1972, and was on the *School Library Journal* list.

- *The Devil's Storybook* was an ALA Notable Book, on the *School Library Journal's* best-of-the-year list, on the *Horn Book* honor list, and a National Book Award nominee.

- *The Eyes of the Amaryllis* was an ALA Notable Book.

- *Tuck Everlasting* was an ALA Notable Book, on the *Horn Book* honor list, received the Christopher Award for juvenile fiction, was on the International Reading Association choices list, was a U.S. Honor Book, and was chosen for the Congress of the International Board on Books for Young People in 1978.

Natalie Babbitt's writing carries messages which are philosophical statements about "human ways, needs and oddities as visible to children as to adults." She has said, "I believe that children are far more perceptive and wise than American books give them credit for being." This belief underlies all of her writing, which is original and intelligent and appealing to readers of all ages.[1]

[1]Quotes and information taken from *Twentieth-Century Children's Writers,* D. L. Kirkpatrick, Editor, St. Martin's Press, 1978; and *Contemporary Authors New Revision Series, Volume 19,* Linda Metzger, Editor, Gale Research Company, 1987.

Tuck Everlasting

by Natalie Babbitt
(Farrar, Straus, and Giroux, 1985)

Summary

The Tuck family, Angus, Mae, Miles, and Jesse, have a strange and most unusual secret. They have looked the same for the past 87 years! One day a young girl named Winnie Foster accidentally discovers seventeen-year-old Jesse and the source of their secret, a little bubbling spring. In order to keep Winnie from drinking the special water, the Tucks kidnap her and take her to their home.

The Tucks are gentle and kind to Winnie and fully intend to return her to her home the next day. Their only concern is that Winnie understands that living forever may not be the blessing that it seems. Pa Tuck tells Winnie about how it feels to be the same forever. He explains that to live means to constantly grow, move, and change; and part of that changing includes dying. For him, his existence seems like nothing more than being a rock on the side of the road.

After hearing their fantastic story, Winnie understands their concerns about her and what the consequences of drinking from the spring would be. Unfortunately, another stranger, a man in a yellow suit, has overheard the whole story and plots to gain control of the spring in order to make his fortune by selling the water.

When the stranger's plans become clear to the Tucks, Mae accidentally kills him in her effort to stop him. Mae is put in jail by the constable, who had arrived just in time to witness the accident.

Winnie's compassion and belief in the Tucks lead her to decide to help Mae escape. It is Winnie's way of making a difference in the world. The Tucks successfully escape, and Winnie is left to make the decision of her life— whether or not to drink from the spring when she becomes seventeen in order to join Jesse Tuck eternally.

Reading Response Journal

A reading response journal is one way to ensure that the reading of a novel touches each reader in a personal way.

The purpose of the journal is to record thoughts, ideas, observations, and questions as the novel is being read. Each entry should include a brief synopsis of the chapter, highlighting the main events or ideas. Readers should also include reactions, questions, and predictions. Example: I wonder . . .

Assemble lined or unlined three-hole paper inside a fastened report cover. Add more paper as needed. A design may be drawn on the cover as the story unfolds.

Include the following information:

Title of Book _____

Author _____

Publisher _____

Place of Publication _____

Copyright _____

Chapter _____

_____

_____

_____

_____

Chapter _____

_____

_____

_____

_____

Vocabulary Lists

On this page are vocabulary lists which correspond to each sectional grouping of chapters. Define the words in a glossary for *Tuck Everlasting*. Attach the glossary to the back of the reading response journal. Refer to the glossary when completing the vocabulary practice activities.

Section I
(Chapters 1–5)

tangent	tolerantly
ambled	exasperated
tranquil	self-deprecation
bovine	remnants
contemplation	gall
infinite	disheartened
veered	consolingly
melancholy	plaintively
ceased	staggering
jaunty	seized
reluctantly	intense
brooch	oppressive
gallows	meager
accessible	dimensions
isolation	stationary
intrusions	

Section II
(Chapters 6–11)

troupe	burly
perversely	faltered
elated	receded
reservoirs	indomitable
eddies	perilous
lolled	cavernous
camphor	enveloped
assaults	homely
helter-skelter	kingfisher
disarray	bridle
revolutionary	comprehend
populated	luxurious
source	parson
vanity	vigorous
revived	penetrate
rutted	

Section III
(Chapters 12–18)

disarray	silty
lingered	illiterates
constable	roust
cahoots	stern (boat)
threadbare	peril
searing	silhouettes
rigid	willy-nilly
anguish	ordeal
fragrant	accommodations
wheezed	rapidly
flapjacks	

Section IV
(Chapters 19–25)

petulance	remorseless
acrid	prostrate
gentility	furrowed
ebbed	accomplice
flailing	ignorant
tarnation	custody
mantel	ghastly
hearth	staunchly
wistful	
revulsion	
unflinchingly	

Section V
(Epilogue)

catholic	verandah	curlicues
chrome	swivel	

Vocabulary Practice

Complete the following sentences with the correct words from the vocabulary list.

Section I: Chapters 1–5

1. The _____ music put everyone in a sad mood.

2. The rain _____ just as the band began the concert.

3. The _____ heat of August resulted in _____ electric bills.

4. It _____ me that the bus always arrives late.

5. The constant ringing of the alarm _____ the neighbors.

6. The telephone was easily _____ from the patient's bedside.

7. On a beautiful summer day the elderly couple _____ along the path in the park.

8. The timid student _____ knocked on the principal's door.

9. A huge reward was offered for the stolen diamond _____ which was worth over $100,000.

10. The disruptive prisoner was placed in _____ for one month.

11. The Do Not Disturb sign was posted to prevent any _____ during testing.

12. The _____ meal that was served to the hungry delayed airline passengers, resulting in many complaints.

13. The population remained _____ in New York City for two straight years.

14. The _____ of the new _____ were 18 feet high and 12 feet wide.

15. The car _____ sharply to the left into oncoming traffic.

Vocabulary Practice *(cont.)*

Complete the following sentences with the correct words from the vocabulary list.

Section II: Chapters 6–11

1. The modern dance _____ performed for two consecutive weeks.

2. The children were _____ when the snow began to fall.

3. The _____ are filled to capacity due to all the snow and rainfall this past year.

4. The number of _____ in Detroit has diminished over the last ten years.

5. Everyone ran _____ when the blazing fire erupted.

6. Home personal computers are a _____ technological advance connecting the world.

7. The rural areas of this country are sparsely _____ .

8. The chamber of commerce _____ the downtown shopping area by building a new mall.

9. The east coast shoreline has _____ after the winter blizzards and the summer hurricanes.

10. All the stores in the shopping center were _____ with smoke when the fire erupted in the restaurant.

11. The new _____ delivered his sermon to a chapel filled with all the congregants.

12. It was difficult to _____ all the steps in the algebra and probability problems.

13. The young equestrian gently placed the _____ around the horse's face before mounting him.

14. The _____ balls prevented the moths from destroying the woolen clothing during the summer.

15. The boys always have a _____ workout during football practice.

16. The soldiers held off the enemy so they could not _____ the front lines.

Vocabulary Practice *(cont.)*

Complete the following sentences with the correct words from the vocabulary list.

Section III: Chapters 12–18

1. It was almost impossible to _____ the teenager each morning in order to catch the school bus.

2. The county _____ arrested five speeders over the holiday weekend.

3. The two friends were in _____ to rob the grocery store.

4. The fraternity house was in _____ after the party.

5. The _____ at the hotel were excellent.

6. During the winter the Salvation Army tries to replace coats that are _____ with warm ones for the homeless.

7. The _____ scent of freshly cut grass is a summer delight.

8. The young child _____ all night long due to his asthma.

9. The blueberry _____ and scrambled eggs were a welcome breakfast treat.

10. The county has set up a special program for adult _____ to teach them to read.

11. It was quite an _____ for the mountain climbers to get down the snow-covered mountain after the avalanche.

12. The toddler _____ in front of the candy counter while his mother was shopping for groceries.

13. The girl had to hold her leg in a _____ position so it could be placed in a brace.

14. The bus accident caused much _____ for the worried parents.

15. The scouting troop was in great _____ crossing the wobbling bridge.

Vocabulary Practice *(cont.)*

Complete the following sentences with the correct words from the vocabulary list.

Sections IV and V: Chapters 19–Epilogue

1. The children love to turn in the _____ chair.

2. Each night the family sits on the _____ after dinner, admiring the sunset.

3. The child's arms were _____ wildly, trying to avoid the vaccination from the pediatrician.

4. The elderly man fell _____ on the couch after mowing the lawn in the afternoon sun.

5. At first, a feeling of _____ used to overcome the nursing student at the sight of blood.

6. The _____ to a crime is as guilty as the person who commits it.

7. There was a bitter _____ battle between the divorcing parents over the children.

8. A beautiful clock was placed on the _____ above the fireplace.

9. The woman's brow was _____ with wrinkles.

10. If you drive a car, you may not claim to be _____ of the rules of safety.

11. The lawyer _____ defended his client at the courthouse.

12. The family was _____ as they stared at the headstone above the grave.

13. The fire in the _____ warmed the entire room.

14. What in _____ do you mean?

15. The _____ killer was sentenced to the death penalty.

About the Author Activity

After reading about Natalie Babbitt, answer the questions below in complete sentences.

1. When and where was Natalie Babbitt born?_____

   _____

2. From which college did Natalie Babbitt graduate and when? _____

   _____

3. Who did Babbitt marry? What was his occupation? _____

   _____

4. How did Babbitt begin her career? _____

   _____

5. What prompted Babbitt herself to begin writing?_____

   _____

6. How many books has Babbitt Babbitt written?_____

   _____

7. List the titles of the books written by Natalie Babbitt.

   _____

   _____

   _____

   _____

8. Which books received an ALA Notable Book award and also were placed on the *Horn Book* honors list?

   _____

   _____

9. How many awards did Babbitt receive for *Tuck Everlasting?*

   _____

10. Babbitt has said, "Children are far more perceptive and wise than American books give them credit for being." How do you think this belief has influenced her writing?

   _____

Comprehension Check

(Section I)

1. On the back of this paper, write a description of each of the characters introduced in this section. Provide as much detail as possible about their physical characteristics, relationships, and personalities.

2. What does the "touch-me-not appearance" of the cottage mean?

    _____

    _____

3. Describe the woods next to the cottage.

    _____

    _____

4. What amazing fact about the Tucks is revealed?

    _____

5. Describe Mae's one special object.

    _____

    _____

6. Why is Winnie thinking about running away?

    _____

    _____

7. What two comments did Winnie's grandmother make about the music coming from the wood?

    _____

8. What do you think the man in the yellow suit wants?

    _____

9. What happened in the wood when Winnie went there in the morning?

    _____

10. What do you think Mae Tuck meant when she said, "Well, boys, here it is. The worst is happening at last"?

    _____

    _____

Comprehension Check *(cont.)*

(Section II)

1. What was unusual about Winnie's kidnapping?

   _____

   _____

2. What would you have done in Winnie's place?

   _____

   _____

3. What did Winnie discover about the music she had heard the night before?

   _____

   _____

4. What was the fantastic secret the Tucks told Winnie?

   _____

   _____

5. On the back of this page, list at least five of the nine events that the Tucks revealed as support for their incredible story.

   _____

   _____

6. Why didn't the Tucks want Winnie to drink from the spring that morning?

   _____

   _____

7. Why do you think the man with the yellow suit was smiling?

   _____

   _____

8. How do Jesse's and Miles' views about the spring differ?

   _____

   _____

9. How was the home lifestyle of the Tucks different from that of the Fosters?

   _____

   _____

10. Why can't the Tucks stay in any one place for very long?

   _____

   _____

Comprehension Check *(cont.)*

(Section III)

1. How have Winnie's feelings changed? _____

_____

2. Describe Angus Tuck. _____

_____

3. In one sentence tell what Angus Tuck was trying to explain to Winnie at the pond.

_____

_____

4. Why did Angus Tuck say that they are "like rocks beside the road"?

_____

_____

5. What did Angus Tuck say might happen if everyone found out about the special spring?

_____

_____

6. Why do you think the Tucks are so excited and pleased about having Winnie with them?

_____

_____

7. What did Jesse ask Winnie to do?_____

_____

8. Why hadn't Miles taken his wife and children to drink the special water?

_____

_____

9. What would happen if nothing ever died?

_____

_____

10. What bargain did the man with the yellow suit make with the Fosters?

_____

Comprehension Check *(cont.)*

(Section IV)

1. On the back of this paper, write a summary of the events that occurred in this part of the story.

2. How did the man in the yellow suit know about the Tucks? _____
   _____

3. What clue made it possible for the man to recognize the Tucks? _____
   _____

4. What do you think about the plans of the man in the yellow suit?
   _____
   _____

5. Why did Mae hit the man in the yellow suit?
   _____
   _____

6. Why had Angus Tuck looked at the body of the man on the ground almost enviously?
   _____
   _____

7. Why was it so important that Mae not go to the gallows?
   _____
   _____

8. How did Winnie feel about all that had happened?
   _____
   _____

9. How had Winnie changed since we first met her at the beginning of the book?
   _____
   _____

10. Do you agree with the constable that Winnie is a criminal because she had been an accomplice in freeing Mae from jail? Should she be punished? Give reasons for your opinions.
    _____
    _____

Comprehension Check *(cont.)*

(Section V)

1. Explain what Winnie did to "make a difference in the world."

_____

_____

_____

2.   *"Stone walls do not a prison make,*
          Nor iron bars a cage."

   What do you think these lines mean in reference to the Tucks?

   _____

   _____

   _____

3. At the end of the story, we see that the toad is still around. By saving the toad from the dog and pouring the special water on it, Winnie was doing something she thought was good. Compare that to what the man with the yellow suit wanted to do.

   _____

   _____

   _____

4. Why do you think that Winnie did not drink from the special spring herself?

   _____

   _____

   _____

5. Explain why Tuck said, "Good girl."

   _____

   _____

   _____

6. What do you think Winnie did the rest of her life?

   _____

   _____

Character Traits

Character traits are those qualities about a person which define his or her personality. They are the characteristics or features which distinguish the person from others. Some character traits are negative, while others are positive. Many times characters change their traits as they grow and mature or have to adapt to new and changing environments. Examples of terms describing character traits include resourceful, kind, sinister, naive, immature, determined, easygoing, etc.

In the activity below, examine and identify the character traits for each of the four main characters of the novel *Tuck Everlasting*. Then provide examples of supporting details from the novel which illustrate those characteristics.

Character	Trait	Supporting Details
Winnie Foster	• determined • loyal • brave • _____	_____ _____ _____ _____
The Stranger	• clever • greedy • evil • _____	_____ _____ _____ _____
Mae Tuck	• kind, caring • easy going • strong willed • _____	_____ _____ _____ _____
Angus Tuck	• intelligent • sensitive • envious • _____	_____ _____ _____ _____

Continue the above activity with the other characters. Choose two of the following characters and identify two traits and supporting details: Jesse, Miles, the grandmother, the constable.

_____   • _____   _____

                       • _____   _____

                       • _____   _____

_____   • _____   _____

                       • _____   _____

                       • _____   _____

Writing Options

Choose one of the following writing activities as a culminating exercise after reading *Tuck Everlasting*.

Develop the essay with an introduction, body, and conclusion. Use the back of this page to plan your essay. Write a rough draft. Then revise and edit.

Check for mechanics: *paragraphs, capitals, punctuation, spelling,* and *good sentence structure.* Try to vary your sentences and use expressive language.

Essay #1:

Write an essay comparing two of the characters from the novel *Tuck Everlasting*.

- Describe each character in appearance and personality. You may use your visual organizer about the characters and their character traits.

- Explain two ways in which the characters are similar and two ways in which they differ. Be sure to include specific characteristics and illustrate the examples with supporting details from the novel. The details may include actions, feelings, and/or words.

- Explain which character you would choose as a friend and why.

Essay #2:

Winnie Foster, the main character in the novel *Tuck Everlasting*, changes and grows. Discuss at least four different ways in which Winnie changes as a result of meeting the Tucks. Be sure to use specific examples from the novel as supporting details.

Essay #3:

One of the main themes of the novel *Tuck Everlasting* is "the wheel of life."

- What is the "wheel of life"? How is it explained in the novel? What is a person's place in the natural order of the world?

- How do the Tuck family members react or feel about their special circumstances?

- How does Winnie's decision at the end of the novel relate to her understanding of what Angus told her about life? Do you feel she made the right decision?

- What would you do if you had the opportunity to drink from the spring in the Foster wood? Explain why.

Sequence of Events/In the News

Some of the events from *Tuck Everlasting* are listed below. Rewrite them on the lines in correct chronological order.

- Winnie Foster is found unharmed.

- Mae Tuck escapes.

- A horse is stolen outside of Treegap.

- Winnie Foster disappears.

- Mysterious activity takes place in the Foster wood.

- Winnie Foster, age 78, dies.

- A stranger dressed in a yellow suit arrives in Treegap.

- The Fosters sell their wood.

- Mae Tuck is put in jail for murder.

- An unusual summer storm hits Treegap.

_____

_____

_____

_____

_____

_____

_____

_____

_____

_____

_____

_____

Extension: Choose one of the events listed above or think of another event to use as a news flash. Write a news report about the event. Make sure to use accurate information from the story in developing the five Ws: *who, what, where, when, or why.*

Create a classroom newsletter or newscast to be videotaped for broadcasting.

Story Diagram

There is often a basic pattern to the action of a story line. One such pattern can be shown as a W:

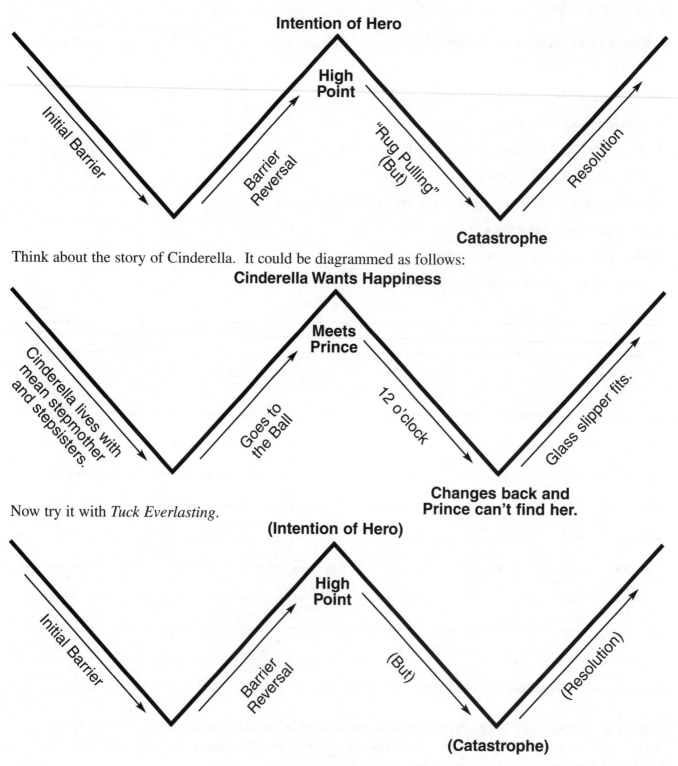

Think about the story of Cinderella. It could be diagrammed as follows:

Now try it with *Tuck Everlasting*.

Language Arts: Figurative Language

Tuck Everlasting is made interesting both by its exciting plot and by its use of figurative language. The story is enriched with similes, metaphors, and personification.

A *simile* compares things to one another by using the word *as* or *like*. It helps to better describe how something looks, feels, smells, tastes, or sounds by comparing the object to something else with which we are familiar.

Example: "*. . . this weary old earth . . . would have trembled on its axis like a beetle on a pin.*"

A *metaphor* also compares two different things, but it does not use a word of comparison such as *like* or *as*.

Example: "*At this, the toad stirred and blinked. It gave a heave of muscles and plopped its heavy mudball of a body a few inches farther away from her.*"

Personification is a form of figurative language in which an animal or object is given human characteristics.

Example: "*The graceful arms of the pines stretched out protectively in every direction . . . .*"

Listed below are examples of figurative language found in *Tuck Everlasting*. On the space provided by each example, write the name of the type of figurative language.

1. _____ ". . . a stack of wooden bowls, their sides smoothed to velvet."

2. _____ ". . . her backbone felt like a pipe full of cold running water..."

3. _____ "'I'm about dry as dust.'"

4. _____ "So the road went humbly by and made its way . . . ."

5. _____ "But at the same time he had a kind of grace, like a well-oiled marionette."

6. _____ "The sun was only just opening its own eye . . . ."

7. _____ "It (the music) was like a ribbon tying her to familiar things."

8. _____ "The last stains of sunset had melted away . . . ."

9. _____ ". . . enclosed by a capable iron fence some four feet high which clearly said, 'Move on—we don't want you here.'"

10. _____ " . . . the wrinkled surface of a tiny lake . . . ."

11. _____ "The sun was dropping fast now, a soft red sliding egg yolk, ..."

12. _____ " . . . they gathered around her like children at their mother's knee."

Challenge: Find and identify other examples of figurative language from the book.

Analyzing Poetry

Miles said to Winnie, "People got to do something useful if they're going to take up space in the world." "Doing something useful" does not always have to mean being the greatest of leaders in the world, just as long as it is being the best that you can be. Read the following poem:

A Little Fellow Follows Me*

A careful man I want to be,
    A little fellow follows me;
I do not dare to go astray,
    For fear he'll go the self-same way.

I cannot once escape his eyes,
    Whate'er he sees me do, he tries;
Like me he says he's going to be,
    The little chap who follows me.

He thinks that I am good and fine,
    Believes in every word of mine;
The base in me he must not see,
    The little chap who follows me.

I must remember as I go,
    Through summer's sun and winter's snow,
I am building for the years to be
    That little chap who follows me.

---

1. Who might the "little fellow" be? _____

   _____

2. What does the "little chap" do?_____

   _____

3. How does the "little chap" feel about the poet? _____

   _____

4. Why must the poet be a careful man?_____

   _____

5. How will the poet make a difference in the world? _____

   _____

6. How did Winnie make a difference in *Tuck Everlasting*?_____

   _____

7. How could you make a difference in the world?

       short-term goal(s) _____

       long-term goal(s) _____

8. How many stanzas are in the poem?_____

9. What type of rhyming pattern does the poet use?_____

   _____

10. Is this poem told in first person or third person? _____

*Taken from John Wooden's favorite poems in his *Player's Notebook* for Basketball Fundamentals Camp. Reprinted with permission.

Acrostics

In an acrostic, the letters of a word or name are written to provide the structure for the poem.

Make an acrostic for each person or place from the story. Think about what each is like. Then write a word that fits the person or place for each letter of the name. Use a thesaurus and/or a dictionary to help you out.

J oyful _____

E nthusiastic _____

S weet on Winnie _____

S eventeen _____

E ager _____

T hin _____

U nsettled _____

C urly hair _____

K ind _____

W _____

I _____

N _____

N _____

I _____

E _____

F _____

O _____

S _____

T _____

E _____

R _____

M _____

I _____

L _____

E _____

S _____

T _____

U _____

C _____

K _____

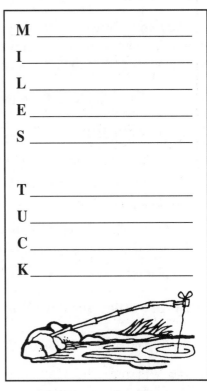

T _____

R _____

E _____

E _____

G _____

A _____

P _____

M _____

A _____

E _____

T _____

U _____

C _____

K _____

A _____

N _____

G _____

U _____

S _____

T _____

U _____

C _____

K _____

Terrarium

In Chapter 12 Tuck and Winnie go out on the pond to talk about the cycle of life. He says, "Everlasting's a wheel, turning, never stopping. The frogs is part of it, and the bugs, and the fish, and the wood thrush, too. And people." Tuck is talking about the interrelationships between living things and their environment. The natural balance of all things on earth keeps everything moving and alive. It is an ecosystem.

Make a miniature ecosystem by creating a terrarium. Within the terrarium, all conditions such as humidity, temperature, and soil nutrients are controlled and self-sustaining so that the glass or plastic container becomes the ecosystem for the plants inside it.

Choose plants that have the same kinds of requirements to flourish together inside your terrarium.

Materials Needed

- a glass container such as a fishbowl, an old aquarium, a brandy snifter, or a large jar
- a cover for the container which can be made of plastic wrap or glass
- coarse gravel
- small plastic screen or charcoal chips
- soil made up of humus, leaf mold, and loam (Packaged potting soil works well.)
- plants; water mister

Steps in Putting Together Your Terrarium

1. Spread a layer of coarse gravel at the bottom of the container to keep water from settling in the soil.

2. Place a plastic screen or charcoal chips on top of the gravel to separate the soil from the gravel. Charcoal chips will help to keep the soil clean.

3. Decide where you want the plants and carefully place them in the soil with a little clump of their own soil. Plants need to have enough space to grow, so avoid overcrowding.

4. Add moisture by spraying water on the plant leaves with a mister (any spray bottle will do). The soil should be moist but not soggy.

5. Put on the cover and watch the terrarium for a few days to adjust the moisture. If it seems too dry, add some mist. If it is too damp and water drops form on the container, then wipe off the glass and leave the cover off for awhile to dry it out.

6. Place your terrarium where it will get the appropriate amount of light but won't get too hot.

Once it is established, your terrarium should be able to thrive on its own, and you can enjoy your miniature ecosystem.

Music Boxes

Mae Tuck had a little music box which she took with her wherever she went. It was very special to her. Swiss music boxes of the late 1800s, like Mae's, can be considered one of the earliest types of mechanical instruments for the home. In 1877, Thomas Edison invented the speaking phonograph, which recorded and reproduced voices at home. It used a cylinder similar to the one in the music box, but instead of pins attached, grooves were made as one cranked the cylinder and talked. Because the music boxes were expensive and limited to only a few tunes, by the early 1900s people were using disc phonographs and talking machines, which led to record players, tape recorders, and all the electronic instruments we use today.

Nevertheless, music boxes have remained popular as collector items. There is something enchanting about music boxes which makes them appealing to people of all ages. They come in all shapes, sizes, and sounds. Learn how they are made. What makes the music? How does it work? Consider a player piano—is it a giant music box?

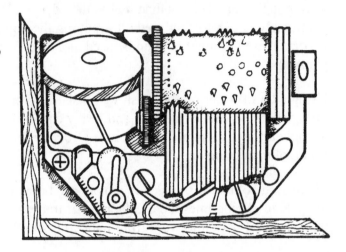

Challenge students to make their own music "boxes." Encourage creativity. These can be as simple as a music box made from rubber bands or as elaborate as a decorated box housing an instrument or radio. Have a Music Box Show. Each student brings in a music box. Music boxes can be the ones that students made or real ones. Display them. Group the student-made music boxes into categories such as most creative, most beautiful, best music, etc. Group the "real" ones into categories such as ceramic, wood, children's toys, holidays, size, type of music, or any other appropriate category. Have students give demonstrations of their music boxes. Let each talk about where it came from and whether it has a special meaning.

Watercolors

Reread the description of the woods at the beginning of Chapter 5. Close your eyes and envision what it looks like. Paint your idea of the woods, using watercolors.

Using watercolors is a technique that is free and enjoyable. Its beauty lies in the transparency of colors and the appearance of spontaneity. Before painting the impressions of the Treegap woods, you may want to review and practice some watercolor techniques which the students can use in their pictures.

There are two paper methods of using watercolor paints: wet and dry. The wet-paper method requires putting on a clear water wash before adding the color. This method makes the edges of the color very soft. Conversely, the dry-paper method is putting the colors directly on dry paper. These two methods can be used alone or together in the same paintings.

Using a lot of water on the brush will make a color transparent while a little dampness will create bold and heavy colors. Allowing white paper to show through as part of a picture is also an effective technique in watercolor painting.

In creating colors for the picture, colors can be blended right on the picture as well as beforehand on the palette. Sometimes the overlapping of transparent colors will automatically create a new color. For this reason, it is best to work from light colors to dark.

Have students try out different strokes, colors, and methods on practice paper in order to become comfortable with the medium. Then, as they get started with their painting, remind them that if they use pencil underdrawings, they should keep them very light and simple because they will show through. Change the dipping water frequently to keep the colors pure. And finally, the best watercolor paintings look as if they were painted very quickly, even though a great deal of thought and planning went into them.

Travel Brochure

Have students bring in travel brochures that they might have at home. Examine them together and decide on some common characteristics found in all of them, such as pictures, positive features of the area, things to do, places to stay, special activities, maps, advertisements, and endorsements.

From reading the descriptions of Treegap and its surrounding areas, make a travel brochure that would entice tourists to visit the area. Remember to include those things discussed that make a good travel brochure. Use your imagination to expand on the information you have from the story to make people want to take a vacation in Treegap.

Your Future City

Treegap certainly has changed from the small town at the beginning of the book to the growing city at the end. What causes cities to change? Population, technology, money, and needs of the people are a few reasons. Can you add to the list?

If you could plan your own city, what are the things you would want to include? Here are a few ideas to consider:

- public sectors
- private sectors
- entertainment
- recreation
- transportation
- shopping

- communication
- energy sources
- water
- food
- waste disposal
- government

Use your imagination. The city does not necessarily have to be on land as we know it today. Consider the ocean, space, moon, or even other planets.

Make a model of your city, using cardboard, clay, wood, sticks, boxes, plastic articles, paints, toys, and whatever else you can find to create your ideal city. Be prepared to give an oral explanation of its location, power sources, and environment.

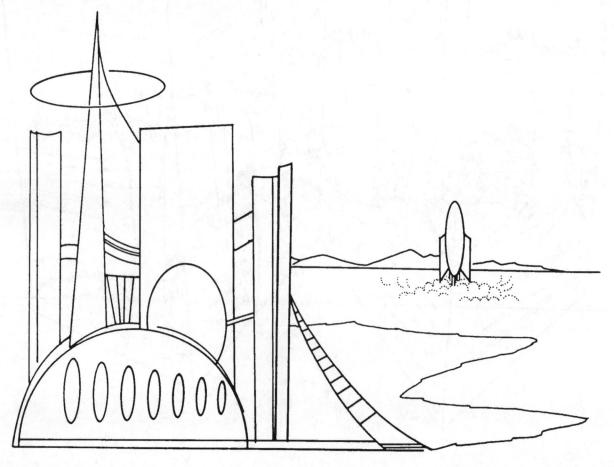

Unit Test

Matching: Match these quotes with the characters who said them.

Winnie   Mae   Tuck   Jesse   man in the yellow suit

1. _____ "It's no use having that dream. Nothing's going to change."

2. _____ "I want to grow again, and change. And if that means I got to move on at the end of it, then I want that, too . . . "

3. _____ " . . . Why, heck, Winnie, life's to enjoy yourself, isn't it? What else is it good for?"

4. _____ "I can't think why you're so upset. Did you really believe you could keep that water for yourselves?"

5. _____ "I'm not exactly sure what I'd do, you know, but something interesting—something that's all mine."

True or False: Write *true* or *false* next to each statement. If the statement is false, write it so it is true.

6. _____ Jesse wanted Winnie to wait until she was older to drink from the spring.

7. _____ Miles' wife knew the stranger's grandmother.

8. _____ The Tucks were foolish old people.

9. _____ The stranger had a good idea.

10. _____ Winnie was able to make a difference.

Short Answer: Provide a short answer for each of these questions.

11. When Winnie was first taken away by the Tucks, what helped to calm her down?

_____

12. How did the Tucks know that it was the water from the spring that caused them to stop changing?

_____

13. How did the man in the yellow suit find Winnie?

_____

14. How did the constable know that Mae should be arrested?

_____

15. What helped the escape plan to work?

_____

Unit Test

Contrasts: *Tuck Everlasting* deals with many contrasting elements. Write specifics from the story which support the contrasts listed.

Example: *life*—The Tucks were alive; they could not die.

        death—Eventually Winnie died.

16. *right* _____

     wrong _____

17. *neat* _____

     messy _____

18. *love* _____

     hate _____

19. *happy* _____

     sad _____

20. *choice* _____

     no choice _____

Responses: Explain the meanings of the following quotations from *Tuck Everlasting*.

21. "I'm not exactly sure what I'd do, you know, but something interesting—something that's all mine. Something that would make some kind of difference in the world."

     _____

     _____

22. "Being part of the whole thing, that's the blessing." _____

     _____

     _____

23. "I've got what you want, and you've got what I want."

     _____

24. "Mae Tuck must never go to the gallows."

     _____

25. "When she was seventeen—would she?"

     _____

Essay: Answer each of the following questions in well-developed paragraphs.

26. Do you think Winnie made the right decision? Why or why not? What is the author's point of view? Support your answers with specifics from the book.

27. What do you think Winnie gained from her experience? How did it change her?

Vocabulary Test

Multiple Choice: Choose the word which matches the definition.

1. A place where a criminal is hanged is called the _____ .
   (a) bovine   (b) gall   (c) gallows   (d) hearth

2. To be separated and alone is to be in _____ .
   (a) infinite   (b) intrusions   (c) indomitable   d) isolation

3. Elated is the opposite of _____ .
   (a) happy   (b) melancholy   (c) ecstatic   (d) remorseless

4. People who cannot read are _____ .
   (a) illiterates   (b) intense   (c) ignorant   (d) furrowed

5. Constable is to sheriff as minister is to _____ .
   (a) veranda   (b) parson   (c) swivel   (d) camphor

6. When someone is annoyed or irritated, he is _____ .
   (a) stationary   (b) threadbare   (c) exasperated   (d) accomplice

7. When something is hard to take or is a burden, it is _____ .
   (a) oppressive   (b) custody   (c) seized   (d) tranquil

8. A synonym for lodgings or a place to stay is _____ .
   (a) fragrant   (b) accommodations (c) brooch   (d) meager

9. When things are out of order, they are in _____ .
   (a) cahoots   (b) staggering   (c) revulsion   (d) disarray

10. Strong, energetic, and active are words that mean _____ .
    (a) luxurious   (b) comprehend   (c) vigorous   (d) vanity

Match the word to its definition.

_____ 11. bridle   A. get into, pierce, or soak through

_____ 12. rigid   B. easy to get to

_____ 13. penetrate   C. not flexible, stiff

_____ 14. accessible   D. a difficult experience

_____ 15. ordeal   E. harness that fits around the horse's head

Write a sentence with the word *reluctant* or *reluctantly*.

16. _____

_____

The Cay

by
Theodore Taylor

Table of Contents

About the Author

Theodore Taylor was born on June 23, 1921, in the southern town of Statesville, North Carolina. His father was Edward Riley Taylor, and his mother was Elmora Langhans Taylor.

Mr. Taylor attended Craddock Elementary School in Craddock, a workingman's town a few miles from Norfolk, Virginia. The elementary school was part of a larger building which served as the high school as well. While he received straight A's in English and history, problems in math caused him to graduate from high school a year late.

Mr. Taylor's writing career began early, while he was in high school. He was a cub reporter for the Portsmouth, Virginia, *Evening Star* from 1934–1939. He continued there as a sports editor until 1942.

His adult education included attendance at the U.S. Merchant Marine Academy at King's Point, New York, and Columbia University where he studied in the American Theater Wing.

When World War II came in 1942, he joined the merchant marines where he was an able-bodied seaman aboard a gasoline tanker in the Atlantic and Pacific Oceans. Later he was promoted to third mate. By the fall of 1944, he was drafted by the U.S. Navy as a cargo officer.

After his university studies in New York in 1955, he moved to Laguna Beach, California, so he could become active in the film industry. He made several film documentaries which took him all over the world. While on these trips, he continued to write articles for *McCall's, Redbook,* and *The Saturday Evening Post.*

Mr. Taylor wrote *The Cay* in 1969 and won 11 literary awards for it. It was featured as the Bell Telephone Special on NBC in 1974. Some awards for his writings include Commonwealth Club of California Silver Medal; Best Book Award, University of California, Irvine, in 1970 for *The Cay; The New York Times* Outstanding Books for the year of 1976 for *Battle in the Arctic Seas;* and Jefferson Cup Honor Book Award from the Virginia Library Association in 1987 for *Walking up a Rainbow.* Other books written by Theodore Taylor are *The Maldonado Miracle, The Trouble with Tuck, Tuck Triumphant,* and *The Teetoncey Trilogy.*

He has also written a prequel/sequel to *The Cay* titled *Timothy of the Cay.*

The Cay

by Theodore Taylor

(Avon Camelot, 1970)

(Available in Canada, Dell Seal; UK, Doubleday Bantam Dell; Australia,
Transworld Publishers)

Summary

Phillip Enright is a young boy happily living on an island in the Caribbean. The story takes place on the island of Curaçao, the largest of the Dutch islands off the Venezuelan coast. Phillip and his friends have great times pretending that they are saving their town from pirates of old or from raids by the tall-masted ships coming over the horizon. They like to pretend that these ships are Spanish galleons coming to bombard and pillage their town of Willemstad.

One day their wildest imaginings come true and create a nightmare for the boys and the people of the local islands. In February of 1942, German navy submarines appear. The towns of Saint Nicholas and Aruba are hit by shells. Next the Germans focus on Phillip's town of Willemstad, where the large oil refineries are making fuel to help the Allies in the fight against Germany. The people of Willemstad watch as the German U-boats sink tanker after tanker in an attempt to shut down the refineries and stop the oil from being sent to England.

The fighting becomes so intense that Phillip and his mother board a ship to return to the United States while his father stays in Willemstad at his job to help in fuel production. When Phillip's ship is torpedoed and sinks, he finds himself on a small raft with a black dockman named Timothy. Hours later, Phillip awakens and realizes he is blind as a result of a head injury. He must learn to work with Timothy in order to survive with very little food and water.

As the raft floats to a small cay, a new stage of adventure begins. Timothy's ingenuity as a survivor and provider leads Phillip to respect and trust him. Although he is blind, Phillip learns to fish and gather food to survive on the cay. Together they make plans to attract attention if airplanes are out looking for them.

Timothy protects Phillip when the cay is ravaged by a hurricane, but when the storm is over, Timothy is dead. Phillip survives alone until he is finally rescued by American sailors. It has been over four months since the ship he left Willemstad on sank. Phillip is reunited with his parents and eventually returns to live in the Dutch islands. His experiences on the cay with Timothy have changed his outlook on life in many ways.

Reading Response Journal

A reading response journal is one way to ensure that the reading of a novel touches each reader in a personal way.

The purpose of the journal is to record thoughts, ideas, observations, and questions as the novel is being read. Each entry should include a brief synopsis of the chapter, highlighting the main events or ideas. Readers should also include reactions, questions, and predictions. Example: I wonder . . . .

Assemble lined or unlined three-hole paper inside a fastened report cover. Add more paper as needed. A design may be drawn on the cover as the story unfolds.

Include the following information:

Title of Book _____

Author _____

Publisher _____

Place of Publication _____

Copyright _____

Chapter _____

_____

_____

_____

_____

_____

Chapter _____

_____

_____

_____

_____

_____

Vocabulary Lists

Define each of the vocabulary words in a self-made glossary for *The Cay*. Attach the glossary at the end of the reading response journal.

Section I
(Chapters 1–3)

alabaster	destroyer	distilled	calypso	channel
cleats	mutiny	Nazi	flimsy	hinged
hurricane	pitch	pontoon bridge	oil refinery	parched
pilot boat	stubborn	submarine	schooner	sextant
stern	ballast	U-boat	tanker	torpedo

Section II
(Chapters 4–7)

anxiously	Denmark	dishearten	doused	ebony
gasping	glare	harass	haze	drone
langosta	Panama	plunge	scan	ignore
spicy	steel	tensely	triangle	shudder
biscuit	bucking	clammy	cay	lulled

Section III
(Chapters 8–10)

bamboo	carnival	catchment	crowing	miserable
driftwood	funnel	hum	patient	rare
murmur	mussels	palm fronds	smoldering	squall
reef	satisfaction	scorpions	vines	weaving
recollection	supports	urchins	dawn	malaria

Section IV
(Chapters 11–14)

abrupt	bearing	cane	convince	coral
sensation	dependent	diameter	echo	faint
foundations	grindstone	harsh	damp	keg
melon	salvage	fashioned	skate	slope
sinkers	stranded	tethered	treacherous	voodoo

Section V
(Chapters 15–19)

bleat	burrow	frame	fury	groped
described	flayed	inspect	lee	jab
gusted	howl	moray eel	rattle	receded
locate	limp	slithering	swirl	tatters
scallop	screech	consciousness	debris	honing

Vocabulary Practice

Complete the sentences using the terms on the vocabulary list.

Section I (Chapters 1–3)

1. While submerged, the crew on the _____ viewed the enemy through the periscope.

2. A _____ exploded upon impact.

3. The _____ hit an embankment while sailing.

4. The ocean liner was able to pass through the _____ .

5. The joyous _____ music filled the air.

6. The intense heat from the sun _____ the boy's throat.

7. The approaching _____ brought strong winds.

8. The _____ building was destroyed during the storm.

9. The boys stood on the _____ , gazing at the sunset.

10. The sight of the _____ off the coast caused fear and anxiety on the island.

11. The _____ destroyers were firing at the American boats.

12. The explosion at the _____ caused an immense glow in the sky.

13. The _____ sailors could not be swayed to come ashore.

14. The crew planned a _____ against the officer in charge.

15. The _____ was filled with oil before leaving the harbor.

16. The detective's ability to solve the crime _____ upon one clue.

17. The reading on the _____ helped to determine the longitude and latitude.

18. The captain stood at the _____ of the ship, looking forward to the bow.

Section II (Chapters 4–7)

19. The _____ is a delicious meal from the sea.

Vocabulary Practice *(cont.)*

20. The _____ were iced with a sugary topping.

21. The diver stood _____ at the edge of the board.

22. The lifeguard _____ into the pool to save the infant.

23. The island was surrounded by a foggy _____ , preventing it from being seen.

24. The _____ of the airplane was heard from offshore.

25. The parent could no longer _____ the baby's crying.

26. The fireman _____ the fire before the flames spread.

27. Due to his asthma, the boy was _____ for air.

28. Mexican food is known for being _____ .

29. The girl was _____ awaiting an important phone call.

30. The uninhabited _____ was so small it did not appear on any map.

31. The canal in _____ was built and was controlled for a long time by the United States.

32. The capital of _____ is Copenhagen.

33. Mosquitoes and torrid heat will _____ the hikers.

34. Another illness will _____ the elderly patient.

Section III (Chapters 8–10)

35. A coral _____ is often found in tropical seas and oceans.

36. _____ branches were used as fishing poles.

37. Walls _____ the roof of the building.

38. Buttons are made from the shells of freshwater _____ .

39. The sting from a _____ is poisonous.

40. The _____ was carved into an interesting sculpture.

41. The fire was kept _____ all night long.

Vocabulary Practice *(cont.)*

42. The _____ can be used as a covering on a hut.

43. The _____ can be twisted into a long rope.

44. They built a _____ to capture the rainwater.

45. The clerk used a _____ to transfer the milk back into the bottle.

46. You must be _____ while waiting in line at the movies.

47. The sudden _____ brought much snow to the city.

48. It gave the teacher much _____ to learn that all the students passed the test.

49. When the _____ came to town, the streets were lined with tourists.

50. The infant was _____ due to the high fever.

Sections IV (Chapters 11–14)

51. The boys were _____ off the coast when their boat capsized.

52. Their _____ cries for help were unheeded because they could not be heard.

53. An _____ change in the weather forced the airports to close.

54. _____ road conditions made car travel unsafe.

55. Cantaloupes, honeydews, and watermelons are different kinds of _____ .

56. The _____ of the mountainside was perfect for sledding.

57. The fishing poles were _____ to the tree to prevent their loss during a storm.

58. The hikers always bring a _____ of fresh water along.

59. His belief in _____ caused him to be very superstitious.

60. The police were _____ the killer was a female.

Vocabulary Practice *(cont.)*

61. Children are _____ upon their parents until they can earn a living on their own.

62. The _____ for learning are established early in life.

63. The _____ of a circle is equal to twice the radius.

64. The children removed their _____ clothing to prevent a chill.

65. The _____ was seen swimming close to shore.

66. The _____ reverberated throughout the caverns.

Section V (Chapters 15–19)

67. The _____ of the storm littered the beach with _____ .

68. Can you _____ the snake by listening for its _____ ?

69. When the winds _____ , the explorers were able to _____ the island.

70. The boy _____ through the sand in search of his lost ring.

71. _____ , clams, muscles, and oysters are all bivalves.

72. The sting from the _____ was paralyzing.

73. His clothes were in _____ after he survived the tornado.

74. The squirrel will _____ a hole in which to place his supply of acorns for the winter.

75. The swimmer was _____ from exhaustion after the five-mile race.

76. The _____ of the owl could be heard for miles.

77. The noise from the plane's engines made my head _____ .

78. The wind _____ at a speed of 75 miles per hour during the hurricane.

79. The actor is _____ as tall, dark, and handsome.

80. The _____ snake climbed along the branches of the palm trees.

About the Author Activity

After reading about Theodore Taylor, complete the following outline.

I. Early Life
    A. Birthdate and place _____
    B. Parents _____

II. Education
    A. Elementary _____
    B. High School _____
        1. marks
            a. English   _____
            b. history   _____
            c. math   _____
        2. graduation
    C. High school activities
        1. 1934–1939 _____
        2. 1939–1942 _____
    D. College
        1. _____
        2. _____

III. First Career
    A. 1942
    B. Positions
        1. _____
        2. _____
    C. 1944 _____

IV. Second Career
    A. 1955
    B. Writer for magazines
        1. _____
        2. _____
        3. _____

V. Accomplishments
    A. 1969–1970: Eleven literary awards for *The Cay*, including the following:
        1. _____
        2. _____
    B. 1976—*New York Times* Outstanding Book Award for _____
    C. 1987—Jefferson Cup Award for _____
    D. Other books
        1. _____
        2. _____
        3. _____
        4. _____
        5. _____

Comprehension Check

Section I: Chapters 1–3

1. In your response journal, write a one-paragraph summary of the major events in each chapter of this section. Then complete the rest of the questions on this page.

2. In the beginning of the story, why are the residents of Willemstad worried and fearful?

   _____

   _____

3. Why have the Germans come to these islands all the way from Europe? What do they want?

   _____

   _____

4. What is Phillip's father's job at the refinery?

   _____

   _____

5. Why doesn't Phillip's mother particularly like it in Willemstad?

   _____

   _____

6. Where are Phillip and his mother attempting to go to escape the threat of the Germans? Why do they choose to go there instead of somewhere else?

   _____

   _____

7. What happens that prevents Phillip and his mother from reaching their destination?

   _____

   _____

8. Who is Phillip's shipmate at sea? Describe him.

   _____

   _____

9. From what you have read so far about Phillip's mother, how do you think she might feel about Timothy?

   _____

   _____

10. Describe Phillip's feelings toward Timothy when they are on the raft.

    _____

    _____

Comprehension Check *(cont.)*

Section II: Chapters 4–7

1. In your response journal, write a one-paragraph summary of the major events in each chapter of this section. Then complete the rest of the questions on this page.

2. Where is Timothy from? Why does Phillip think he is from Africa?

   _____

3. In a well-written sentence, describe what suddenly happens to Phillip that makes Timothy feel even more responsible for him.

   _____

   _____

4. Why does Phillip become angry with Timothy and his mother?

   _____

   _____

5. In a few well-written sentences, characterize Phillip in this section. Include his emotions as part of your characterization.

   _____

   _____

6. Why does Timothy tell Phillip to keep away from the edge of the raft?

   _____

   _____

7. How does Timothy attempt to signal an airplane?

   _____

   _____

8. After Timothy sights the cay, what happens to Phillip that enrages Timothy?

   _____

   _____

9. Why does Timothy decide to abandon the raft and go to the desolate island that contains no drinking water?

   _____

   _____

10. In a well-written sentence, tell what you think prevents Timothy from killing the cat.

   _____

   _____

Comprehension Check *(cont.)*

Section III: Chapters 8–10

1. In your response journal, write a one-paragraph summary of the major events in each chapter of this section. Then complete the rest of the questions on this page.

2. Phillip assumes that his father and other men in boats are searching for him, but what does he fail to understand?

   _____

   _____

3. What does Timothy make that he proudly shows to Phillip?

   _____

   _____

4. Phillip is concerned about which two deadly inhabitants that might be on the island?

   _____

   _____

5. Why does Phillip refuse to speak to Timothy when Timothy shows up with three lobsters?

   _____

   _____

6. What does it mean when Timothy tells Phillip, "Young bahss, be an outrageous mahn if you like, but 'ere I'm all you got"?

   _____

   _____

7. What are the two things that Timothy does to help them get rescued from the island?

   _____

   _____

8. Phillip feels good because he discovers that he can do something that Timothy cannot do. What is it?

   _____

   _____

9. What causes Timothy to strike Phillip in the face?

   _____

   _____

10. What does Phillip discover about Timothy that makes him begin to change and to say, "I want to be your friend"?

    _____

    _____

Comprehension Check *(cont.)*

Section IV: Chapters 11–14

1. In your response journal, write a one-paragraph summary of the major events in each chapter of this section. Then complete the rest of the questions on this page.

2. What does Phillip do so that he can walk around the whole island without Timothy's help?

    _____

    _____

3. Why does Phillip think that Timothy is trying to make him independent?

    _____

    _____

4. In a well-written sentence, describe what Timothy says is the cause of all of their troubles.

    _____

    _____

5. What does Timothy finally do to stop the "evil jumbi"?

    _____

    _____

6. What happens to Timothy when he gets that "devil, d'fever"?

    _____

    _____

7. After the fever, what steps does Timothy take to make Phillip even more self-reliant?

    _____

    _____

8. What does Phillip do that convinces Timothy that he is becoming self-reliant?

    _____

    _____

9. What sounds does Timothy hear which indicate that a storm is coming?

    _____

    _____

10. List three precautionary things that Timothy does before the storm hits the cay.

    _____

    _____

Comprehension Check *(cont.)*

Section V: Chapters 15–19

1. In your response journal, write a one-paragraph summary of the major events in each chapter of this section. Then complete the rest of the questions on this page.

2. In a few sentences, describe the storm that hit Timothy and Phillip's island.

   _____

   _____

3. How does Timothy prevent Phillip from becoming seriously injured?

   _____

   _____

4. Why does the storm stop for about 30 minutes?

   _____

   _____

5. What happens to Timothy during the storm, and what was the consequence?

   _____

   _____

6. What does Phillip find when he looks for the fishing poles?

   _____

   _____

7. In a well-written sentence, explain why the birds attack Phillip.

   _____

   _____

8. While he is diving for lobster, what happens to Phillip?

   _____

   _____

9. What does Phillip do to solve the problem of his rescue smoke not being seen?

   _____

   _____

10. In a paragraph, describe the ways that Phillip changes while he is on the cay.

   _____

   _____

"Dat Be True"

Phillip found Timothy's beautiful West Indies accent to be unclear at times. Below are some sentences from the story. Rewrite them in standard English, in the way you would say them.

1. "D'mahn who feeshes follows d'feesh. Sartainly, d'feesh be 'ere . . . ." _____

    _____

2. "Timothy, my own self, long ago could climb d'palm veree easy."

    _____

    _____

3. "Dis be a western starm, I b'guessin'. Dey outrageous strong when dey come."

    _____

    _____

4. "D'islan' is 'bout one mile long, an' a half wide, shaped like d'melon."

    _____

    _____

5. "Phill-eep, 'as it evah come into your own self that I might be poorly again some marnin'?"

    _____

    _____

6. "Do not be despair, young bahss. Someone will fin' us. Many schooner go by dis way, an' dis also be d'ship track to Jamaica, an' on."

    _____

    _____

    _____

7. "We 'ave rare good luck, young bahss. D'wattah kag did not bus' when d' reff was launch, an' we 'have a few biscuit, some cholade, an' d' matches in d' tin is dry. So we 'ave rare good luck."

    _____

    _____

    _____

    _____

    _____

Who? What? Where? When?

Throughout *The Cay*, Theodore Taylor uses descriptive writing to present detailed settings to enable the reader to visualize the scene.

Match the terms which answer *who, what, where,* and *when* to the descriptions below.

- Henrik
- the hut
- Phillip's father
- Phillip

- malaria fever
- Phillip's mother
- the palm tree
- S.S. *Hato* explosion

- the cay
- before the storm
- Virginia
- the sea before the storm

- Stew Cat
- Timothy
- the rain
- Chinese sailors

1 It was so still over our cay that we could hear nothing but the rustling of the lizards.	**2** His face was round and he was chubby. His hair was straw colored and his cheeks were always red.	**3** They are very frightened, and some of the people who are angry with them would not sail the little ships either.	**4** Everything was bright red and there were great crackling noises. Heat from the fire washed over us.
5 It was two feet in diameter because I could easily put my hands around to the back . . . The bark was rough against my hands and feet.	**6** No people. No water. No food. No phones. It was not any better than the raft.	**7** She pulled me up against her body. She was like that. One minute, shaking me; the next holding me.	**8** A crack like d'rifle...It can make d'shot all right.
9 Timothy began to mumble and laugh . . . He began to shiver again . . . He never really regained his strength.	**10** I liked it because it was something I could hear and feel: not something I must see.	**11** Something brushed against my arm, and I yelled out in terror.	**12** It was about eight feet wide and six feet deep, with supports made of wood picked off the beach.
13 He didn't just order her to stay. But he wasn't that kind of a man.	**14** He was ugly. His nose was flat and his face was broad: his head was a mass of wiry gray hair.	**15** You are very brown and very lean.	**16** I remembered the summers with lightning bugs and honeysuckle smells; the cold winters when the fields would all be brown.

Sequencing

Some of the events from the story are listed below. Rewrite them on the lines in correct chronological order.

- Timothy dies.
- The S.S. *Hato,* with Phillip and his mother on board, is torpedoed.
- Timothy makes a vine rope to guide Phillip to the beach.
- Phillip and Henrik go to Punda to watch the war preparations.
- Timothy teaches Phillip how to weave mats.
- Phillip is bitten by a moray eel.
- Timothy pulls Phillip onto a raft.
- Phillip is reunited with his parents.
- Phillip loses his eyesight.
- A hurricane blows over the island.

1. _____

2. _____

3. _____

4. _____

5. _____

6. _____

7. _____

8. _____

9. _____

10. _____

Character Traits

Character traits are those qualities about a person which define his or her personality. They are the characteristics or features which distinguish the person from others. Some character traits are negative, while others are positive. In life, people generally attempt to change the negative qualities into positive ones.

Timothy and Phillip, the two main characters in the novel *The Cay*, exhibited different character traits. However, both characters did share some personality characteristics which enabled them to develop a bond of friendship.

Below each heading, write the character trait which best applies to Timothy or Phillip. If the trait applies to both, write it below each name. Be able to cite examples which illustrate each trait.

Traits

- self-centered
- prejudiced
- good-natured
- illiterate
- young
- flexible
- caring

- experienced
- stubborn
- nurturing
- rich
- forgiving
- quick learner
- strong

- independent
- agile
- educated
- poor
- old
- knowledgeable
- smart

Timothy	Phillip

Explain two ways in which Phillip changed physically and emotionally.

Physically   **Emotionally**

_____   _____

_____   _____

On the Map

Willemstad, Curaçao, is the opening setting of *The Cay*. Find out more about this island by reading the map and filling in the blanks below.

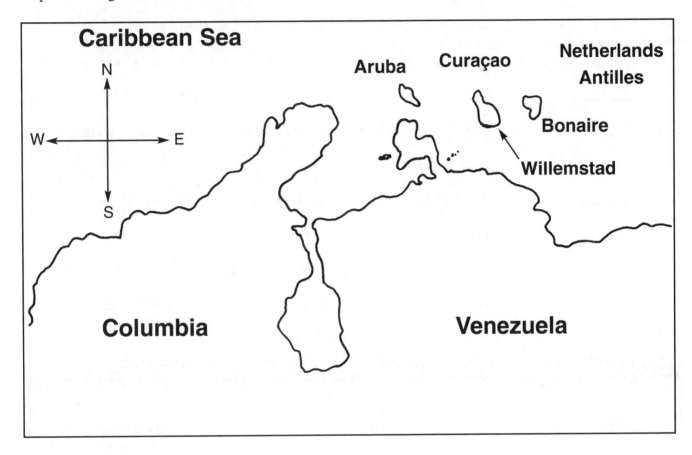

1. _____ is the island west of Curaçao.

2. The sea surrounding Curaçao is the _____ .

3. The country directly south of Curaçao is _____ .

4. The capital of Venezuela is _____ .

5. _____ is the country west of Venezuela.

6. Curaçao and Bonaire make up the _____ Antilles.

7. Curaçao is this direction from Colombia. _____ .

8. _____ is the capital of Curaçao.

Extensions:

Find out about Curaçao. Write a short report or make a web that contains the following information about the island: the type of government, its predominant religion, language(s) spoken there, way of life, education, climate, and history.

Sea Life of the Cay

Timothy and Phillip encountered many types of sea life on their small island. See if you can remember them. Write the correct name next to each description, using the word bank for help.

1. _____ These small, black, round sea animals have sharp, poisonous spines.

2. _____ Phillip learned to pry these loose and use them as bait to catch fish.

3. _____ First they were boiled in sea water; then they were cooked in fresh water.

4. _____ This animal bit Phillip when he dived into the hole to catch a lobster.

5. _____ They flopped right onto the raft. Timothy and Phillip ate them raw.

6. _____ When Phillip fell off the raft, Timothy rescued Phillip from these.

7. _____ This small fish was speared on the reef and boiled over a low fire.

8. _____ Timothy tried to make a stew from this plant, but it was too bitter to eat.

9. _____ These sea creatures could be seen in the clear water around the cay.

10. _____ Timothy had to dive to catch these lobsters.

Word Bank

• sharks	• seaweed	• flying fish
• mussels	• moray eel	• organpipe coral
• sea urchins	• langosta	• sea grape leaves
	• pompano	

Extension: Place the words in the word bank in alphabetical order below.

1. _____   6. _____

2. _____   7. _____

3. _____   8. _____

4. _____   9. _____

5. _____   10. _____

Unit Test

Matching: Match these quotes with the characters who said them.

• Mr. Enright	• Mrs. Enright	• Phillip	• Timothy	• sailor

_____ 1. "There is more danger in the trip back than there is in staying here."

_____ 2. "They are not the same as you, Phillip. They are different, and they live
                             differently. That's the way it must be."

_____ 3. "Young bahss, d' wind 'as shift. You'll be warmer on dis side."

_____ 4. "Something happened to me that day on the cay. I'm not quite sure what
                             it was even now, but I had begun to change."

_____ 5. "You wouldn't believe what's up there."

True or False: Write *true* or *false* next to each statement below. Correct the false statements so that
they are true.

_____ 1. Phillip's mother was not prejudiced.

_____ 2. Mr. Enright and his family boarded the ship S.S. *Hato*.

_____ 3. Phillip, at first, did not like Timothy.

_____ 4. Stew Cat died in the hurricane.

_____ 5. Phillip lived on the island for the rest of his life.

Short Answer: Provide a short answer for each of these questions.

1. Where was the S.S. *Hato* bound? _____

2. Why didn't Mr. Enright go with Phillip and his mother?_____

3. Why did the Germans form an embargo around Curaçao? _____

4. Where did Timothy hide Stew Cat while he was killing the "evil jumbi"? _____

5. After Phillip was listed as officially lost at sea, what did his mother do? _____

   _____

6. Describe two problems that Phillip had. _____

   _____

7. How did the story end? _____

8. Name two ways that Phillip helped Timothy. _____

9. Name two ways that Timothy helped Phillip. _____

10. Survival is a theme in *The Cay*. Give three examples of survival techniques that either Phillip or
    Timothy used.

   _____

Vocabulary Test

Match the word to the definition.

_____	1. fronds	A. something that catches water
_____	2. reef	B. smoking without flames
_____	3. smoldering	C. ridge of rock or sand
_____	4. moray eel	D. leaves of a palm tree
_____	5. catchment	E. dangerous snake-like fish

_____	6. malaria	A. witchcraft
_____	7. submerged	B. disease from mosquitoes
_____	8. lulled	C. black
_____	9. ebony	D. put to sleep
_____	10. voodoo	E. underwater

_____	11. fashioned	A. type of wind
_____	12. squall	B. tied up
_____	13. tatters	C. created
_____	14. tethered	D. tropical storm with an eye
_____	15. hurricane	E. ragged

Complete the sentences using correct words from the word bank.

Word Bank	
A. recollection	F. honing
B. sextant	G. sensation
C. mutiny	H. patient
D. harass	I. schooners
E. debris	J. anxiously

_____ 16. "Tis a good ting not to _____ d'soul ovah dis."

_____ 17. I accomplished a lot in three days, even putting a new edge on Timothy's knife by _____ it on coral.

_____ 18. The _____ were quiet against the docks inside the channel.

_____ 19. If you are blind, the _____ of falling can be terrifying.

_____ 20. He shook his head. "I 'ave no _____ o' anythin 'cept dese islands.

Baseball Terminology

Write each spelling word three times. Use cursive writing.

1. pitcher _____ _____ _____
2. shortstop _____ _____ _____
3. outfield _____ _____ _____
4. league _____ _____ _____
5. catcher _____ _____ _____
6. home run _____ _____ _____
7. stadium _____ _____ _____
8. baseman _____ _____ _____
9. double _____ _____ _____
10. triple _____ _____ _____
11. cleats _____ _____ _____
12. summer _____ _____ _____
13. glove _____ _____ _____
14. mitt _____ _____ _____
15. steal _____ _____ _____
16. dugout _____ _____ _____

Use the spelling list to complete the puzzles.

1.
2.
3.
4.
5.
6.
7.
8.

9.
10.
11.
12.
13.
14.
15.
16.

Baseball Terminology (cont.)

• pitcher	• league	• outfield	• shortstop
• catcher	• baseman	• stadium	• home run
• triple	• double	• cleats	• mitt
• glove	• summer	• dugout	• steal

Arrange the spelling words in alphabetical order.

1. _____

2. _____

3. _____

4. _____

5. _____

6. _____

7. _____

8. _____

9. _____

10. _____

11. _____

12. _____

13. _____

14. _____

15. _____

16. _____

Dictionary Usage

Pitch*er [pĭch r] n. The baseball player who pitches the ball to the batter.

Pitch*er [pĭch r] n. 1. The container used to hold and pour out liquids, having a handle on one side and a lip or spout on the other. 2. a. A pitcher with something in it: a pitcher of milk. b. The amount that a pitcher holds.

Pronunciation Key

ă pat / ā pay / â care / ä father / ĕ pet /
ē be / ĭ it pit / ī pie / i fierce / ŏ pot /
ō go / ô paw, for / oi oil / o͝o book /
o͞o boot / ou out / ŭ cut / û fur /
th the / th thin / *hw* which / *zh* vision /
ə *a*go, it*e*m, penc*i*l, at*o*m, circ*u*s

1. How many syllables are in the word *pitcher?*_____

2. In the respelling, after which syllable is the accent mark placed? _____

3. What part of speech is the word pitcher? _____

4. Which entry of pitcher is being referred to in the following sentence?
    The pitcher's fastball travels at a speed of 70 miles per hour. _____

5. The *i* in pitcher is pronounced like the *i* in which word in the pronunciation key?_____

Baseball Terminology *(cont.)*

Definitions: Match the spelling words to correct definitions. Use a dictionary to help you.

_____ 1. pitcher

a. grass-covered playing area from the diamond to the end of the field

_____ 2. league

b. position between second and third bases

_____ 3. outfield

c. player stationed behind home plate

_____ 4. shortstop

d. one of three players who play defensively at the bases

_____ 5. catcher

e. large, often unroofed structure in which athletic events are held

_____ 6. baseman

f. long hit that travels over the outfield, allowing batter to score a run

_____ 7. stadium

g. hit that enables the batter to reach third base

_____ 8. home run

h. hit that enables batter to reach second base

_____ 9. triple

i. pieces of iron, rubber, or leather attached to soles of shoes to prevent slipping

_____ 10. double

j. large, padded leather mitten or glove worn to protect the hand when catching a baseball, usually by catchers

_____ 11. cleats

k. season of year between spring and autumn

_____ 12. mitt

l. long, low shelter at the side of a baseball field for players

_____ 13. glove

m. to gain another base without the ball being batted while the ball is being pitched

_____ 14. summer

n. player who pitches the ball to the batter

_____ 15. dugout

o. association of sport teams from the same area

_____ 16. steal

p. padded leather covering with room for fingers, worn over hand to aid in catching ball

Test Yourself—Unit One

Circle the correctly spelled word. Rewrite it in cursive on the line.

1.	pitcher	piture	pitchur	_____
2.	leegue	league	leage	_____
3.	outfeeld	out field	outfield	_____
4.	shorstop	shortstop	sortstop	_____
5.	catcher	cacher	catzure	_____
6.	baseman	basman	base man	_____
7.	staydium	stayedeum	stadium	_____
8.	triple	tripel	tripple	_____
9.	homerun	home run	hoanrum	_____
10.	dubble	doubel	double	_____
11.	cleets	cleats	cleetz	_____
12.	mit	mutt	mitt	_____
13.	glouve	glove	glouve	_____
14.	sumer	summor	summer	_____
15.	dug out	dugout	duugout	_____
16.	steal	steel	stiel	_____

Circle the word which completes the sentence properly.

1. The (pitcher, picture) stayed in the game for five innings.

2. Can the runner (steal, steel) home?

3. The team at bat waited in the (outfield, dugout).

4. The (catcher, shortstop) caught the ground ball.

5. The second (catcher, baseman) made a (double, home run) play.

6. (Cleats, A glove) help the players get more traction while running.

7. A catcher is protected with special equipment and uses a (mitt, glove) to catch the ball.

8. When a batter hits a (triple, summer), he rounds the bases and stops at third base.

Words from Tuck Everlasting

Directions: Write each word three times in cursive on the lines provided.

1. lingered   _____   _____   _____

2. rigid   _____   _____   _____

3. fragrant   _____   _____   _____

4. illiterate   _____   _____   _____

5. ordeal   _____   _____   _____

6. accommodations   _____   _____   _____

7. flailing   _____   _____   _____

8. revulsion   _____   _____   _____

9. remorse   _____   _____   _____

10. accomplice   _____   _____   _____

11 ignorant   _____   _____   _____

12. custody   _____   _____   _____

13. staunch   _____   _____   _____

14. ghastly   _____   _____   _____

15. verandah   _____   _____   _____

Words from Tuck Everlasting *(cont.)*

Directions: Place the words from page 95 in alphabetical order in column one. In column two, divide each word into syllables. Then, in column three, place the accent mark at the end of the most heavily stressed syllables.

	Column 1	**Column 2**	**Column 3**
1.			
2.			
3.			
4.			
5.			
6.			
7.			
8.			
9.			
10.			
11.			
12.			
13.			
14.			
15.			

Directions: Use the exercise to help you answer the following questions.

1. What word had one syllable? _____

2. What words had two syllables?

   _____   _____   _____

   _____   _____   _____

   _____

3. What words had three syllables?

   _____   _____   _____

   _____   _____   _____

4. What word has five syllables?

   _____

Words from Tuck Everlasting *(cont.)*

Complete the following crossword puzzle with the words from page 95.

Across

3. a difficult or painful experience
6. firm, strong
9. someone who aids a lawbreaker in a crime
12. unable to read or write
14. a roofed porch or balcony
15. stiff, inflexible, unbending

Down

1. the act of right of caring for; guarding
2. without education or knowledge
4. bitter regret or guilt
5. terrifying; dreadful
7. living space or lodging
8. wildly moving arms or legs
10. having a pleasant odor
11. a feeling of strong disgust or loathing
13. remained in place longer than usual

Test Yourself—Unit Two

Circle the word that is spelled correctly.

	A	B	C	D
1.	revultion	revulshun	revulsion	revolsion
2.	remorse	remores	renorse	remoarse
3.	flaling	flaileing	flailing	flayling
4.	accommplish	acomplish	acommplish	accomplice
5.	accomodations	accommodations	acomodations	acomodshun
6.	ordeal	oardeal	ordeel	ordele
7.	ignoreant	ignoraunt	ogknorant	ignorant
8.	iliterate	illiterate	illitterate	illitrate
9.	custode	custoady	custody	kustody
10.	fragrant	fraygrant	phragrant	fragrunt
11.	stanch	staunch	stounch	staunnch
12.	riggid	riged	reggid	rigid
13.	gastly	ghastly	hasthly	ghasly
14.	lingered	lingred	lignered	lengered
15.	veranda	vernada	viranda	verandah

Write a sentence with each of the following words.

16. accomplish _____

_____

17. accommodations _____

_____

18. ignorant _____

_____

19. illiterate _____

_____

20. ordeal _____

_____

More Words from Tuck Everlasting

Write each word three times in cursive on the lines provided.

1. tangent   _____   _____   _____

2. ambled   _____   _____   _____

3. tranquil   _____   _____   _____

4. infinite   _____   _____   _____

5. melancholy   _____   _____   _____

6. ceased   _____   _____   _____

7. reluctantly   _____   _____   _____

8. gallows   _____   _____   _____

9. isolation   _____   _____   _____

10. intrusion   _____   _____   _____

11. elated   _____   _____   _____

12. disarray   _____   _____   _____

13. vanity   _____   _____   _____

14. enveloped   _____   _____   _____

15. receded   _____   _____   _____

More Words from *Tuck Everlasting* (cont.)

Place the words on page 99 in alphabetical order in column I. In column II divide the word into syllables. Then place the accent mark at the end of the most heavily stressed syllable. Refer to a dictionary if necessary.

Column I	**Column II**
1. _____	_____
2. _____	_____
3. _____	_____
4. _____	_____
5. _____	_____
6. _____	_____
7. _____	_____
8. _____	_____
9. _____	_____
10. _____	_____
11. _____	_____
12. _____	_____
13. _____	_____
14. _____	_____
15. _____	_____

Which word has only one syllable? _____

List the words with two syllables. _____

_____   _____   _____

List the words with three syllables. _____   _____

_____   _____   _____

_____   _____

List the words with four syllables. _____   _____

More Words from Tuck Everlasting *(cont.)*

Complete each sentence with the correct spelling word. Check the dictionary for definitions.

1. The boy _____ lent his new bike to his cousin.

2. A _____ feeling pervaded the room when the report of the accident was given.

3. The gentle breeze whispered through the grass, making the peaceful, _____ spring day cool and comfortable.

4. The cows _____ slowly along the path.

5. There were an _____ number of correct answers to the question.

6. The clown _____ his acrobatics when the curtain came down on the stage.

7. The new _____ were constructed behind the old jail.

8. Due to all the questions, the professor drifted off on a _____ while lecturing to the class.

9. After the storm, the river _____ to its normal water level.

10. The whole school was _____ with smoke after the fire.

11. The house was in _____ after the guests left.

12. She displays her _____ by staring at herself each time she passes a mirror.

13. The contagious disease caused the girl to be placed in _____ in the hospital.

14. The English class was _____ when they heard there would be no test.

15. Some questions can be an _____ into a person's privacy.

Test Yourself—Unit Three

Circle the word that is spelled correctly.

	A	B	C	D
1.	tangentt	tangant	tangent	tangente
2.	ambeld	ambeled	embled	ambled
3.	trankwil	tranquil	tanquil	trainquil
4.	receed	receeded	reseded	receded
5.	vanity	vanete	vanety	vanitie
6.	inveloped	enveloped	envelloped	envelopeed
7.	disaray	desarray	disarray	dissaray
8.	elated	ellated	elayted	elatid
9.	introosion	intrusion	intrution	intrushun
10.	galows	galous	glowers	gallows
11.	reluctently	relucktently	reluctantly	relucktantly
12.	isolation	isolasion	isolashun	icolation
13.	cessed	ceased	seased	ceassed
14.	meloncollie	melancollie	melancholy	melancolly
15.	infinete	enfinite	infinit	infinite

16. List which of the following spelling words would appear on a dictionary page with the guide words "**indefinite – – – intrude**."

disarray   isolation   intrusion   infinite   envelope   interest

_____

Write the base word of each of the following words.

17. enveloped _____   19. elated _____

18. receded _____   20. ambled _____

What general rule could be applied to each of the above words?

_____

_____

Words from The Cay

Write each word three times in cursive on the lines provided.

1. hurricane _____ _____ _____

2. mutiny _____ _____ _____

3. stubborn _____ _____ _____

4. ballast _____ _____ _____

5. submarine _____ _____ _____

6. channel _____ _____ _____

7. torpedo _____ _____ _____

8. anxious _____ _____ _____

9. drone _____ _____ _____

10. satisfaction _____ _____ _____

11. smolder _____ _____ _____

12. treacherous _____ _____ _____

13. conscious _____ _____ _____

14. debris _____ _____ _____

15. describe _____ _____ _____

Words from The Cay *(cont.)*

Place the words from page 103 in alphabetical order in column I. In column II divide the word into syllables. Then place the accent mark at the end of the most heavily stressed syllable. Refer to a dictionary if necessary.

Column I   **Column II**

1. _____   _____
2. _____   _____
3. _____   _____
4. _____   _____
5. _____   _____
6. _____   _____
7. _____   _____
8. _____   _____
9. _____   _____
10. _____   _____
11. _____   _____
12. _____   _____
13. _____   _____
14. _____   _____
15. _____   _____

Which word has only one syllable? _____

List the words with two syllables.   _____   _____

_____   _____   _____

_____   _____   _____

List the words with three syllables.   _____   _____

_____   _____   _____

List the words with four syllables. _____

How many accent marks are printed for this word? _____

Which syllable is stressed most heavily? _____

Words from The Cay *(cont.)*

Replace the italicized words in each sentence with one of the spelling words. Write the words on the lines below. Check the dictionary for definitions.

1. The *continuous humming* of the airplane was heard over the sound of the thunder.

2. Mrs. Block *explained* the theme of the novel.

3. The streets were covered with *ruins and rubbish* after the missiles targeted the city.

4. The sailors committed *open rebellion* against their captain while out at sea.

5. A *tropical storm* is developing off the coast of Florida and is heading up the coast of the United States.

6. The embers will continue to *burn* all night long to provide some heat and light for the campers.

7. Many *worried* passengers were stranded at the airport overnight due to the flight cancellations brought on by the storm.

8. Driving conditions were *dangerous* during the height of the blizzard.

9. The football player was not *awake* for five minutes after he was tackled by the opposing team.

10. There is much shallow water on both sides of the *deeper waterway* in the river, preventing the ship from passing through that area.

11. Cargo was used as a *balance* to steady the ship at sea.

12. *Boats that go underwater* can attack enemy ships using radar to launch missiles.

13. Aircraft can launch *large, cigar-shaped metal tubes with explosives* to destroy enemy ships.

14. The *insistent* customer refused to take no for an answer when attempting to return the damaged merchandise.

15. It gives parents great *pleasure* to see their children succeed in school.

1. _____   6. _____   11. _____

2. _____   7. _____   12. _____

3. _____   8. _____   13. _____

4. _____   9. _____   14. _____

5. _____   10. _____   15. _____

Test Yourself—Unit Four

Circle the word that is spelled correctly.

	A	B	C	D
1.	torepedo	torpedoe	torpedo	torpeto
2.	drone	drune	dron	dorne
3.	smoder	smoldre	smoleder	smolder
4.	conscious	consious	concious	conscous
5.	debree	debrie	debris	dibris
6.	descryb	decribe	describe	describe
7.	anxious	ancshus	angshus	anxous
8.	satisfacsion	satisfaction	sattisfacsion	sattisfaction
9.	chanel	channel	chanil	chennil
10.	submrine	submarin	submarine	subarine
11.	stuborn	stuburn	stubburn	stubborn
12.	ballast	ballust	ballas	balast
13.	mewtine	mutine	muttiny	mutiny
14.	hericane	hurrycane	huricane	hurricane
15.	tretchorous	treacherous	treatcherus	treachrous

Write the spelling word from above that matches the synonym below.

16. explain _____

17. waterway _____

18. storm _____

19. nervous _____

20. garbage _____

Words from Social Studies

Write each word three times in cursive on the lines provided.

1. latitude   _____   _____   _____

2. longitude   _____   _____   _____

3. equator   _____   _____   _____

4. hemisphere   _____   _____   _____

5. meridian   _____   _____   _____

6. continents   _____   _____   _____

7. America   _____   _____   _____

8. Asia   _____   _____   _____

9. Africa   _____   _____   _____

10. Europe   _____   _____   _____

11. Antarctica   _____   _____   _____

12. oceans   _____   _____   _____

13. Pacific   _____   _____   _____

14. Atlantic   _____   _____   _____

15. Indian   _____   _____   _____

16. Arctic   _____   _____   _____

As part of any social studies curriculum, all the above spelling words are important to better understand the world around us.

Words from Social Studies *(cont.)*

Label the world map with the terms in the word bank.

Word Bank

- North America
- Asia
- Africa
- Atlantic Ocean

- South America
- Australia
- Indian Ocean
- Arctic Ocean

- Europe
- Antarctica
- Pacific Ocean
- equator

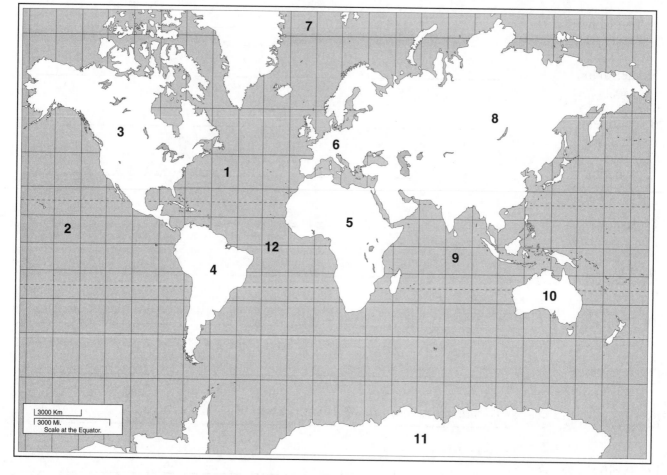

On the lines below indicate which continent or ocean matches the number on the map.

1. _____   7. _____

2. _____   8. _____

3. _____   9. _____

4. _____   10. _____

5. _____   11. _____

6. _____   12. _____

Words from Social Studies *(cont.)*

Unscramble the letters and write the spelling word correctly.

1. isaa

2. micarea

    E

3. epruoe

4. ttilduea

5. rfiaac

6. cciifap

7. tideugnol

8. cctiar

9. nsoaec

10. deaiimnr

11. antltaci

12. uaeqrot

13. nadini

14. ticantaarc

15. toncinsent

16. eismhpeerh

List the letters in the boxed spaces to find out what you should do.

_____

Write the names of the continents in alphabetical order. Remember to capitalize proper nouns.

_____   _____

_____   _____

_____   _____

_____

List the names of the oceans in alphabetical order. Remember to capitalize proper nouns.

_____   _____   _____   _____

Test Yourself—Unit Five

Circle the word that is spelled correctly.

	A	B	C	D
1.	Indian	Indien	Idnian	Indaan
2.	Atlandic	AtlanticK	Atlantic	Adlantic
3.	arktic	Arctick	Ardic	Arctic
4.	Pacific	Paciphic	Pacefic	Pasific
5.	oshins	oceans	oseans	ocens
6.	Europe	Eurup	Earupe	Earope
7.	Antartica	Antarktica	Andarctia	Antarctica
8.	Australia	Astraylia	Australia	Astralia
9.	Affrica	Afrika	Afria	Africa
10.	Amica	Amereia	America	Amereca
11.	meridian	miridian	meridien	meredian
12.	ekator	eqator	equador	equator
13.	lonitood	longetud	longitude	longetude
14.	hemisfere	hemisphere	hemispher	hemispere
15.	lattidue	latitude	lattitude	latitood
16.	condidents	contients	continents	coninents

Complete each sentence with the correct spelling word.

17. A line of _____ , measured in degrees, is the distance east or west from a certain meridian, usually the one in Greenwich, England.

18. The four main _____ cover almost three-fourths of the earth's surface.

19. There are seven main masses of land, or _____ , on earth.

20. A degree of _____ measures about 69 miles north or south of the equator.

Words from Mathematics

Write each word three times in cursive on the lines provided.

1. mathematics _____ _____ _____

2. addition _____ _____ _____

3. subtraction _____ _____ _____

4. multiplication _____ _____ _____

5. division _____ _____ _____

6. addends _____ _____ _____

7. divisor _____ _____ _____

8. dividend _____ _____ _____

9. quotient _____ _____ _____

10. sum _____ _____ _____

11. product _____ _____ _____

12. factors _____ _____ _____

13. numerator _____ _____ _____

14. denominator _____ _____ _____

15. fractions _____ _____ _____

16. difference _____ _____ _____

Knowing the spelling and meaning of mathematical terms helps in computation and problem solving.

Words from Mathematics *(cont.)*

Place the words from page 111 in alphabetical order in column 1. In column 2 divide the word into syllables. Then place the accent mark at the end of the most heavily stressed syllable. Refer to a dictionary if necessary.

	Column 1	**Column 2**
1.		
2.		
3.		
4.		
5.		
6.		
7.		
8.		
9.		
10.		
11.		
12.		
13.		
14.		
15.		
16.		

Which word has only one syllable? _____

List the words with two syllables. _____ _____

_____ _____ _____ _____

List the words with three syllables. _____ _____

_____ _____ _____ _____

Which words have four syllables? _____ _____

Which words have five syllables? _____ _____

How many accent marks are printed for these words? _____

Words from Mathematics (cont.)

Match the mathematical term in column B that is associated with the ringed item in column A.

Column A	Column B

_____ 1.　　　345
　　　　　　　　　− 123
　　　　　　　　　◯

A. product

_____ 2.　◯ x 7 = 35

B. sum

_____ 3.　72 ÷ 8 = ◯

C. addend

_____ 4.　◯
　　　　　　　+ 2345
　　　　　　　　5889

D. difference

_____ 5. 22 x 4 = ◯

E. factor

_____ 6. 35 + 43 = ◯

F. quotient

_____ 7. $\frac{3}{4}$

G. numerator

_____ 8. $\frac{3}{5}$ (3 ringed)

H. fraction

_____ 9. $\frac{7}{12}$ (12 ringed)

I. division

_____ 10. addition : subtraction :: multiplication:

J. denominator

Test Yourself–Unit Six

Circle the word that is spelled correctly.

	A	B	C	D
1.	diviser	dividend	divisor	divishun
2.	mathmatics	quoshun	mathematics	som
3.	numerater	denominater	dinominator	denominator
4.	adends	numerator	facors	addeds
5.	diffrence	differance	defference	difference
6.	produt	product	addishum	multiplikashon

Circle the word that is *not* spelled correctly.

	A	B	C	D
7.	subtraction	addition	multiplicasion	division
8.	quotient	sum	differance	product
9.	dividend	diviser	addend	factor
10.	numerator	denominator	mathematics	mathmatics

Match the word to its correct meaning.

_____ 11. sum   A.   answer in subtraction

_____ 12. product   B.   answer in division

_____ 13. quotient   C.   answer in addition

_____ 14. difference   D.   answer in multiplication

Fill in the blanks with the correct spelling word.

In (15) _____ students need to be able to find the answers to arithmetic

problems and also be able to solve word problems. A student needs to know that the word

(16) _____ indicates that a student is to subtract. Knowing the meaning of

divisor and dividend helps the problem solver to find the (17) _____ in a

division problem. It is important to know that the (18) _____ is the number

above or to the left of the line in a fraction. Students should know that (19)

_____ is the opposite of subtraction and that multiplication is the opposite of

(20) _____ .

Words from English Grammar

Write each word three times in cursive on the lines provided.

1. subject   _____   _____   _____

2. predicate   _____   _____   _____

3. noun   _____   _____   _____

4. verb   _____   _____   _____

5. adverb   _____   _____   _____

6. adjective   _____   _____   _____

7. pronoun   _____   _____   _____

8. preposition   _____   _____   _____

9. conjunction   _____   _____   _____

10. sentence   _____   _____   _____

11. fragment   _____   _____   _____

12. capital   _____   _____   _____

13. declarative   _____   _____   _____

14. interrogative   _____   _____   _____

15. imperative   _____   _____   _____

16. exclamatory   _____   _____   _____

Grammatical terms help students express themselves verbally in oral and written communication.

Words from English Grammar (cont.)

Correctly spell the word that is defined.

1. word that shows action   __ __ __ __

2. connecting word   __ __ __ __ __ __ __ __ __ __ __

3. command   __ __ __ __ __ __ __ __ __ __ __ __

4. person, place, thing, or idea   __ __ __ __

5. question   __ __ __ __ __ __ __ __ __ __ __ __

6. modifies noun   __ __ __ __ __ __ __ __ __

7. replaces a noun   __ __ __ __ __ __ __ __

8. statement   __ __ __ __ __ __ __ __ __ __ __

9. groups of words that express a complete thought   __ __ __ __ __ __ __ __

10. tells how, where, when, or to what extent   __ __ __ __ __ __

11. shows surprise   __ __ __ __ __ __ __ __ __ __ __

12. word that shows relation to a noun, pronoun, or phrase that follows it

   __ __ __ __ __ __ __ __ __ __ __

13. group of words   __ __ __ __ __ __ __

14. who or what performs action in a sentence   __ __ __ __ __ __ __

15. type of letter   __ __ __ __ __ __ __

16. tells what the subject did   __ __ __ __ __ __ __ __ __ __

Label the groups of words _F_ for fragment or _S_ for sentence.

_____ 17. Happy boys and girls

_____ 18. ran to the park to play on the swings.

_____ 19. The summer season is a time to relax.

_____ 20. When will all the flowers start to bloom?

Words from English Grammar *(cont.)*

Place the correct category title above each set of words. Use the terms in the word bank.

Word Bank			
• nouns	• verbs	• adjectives	• adverbs
• pronouns	• conjunctions	• prepositions	

1. _____

swim
run
work
plan
type
active

2. _____

student
school
bravery
desk
computer
office

3. _____

beautiful
tall
simple
huge
compact
red

4. _____

and
but
or

5. _____

quickly
outside
soon
very
almost

6. _____

with
beyond
for
under/above
in/out

7. _____

I, you, he she, it, we, they, his,
hers, its, ours, theirs, me, him, her,
it, us, them, himself, ourselves,
myself, themselves

Identify the type of sentence. Write *D* for declaration, *Int* for interrogative, *Imp* for imperative, and *E* for exclamatory.

Also edit for capital letters and correct punctuation.

_____ 8. what a wonderful time we had at the party

_____ 9. did you receive the invitation to the ceremony

_____ 10. park the car in the parking lot

_____ 11. the principal presented awards to the outstanding student athletes

Draw one line under the complete subject. Draw two lines under the complete predicate. Draw a vertical line (|) separating the subject and the predicate.

Example: The new boy | joined the track team.

12. The fluffy white cat slept all afternoon on the soft couch.

13. The little red wagon is filled with apples from the orchard.

Test Yourself—Unit Seven

Circle the word that is spelled correctly.

	A	B	C	D
1.	prepozition	preposition	preosition	prepocition
2.	predicatte	predecate	predicate	preticate
3.	noun	nown	non	noune
4.	adverbe	atverb	advirb	adverb
5.	adjecthive	adjictive	adjective	adjectiv
6.	subject	subjec	suject	subjeckt
7.	capetal	capital	cepital	capitall
8.	frgment	fragmeant	fragment	fragmint
9.	exclammatory	exsclamatory	exsclamatry	exclamatory
10.	imperative	emperative	impirative	imparative
11.	interogative	interrogative	intirogative	intirogative
12.	declairative	deklarative	declairatif	declarative
13.	conjunksion	conjunktion	conjunction	cunjunction
14.	sentense	sentenc	sentens	sentence
15.	pronoun	pronun	pronon	pronown
16.	virb	verbe	verb	vurb

Identify the part of speech that is underlined in the following sentence.

The chestnut <u>stallion</u> <u>galloped</u> <u>quickly</u> <u>around</u> the track.
                  17.   18.   19.   20.

17._____

18._____

19._____

20._____

Words from Science

Write each word three times in cursive on the lines provided.

1. scientific _____ _____ _____

2. method _____ _____ _____

3. problem _____ _____ _____

4. hypothesis _____ _____ _____

5. materials _____ _____ _____

6. manipulated variables _____ _____ _____

7. procedure _____ _____ _____

8. observation _____ _____ _____

9. conclusion _____ _____ _____

10. graph _____ _____ _____

11. data _____ _____ _____

12. chart _____ _____ _____

13. laboratory _____ _____ _____

14. control _____ _____ _____

15. theory _____ _____ _____

16. experiment _____ _____ _____

The scientific method is the orderly procedure by which a scientist conducts and records an experiment.

Words from Science *(cont.)*

Locate the spelling words in the word search below. Words will be found horizontally, vertically, and diagonally.

D	U	D	E	X	P	E	R	I	M	E	N	T
O	O	M	A	P	R	O	B	L	E	M	O	H
N	S	H	A	T	N	S	H	E	Z	B	P	E
O	L	G	T	N	A	Q	P	H	S	A	K	R
I	A	E	B	E	I	U	N	E	R	O	A	U
S	I	H	I	B	M	P	R	G	C	O	D	D
U	R	M	Z	Y	H	V	U	V	S	H	J	E
L	E	T	P	E	A	Y	G	L	O	S	M	C
C	T	S	T	T	R	D	B	T	A	X	J	O
N	A	A	I	O	P	R	M	C	R	T	O	R
O	M	O	E	M	C	N	K	U	O	A	E	P
C	N	H	T	L	O	R	T	N	O	C	H	D
S	T	S	I	S	E	H	T	O	P	Y	H	C

- chart
- conclusion
- control
- data
- experiment
- graph
- hypothesis
- manipulated
- materials
- method
- observations
- problem
- procedure
- theory

Write the spelling words that contain the following scrambled letters.

1. uslc _____

2. vers _____

3. mine _____

4. harp _____

5. hot _____

6. bat _____

7. top _____

8. fit _____

9. rate _____

10. crop _____

Words from Science *(cont.)*

Match the definitions to the words.

_____ 1. information	A. experiment
_____ 2. place to do science work	B. hypothesis
_____ 3. organized system	C. procedure
_____ 4. steps for doing an experiment	D. theory
_____ 5. question to solve	E. chart
_____ 6. educated guess, prediction	F. scientific method
_____ 7. things that remain constant	G. laboratory
_____ 8. things that are seen	H. graph
_____ 9. decision at end of experiment	I. materials
_____ 10. items needed to experiment	J. conclusion
_____ 11. things that change	K. observation
_____ 12. trial or test	L. manipulated variables
_____ 13. picture, line, or bar diagram	M. control
_____ 14. explanation based on much research	N. problem
_____ 15. organized place to record observations	O. data

Match the verb to its noun form.

_____ 16. hypothesis	A. proceed
_____ 17. observation	B. manipulate
_____ 18. conclusion	C. hypothesize
_____ 19. manipulation	D. observe
_____ 20. procedure	E. conclude

Test Yourself—Unit Eight

Circle the word that is spelled correctly.

	A	B	C	D
1.	scientiphic	scientific	sientific	cientific
2.	metod	mithod	methode	method
3.	thery	theorey	theory	theorie
4.	datah	data	cheart	chairt
5.	observation	observeation	obzervation	observasion
6.	graf	graff	graph	greph
7.	labratory	laboratory	laboratry	laboratary
8.	exsperiment	eggsperiment	experiment	echsperiment
9.	procedure	proseedure	procejure	procedjure
10.	materiels	materials	matearials	muterials
11	hipothesis	hypothhisis	hypothesis	highpothesis
12.	promblem	problem	probelm	problim
13.	conclueshun	conclustion	canclushun	conclusion
14.	manipulated	manypulated	manupulated	minipulated
15.	veribles	variabeles	variables	varyables

Write the science spelling word that describes each statement.

_____ 16. You need to gather a ball, a pillow, a desk, a ruler, and a blanket.

_____ 17. Will plants grow better in a dark closet or in sunlight?

_____ 18. I think a Ping-Pong ball bounces higher than a tennis ball.

_____ 19. I saw that Plant A grew 8 cm in the light.

_____ 20. Plant A was placed in light; plant B, in dark.

Homophones

Homophones are words that sound alike but are spelled differently and have different meanings.

Write each of the homophones once in cursive on the lines provided.

1. wear _____ where _____

2. hear _____ here _____

3. steel _____ steal _____

4. rode _____ road _____

5. bore _____ boar _____

6. air _____ heir _____

7. pair _____ pear _____

8. there _____ their, they're _____

9. to _____ too _____

10. so _____ sew _____

11. see _____ sea _____

12. hair _____ hare _____

13. know _____ no _____

14. tail _____ tale _____

15. wood _____ would _____

16. which _____ witch _____

17. groan _____ grown _____

18. roll _____ role _____

19. toe _____ tow _____

20. scene _____ seen _____

21. plain _____ plane _____

22. ate _____ eight _____

Homophones *(cont.)*

Match each homophone to its meaning.

_____ 1. wear   A. also

_____ 2. where   B. to put on your body

_____ 3. their   C. to understand

_____ 4. there   D. towards

_____ 5. they're   E. belonging to them

_____ 6. to   F. they are

_____ 7. two   G. negative

_____ 8. too   H. at the place

_____ 9. know   I. in what place

_____ 10. no   J. 2

Match:

_____ 11. hear   A. ocean

_____ 12. here   B. stitch

_____ 13. sew   C. listen

_____ 14. sea   D. look

_____ 15. road   E. close by

_____ 16. see   F. rabbit

_____ 17. tale   G. past tense of eat

_____ 18. plain   H. story

_____ 19. ate   I. simple

_____ 20. hare   J. street

Match:

_____ 21. tow   A. part in a play

_____ 22. groan   B. pull

_____ 23. role   C. sound expressing pain

_____ 24. witch   D. fruit

_____ 25. pear   E. woman with supernatural powers

Homophones *(cont.)*

Circle the word which best completes the sentence.

1. (Where, Wear) are you going this afternoon?

2. (There, Their, They're) are (eight, ate) students absent today.

3. John broke his (tow, toe) while skateboarding.

4. The youngster has (groan, grown) three inches over the year, according to the pediatrician.

5. (Would, Wood) you like to spend this weekend visiting your grandparents in Florida?

6. Pamela could not decide (which, witch) (role, roll) to eat for lunch.

7. The (hair, hare) on the dog's (tail, tale) was singed in the fire.

8. Do you (know, no) how to (sew, so) on the sewing machine?

9. The (air, heir) that we breathe is a renewable resource that still needs to be conserved.

10. The (rode, road) leading to the (steal, steel) mill is filled with potholes from the winter storms.

11. (Too, To, Two) many ships have been lost at (see, sea) in the Bermuda Triangle.

12. At the (fair, fare) grounds a (pair, pare, pear) of diamond earrings was found.

13. Do you (hear, here) the sound of the (planes, plains) as they approach the runway of the airport?

14. (For, Four) hundred wild (boars, bores) stampeded across the grasslands.

15. (There, They're, Their) going to be (seen scene) by the doctor in a few minutes.

16. Who will play the (roll, role) of the (witch, which) in the Halloween play?

Subjects and Predicates

Every sentence has two parts: the *subject* and the *predicate*. The *complete subject,* all the words that tell *whom* or *what* the sentence is about, is the part about which something is said. The *complete predicate,* all the words that tell what the subject *does* or *did* or what the subject *is* or *was,* is the part of the sentence usually following the subject.

Examples

Subject	Predicate
The tall sailing vessel	*docked at the long pier.*
Many of the trees	*are losing their leaves.*
Spring flowers	*are beautiful signs of a new season.*

Directions: Draw one line under the complete subject and two lines under the complete predicate.

Example: The winner of the competition was awarded a trophy.

1. The snow was falling heavily during the night, depositing one foot on the ground.

2. The streets and highways were closed for many hours.

3. All the schools in the area had delayed opening for two hours.

4. Most of the elementary school students did not attend school at all.

5. Many high school students were stranded on an overturned bus.

6. A helicopter and an ambulance transported the injured students to the hospital.

7. Another major storm pounded the area, dumping another four feet of snow.

8. The board of education decided to close the schools for two weeks.

9. At first the children enjoyed ice skating, building snowmen, and sledding.

10. The regular school year was extended for two weeks into the month of July.

11. The Little League baseball game schedule was revised and altered.

12. The local pools and beaches changed their lifeguard schedules.

13. Many vacation plans needed to be adjusted or cancelled.

14. The highlight of the summer, the county fair, continued as planned.

Simple Subjects and Predicates

The *simple predicate* of a sentence is the most important word or words of the complete predicate. The simple predicate is the *verb* of the sentence. *Action verbs* tell about an action, while *linking* or *state-of-being* verbs tell that something is or was.

> *Example:*   Rain <u>fell</u> from the sky. Johnny <u>skateboarded</u> to the park. (action)
> Baseball <u>is</u> the national pastime. The dark sky <u>looked</u> threatening. (linking)

The *simple subject* is the most important word or words in the complete subject. The simple subject is also referred to as the *subject of the verb.* It is usually a noun or pronoun. The simple subject answers the question *who* or *what.* To find the subject, locate the verb first and then ask who or what.

> *Example:*   The funny clowns at the circus performed three times.
> Verb: *performed*
> Who or what performed? *clowns*

Directions: Draw *one line* under the *complete predicate.* Then circle the simple predicate or verb.

Example: The frightened dog (barked) at the stranger.

1. The heart is the strongest muscle in the body.
2. The brain is enclosed in the skull.
3. The optic nerve attaches the eye to the brain.
4. The boy broke his femur during the basketball game.
5. The baby could distinguish color at an early age.

Directions: Draw *one line* under the *simple subject* and *two lines* under the simple predicate or verb.
Example: The little <u>kitten</u> sipped the warm milk.

1. Crossword puzzles help develop vocabulary.
2. The clues in these puzzles are definitions.
3. Sometimes students check the dictionary.
4. Maryanne always keeps the dictionary by her side.
5. The cryptogram is another type of word game.
6. This word puzzle has words in code.
7. A word search puzzle includes hidden words.
8. The puzzle solver hunts for the hidden word or words.
9. Some children like to make up their own codes.
10. Summertime is a good time to read and exercise.
11. Michael and Joe join the reading program at their local library.
12. Joan read 20 books last summer.
13. Heather was the first-place winner in the swim competition.
14. The lifeguards awarded her a trophy and a plaque.
15. The librarian distributed certificates to all "reading buddies."

Subjects in Different Positions

The subject is usually at the beginning of a declarative sentence, or statement. That word order is considered *natural*. However, sometimes the subject follows the verb. Then the word order is called *inverted*. To find the subject in an inverted word order sentence, first find the verb. Then ask *who* or *what* before the verb.

> *Example:*   **Natural**—The soccer game lasted two hours yesterday.
> Verb: *lasted* Who or what lasted? (game) The subject of *lasted* is *game*.
> **Inverted**—Onto the field dashed the players.
> Verb: *dashed* Who or what dashed? (players) The subject of *dashed* is *players*.

When a sentence begins with *here* or *there*, the subject usually follows the verb.

> *Example:*   Here are the golf balls.
> Verb: *are* Who or what are? (golf balls) The subject of *are* is *golf balls*.

Directions: In the sentences below, draw <u>one line</u> under the subject and <u>two lines</u> under the simple predicate or verb. On the line to the right, write *natural* or *inverted* to describe the word order.

1. Here is the equipment for the game. _____

2. Along the coast are twenty humpback whales. _____

3. With a smile on her face, Susan greeted the guests. _____

4. Into the cage climbed the tiger. _____

Interrogative, exclamatory, and imperative sentences may also have unusual word order. To find the subject in an interrogative or exclamatory sentence, change the word order to a declarative sentence.

Interrogative Sentence: Do some trees lose their leaves in autumn?

Declarative Sentence: Some trees do lose their leaves in autumn.

> **Verb:** *do lose*   **Subject:** *trees*

Exclamatory Sentence: What a great game they played!

Declarative Sentence: They played a great game.

> **Verb:** *played*   **Subject:** *they*

An imperative sentence, or command, does not usually contain a subject. The subject is understood to be you. (You) *Close the garage.* (You) *Brush your teeth.*

If a person is named in an imperative sentence, then the name is the subject.

Mark, walk the dog.   *Mark* is the subject.

Subjects in Different Positions *(cont.)*

Directions: In the sentences below, draw a line under the subject of the verb. If the subject is understood, write (*you*) after the sentence.

1. Please turn the computer off. _____

2. What a wonderful time we had at the party! _____

3. Did you throw a no-hitter during the baseball game? _____

4. Which animals were in the dark and dreary cave? _____

5. Buckle your safety belt before we start the car. _____

6. Draw a map of your bedroom. _____

7. Did your relatives visit for the Fourth of July? _____

8. Did priests make calendars in ancient Babylon and Egypt? _____

9. Jessica, please pass the candy to all the children. _____

10. How many goals did Sam score in the soccer game? _____

11. What a lovely mural is on the subway wall! _____

12. When were the pyramids built in Egypt? _____

Nouns

Nouns are words that name a person, place, thing, or idea.

- **Persons** include both names of people and categories.
  Mr. Blue   *children*   *policemen*   *teacher*   *girl*   *boy*

- **Places** can name both specific and general places.
  New York   *school*   *park*   *department stores*   *homes*

- **Things** refer to objects.
  door   *shoes*   *newspaper*   *table*   *globe*

- **Ideas** tell about feelings or thoughts.
  love   *pain*   *philosophy*   *care*   *liberty*   *freedom*   *belief*   *rules*

Directions: Underline the nouns in the following sentences. The number at the end of the sentence tells how many nouns to look for.

1. Summer is a wonderful time of the year. (3)

2. The weather is hot and many children enjoy swimming. (3)

3. Most schools are closed and people have time to go on vacations. (4)

4. The days are longer and we have more hours of sunlight. (3)

5. It is wonderful to go to the pool, beach, or lake. (3)

6. My teacher, Mr. Dawson, visited the Metropolitan Museum of Art in New York City in July. (5)

7. He said that great care and concern are shown by visitors. (3)

8. My friends, Tim and Carol, went to the Statue of Liberty and to Ellis Island. (5)

9. The scent of beautiful flowers drifts across Central Park as we eat our lunch outside. (4)

10. We like to cook hamburgers on the grill and picnic in the backyard. (3)

Directions: Place each of the following words under the correct heading of person, place, thing, or idea.

- France
- happiness
- clouds
- shoelaces
- bicycles
- science
- city
- Ms. Litz
- sounds
- loyalty
- glasses
- Dr. Forest
- love
- table
- pain
- building
- fairness
- Texas

Person	Place	Thing	Idea

Common and Proper Nouns

Common nouns are words that name any person, place, or thing. They begin with small letters.
  Examples: house   buildings   statues   city   country

Proper nouns are words that name specific people, places, or things. These words begin with a capital letter.
  Examples: White House   Empire State Building   Statue of Liberty   San Francisco   United States

Directions: In the following sentences, put one line under each common noun and two lines under each proper noun.

1. The first president of the United States was George Washington.

2. The Eiffel Tower is a tourist attraction in Paris.

3. John Glenn is well known as a famous astronaut.

4. There are many famous bridges such as the Golden Gate Bridge in California and the George Washington Bridge in New York.

5. The Space Needle is a tourist attraction in Seattle, Washington.

Directions: Match each common noun in column A with a proper noun in column B.

Column A	Column B
_____ 1. city	A. Bingo
_____ 2. river	B. *Titanic*
_____ 3. building	C. Asia
_____ 4. movie	D. Dallas
_____ 5. newspaper	E. French
_____ 6. game	F. Mississippi
_____ 7. continent	G. *New York Times*
_____ 8. ocean	H. Twin Towers
_____ 9. people	I. Pacific
_____ 10. ship	J. *The Little Mermaid*

Directions: Write the letter *C* by each word that is a common noun. If the word is a proper noun, label it with the letter *P*.

1. Mr. Brown _____   6. Mt. Olympus _____

2. sun _____   7. Nile River _____

3. king _____   8. table _____

4. King Charles _____   9. president _____

5. Mickey Mouse _____   10. Aunt Nellie _____

Singular and Plural Nouns

Singular nouns name only one person, one place, or one thing.
> *Example:* dog   house   child

Plural nouns name two or more persons, places, or things.
> *Example:* dogs   houses   children

A. Most plurals are formed by adding the letter *s* to the noun.
> *Example:* dog—dogs

B. If the last two letters of a noun are a vowel (*a, e, i, o, u*) plus the letter *y*, just add the letter *s*.
> *Example:* key—keys

C. If the last two letters of a noun end in a consonant and the letter *y*, change the y to *i* and add the letters *es*.
> *Example:* baby—babies

D. If a noun ends with the letter *f* (or sometimes *fe*), change it to the letter *v* and add *es*.
> *Example:* elf—elves

E. If the last two letters of the noun end in a vowel (*a, e, i, o, u*) plus the letter *o*, just add the letter *s*.
> *Example:* patio—patios

F. If the last two letters end in a consonant and the letter *o*, add the letters *es*.
> *Example:* tomato—tomatoes

G. If a noun ends with *s, z, sh, ch,* or *x*, add the letters *es*.
> *Example:* box—boxes

Directions: Write the plural form of each word.

1. fox   _____
2. knife   _____
3. apple   _____
4. stereo   _____

5. lady   _____
6. family   _____
7. monkey   _____
8. giraffe   _____

Directions: In the following sentences label each underlined word (S) singular or (P) plural.

1. The <u>zookeeper</u> must keep all the <u>animals</u> clean and healthy.
2. Three <u>men</u> used <u>axes</u> to chop the <u>trees</u> down in the <u>forest</u>.
3. The <u>man</u> and <u>woman</u> waited patiently for the next <u>bus</u> to arrive.
4. <u>Cars</u> waited for the <u>children</u> to cross the street.
5. <u>Ponies</u>, <u>monkeys</u>, <u>lions</u>, and <u>bears</u> are attractions at the <u>circus</u>.
6. <u>Leaves</u> fall off <u>trees</u> in autumn.
7. The busy <u>bee</u> buzzes around the beautiful <u>flowers</u> before landing.
8. <u>Flashes</u> of lightning lit the evening <u>sky</u> before a <u>bolt</u> struck the <u>benches</u>.
9. <u>People</u> on <u>farms</u> usually live in rural <u>areas</u>.
10. People in a large <u>city</u> live in a metropolitan <u>area</u>.

Possessive Nouns

Possessive nouns are nouns that are written to show ownership.

A. *Singular nouns* show ownership when an apostrophe plus *s* ('s) are added at the end of the word.
   Example: This book belongs to Dina.
   This is *Dina's* book.

B. Plural nouns that end with the letter *s* show ownership when an apostrophe is added after the ending letter *s*.
   Example: These toys belong to the boys.
   These are the *boys'* toys.

C. Plural nouns that do not end with the letter *s* show ownership when an apostrophe plus *s'* is added at the end of the word.
   Example: This bus belongs to the children.
   This is the *children's* bus.

Directions: Write each underlined word in the possessive form.

1. <u>Mr. Briggs</u> house was the largest on the block. _____

2. The <u>mens</u> coats were hanging in the front closet. _____

3. The <u>birds</u> nest was on the fifth branch of the tree. _____

4. My <u>sisters</u> plant grew taller than mine. _____

5. When the <u>puppies</u> collars slipped off, we put them on again. _____

6. We found the <u>mouses</u> cheese was left uneaten. _____

7. The <u>libraries</u> checkout systems were not working today. _____

8. <u>Womens</u> clothing is located on the second floor. _____

9. <u>Freds</u> ride arrived earlier than expected. _____

10. Mary tuned the <u>guitars</u> strings before each song. _____

Directions: Underline the correct possessive in each of the following sentences.

1. All of the (girls, girl's girls') bookbags were placed on the chairs.

2. The (teachers, teacher's, teachers') notebook contained all the marks for her class.

3. The (babys, baby's, babies') cries in the hospital nursery woke everyone up.

4. All (players, player's, players') hats were new and clean before the game started.

5. The largest (deers, deer's, deers') tracks were easily seen in the freshly fallen snow.

Directions: Write the singular and plural possessive forms for each noun.

Noun	Singular Possessive	Plural Possessive
1. cat	_____	_____
2. mouse	_____	_____
3. runner	_____	_____

Noun Abbreviations

Abbreviations are shortened forms of words, usually nouns. The abbreviation of a proper noun is written with a capital letter. Periods usually follow an abbreviation.

Directions: Write the abbreviations for the following words.

Days of the Week

Sunday _____

Monday _____

Tuesday _____

Wednesday _____

Thursday _____

Friday _____

Saturday _____

Months of the Year

January _____

February _____

March _____

April _____

May _____

June _____

July _____

August _____

September _____

October _____

November _____

December _____

Titles

Mister _____

Doctor _____

Reverend _____

President _____

Senator _____

Governor _____

Captain _____

General _____

Professor _____

Junior _____

Senior _____

Streets

Drive _____

Avenue _____

Road _____

Boulevard _____

Parkway _____

Highway _____

Street _____

Place _____

Lane _____

Places

Fort _____

Mountain _____

River _____

National Park _____

States
(Use zip code abbreviations—no periods.)

New York _____

New Jersey _____

California _____

Texas _____

Wisconsin _____

Illinois _____

Kentucky _____

General

Celsius _____

Fahrenheit _____

United States Navy _____

District Attorney _____

Subject Pronouns

Pronouns are words that are used to take the place of a noun in a sentence.

Subject pronouns are used to take the place of one or more of the nouns in the subject.

    A. Singular Subject Pronouns: B. Plural Subject Pronouns:

      I   *you*   *he*   *she*   *it*   *we*   *you*   *they*

Examples: Mary and Tom went shopping at the mall.
                Mary and he went shopping at the mall.
                She and he went shopping at the mall.

Subject pronouns are used after a state-of-being (linking) verb.

Example: The winners of the race were Tom and Mary.
               The winners of the race were Tom and she.
               The winners of the race were he and she.

Directions: Choose the correct subject pronoun in each of the following sentences.

1. The tallest children in the class are Sally and (I, me).

2. (We, Us) girls decorated the room for the surprise party.

3. Tom and (him, he) will pick up the soda before coming.

4. (They, Them) said that they will be late arriving.

5. The hostesses at the party will be Karen and (she, her).

6. (She, her) and (I, me) will come early to help you.

7. The first guests to arrive were Craig and (him, he).

8. (They, us) said the party was fun.

Directions: Use the correct subject pronoun in place of the words in parentheses.

1. Steffanie and _____ like to go to the museum on Sunday afternoons. (Christine)

2. Christine and _____ made dinner for the whole family. (Kevin)

3. _____ is a beautiful instrument if played well. (the piano)

4. The singers were _____ and I. (John)

5. _____ are scheduled to play basketball on Saturday. (Bob, Larry, Phil, Jack)

Directions: Rewrite this sentence twice. The first time, substitute only one subject pronoun. The next time, substitute two subject pronouns.

Carl and Mike like to water-ski in the summer. _____

_____

Possessive and Reflexive Pronouns

Possessive pronouns show ownership.

A. Singular Possessive Pronouns:
       my   *mine*   *your*   *yours*   *his*   *hers*   *its*

B. Plural Possessive Pronouns:
       our   *ours*   *your*   *yours*   *their*   *theirs*

Reflexive pronouns refer to the subject of the sentence and end with *self* or *selves*.

A. Singular Reflexive Pronouns:
       myself   *yourself*   *himself*   *herself*   *itself*

B. Plural Reflexive Pronouns:
       ourselves   *yourselves*   *themselves*

Directions: Underline the possessive pronouns in the following sentences.

1. My bicycle is the green one in front of Katie's house.

2. The science book is mine, not yours.

3. Your brother can run faster than mine.

4. She had her hair cut at the new salon in town.

5. My mother bought our new shirts at the shopping mall on Thursday.

6. How far away is his house from the school bus stop?

7. Their house is painted white and has green shutters.

8. The children placed their cookies on the kitchen table.

Directions: Complete each of the following sentences with the correct reflexive pronoun. Use the list at the top of the page to help you.

1. They treated _____ to an ice-cream sundae at the soda shop.

2. "We should treat _____ to a good movie tonight."

3. Beth reminded _____ that she had forgotten her math book.

4. Will considers _____ to be the best hockey player on the team.

5. The coach told his players, "Don't upset _____ , or you will not play well."

6. The little girl said that she didn't want her mother to help her get dressed because she could do it _____ .

7. We can call Sarah, or you can call her _____ .

8. We recognized _____ in our class graduation picture.

Object Pronouns

Object pronouns are used to replace nouns.

A. Singular Object Pronouns:
    me   *you*   *him*   *her*   *it*

B. Plural Object Pronouns:
    us   *you*   *them*

Object pronouns can be used as the *direct object* in a sentence. This happens when the word receives the action sent to it by the verb.

    Example: John threw it.
                      John saw him and her.

The verb in the first sentence is *threw*. "It" is the word that received the action. The question you can ask to help find the direct object is "What was thrown?" The answer to this is "it."

The verb in the second sentence is *saw*. What was seen? The answer is *him* and *her*. In this case, there are two answers which make it a *compound object*.

Object pronouns can also be used as the object of the preposition in prepositional phrases.

    Example: Sue and Ellen came with him.

In this sentence *him* is the object in the prepositional phrase *with him*.

Directions: Underline the object pronouns in each of the following sentences.

1. Polly cried all day about it.
2. Her mother helped her look for the missing book.
3. Please help Tim and him with the groceries.
4. Did you see them at the store?
5. Herb joined us on the checkout line.
6. I asked her and him about the game.
7. The teacher gave me the part in the play.
8. You will see us in the play.

Directions: Insert an object pronoun in the blank in each of the following sentences.

1. He found _____ seated in the front of the auditorium. (singular)
2. Would you tell Philip about _____ part in the school play. (singular)
3. We saved _____ some seats. (plural)
4. They must give _____ the tickets to the movie. (plural)
5. I bought the popcorn for _____ . (singular)
6. Did you make arrangements with him or _____ ? (singular)

Pronouns and Antecedents

Pronouns are words that are used to take the place of nouns.

Antecedents are words to which the pronouns refer.

   A. Antecedents are nouns (or sometimes other pronouns) in the sentence.

   B. Antecedents usually come before the pronoun in the same sentence.

   C. Antecedents sometimes appear in the sentence just before the one with the pronoun.

Singular Pronouns:

| I | me | mine | you | your | yours | he |
| she | it | him | her | his | hers | its |

Plural Pronouns:

| we | us | our | ours | you | your |
| yours | they | them | their | theirs |

Examples:

   1. Evan took great care growing his garden. (*His* refers to the antecedent noun *Evan*).

   2. Carl tumbled down the hill. He was badly bruised. (*He* refers to the antecedent *Carl*.)

Directions: Underline the pronoun and circle its antecedent.

   1. Wanda said the library is not far from where she works.

   2. Biking is fun. It is usually done in warm weather.

   3. Craig and Bill came in at three o'clock. They were playing football.

   4. Carla said she didn't feel well.

   5. Louise said her mother would be home soon.

   6. Bob and Jim set everything up for their party.

Directions: Supply the correct pronoun in the following sentences.

   1. Jennifer and Betty brought _____ books with them.

   2. The library was not open. The sign said _____ was closed on Sunday.

   3. The sale at the store ended before Hal got there. _____ was very disappointed.

   4. Debra felt that _____ project was the best in the class.

   5. Margo and Katie took _____ walk at the same time every evening.

   6. Wendy liked the way _____ looked in her new dress.

   7. Baseball players must practice to keep _____ skills sharp.

   8. Jack took the last shot in the basketball game. _____ scored the winning point.

Indefinite Pronouns

Indefinite pronouns are words that do not refer to a specific person or to a specific thing.

A. Singular Indefinite Pronouns:

another	*everything*	*each*	*anybody*	*everyone*
someone	*anything*	*one*	*nobody*	*anyone*
either	*someone*	*everybody*	*neither*	*no one*

B. Plural Indefinite Pronouns:

several	*many*	*few*	*both*

Directions: Underline each indefinite pronoun in the following sentences.

1. Everybody brought his own chair to the outdoor concert.

2. Neither has come with a camera.

3. I don't know if anyone can bring a lunch.

4. Each was given a ticket when he or she paid.

5. Somebody agreed to hold her flowers during the performance.

Directions: Choose the correct pronoun for the indefinite pronoun that is its antecedent.

Example: Everyone missed (their, his) cue to come onto the stage.
Everyone is the antecedent, and *his* is the correct pronoun because *everyone* is singular and the pronoun must agree with its antecedent.

1. I am sure that no one will be willing to pay that much money for (his, their) entry fee.

   Antecedent: _____

   Pronoun: _____

2. One of my friends said that (she, her) read that book last month.

   Antecedent: _____

   Pronoun: _____

3. Each of the children in my family has (his, her, his or her, its, their) own set of roller blades.

   Antecedent: _____

   Pronoun: _____

4. Either of the movie critics can make (their, his, his or her) own choice about the best movie.

   Antecedent: _____

   Pronoun: _____

Verbs

Verbs are words that express action or being.

An *action verb* describes physical action, that which can be seen.

> *Example:*   Tom collected stamps and coins.

Sometimes the verb expresses mental action, that which cannot be seen.

> *Example:*   Candice knew all the answers on the test.

A *linking verb* joins or links the subject of a sentence with a word or words in the predicate. It tells that something *is* or *was*.

> *Example:*   The pot on the stove was hot!

Common Linking Verbs:

am	*be*	*feel*	*has been*	*is*	*been*	*sound*
have been	*are*	*being*	*taste*	*was*	*will be*	*look*
had been	*were*	*become*	*appear*	*seem*		

Directions: In each of the sentences below, underline the verb. Label each verb *action* or *linking*. If the verb is an action verb, write *PA* for physical action or *MA* for mental action.

_____   1. Lightning flashed across the sky.

_____   2. The quarterback raced down the field.

_____   3. The winner is the first person to cross the finish line.

_____   4. The crackling fire looked beautiful!

_____   5. The roasting marshmallows smelled delicious!

_____   6. The hunters captured a turkey and a deer.

_____   7. Hailstones are little ice balls.

_____   8. Fog covered the airport, preventing the planes from landing.

_____   9. Trucks skidded on the snow-covered highways.

_____ 10. Dew formed on the grass in the early morning.

_____ 11. The magician pulled a bouquet of flowers from the scarf.

_____ 12. Mike appears frail after his operation.

_____ 13. Kitty seems to be the fastest runner in the sixth grade.

_____ 14. The young boys became excellent ranch hands.

Main Verbs and Helping Verbs

A *verb* is one word or a group of words. If there are two or more that make up the verb, the last word is the *main verb*. It expresses action or being. The *helping verb* is the verb that helps the main verb express the action.

>   *Example:*   is walking, are racing

The helping verb and the main verb are sometimes separated by other words in the sentence.

>   *Example:*   *Can* chickens *fly*? Joseph *must* not *have heard* the doorbell.

The most common helping verbs are forms of *be, have,* and *do.*

>   **be**—*am, is, are, was, were, will be*
>   **have**—*have, has, had*
>   **do**—*do, does, did*
>   Other common helpers—*could, should, would, can, must*

Directions: In the sentences below, underline the verbs. Then write the parts of the verb in the correct columns. The first example has been completed for you.

	Helping Verb(s)	Main Verb
1. Lois <u>has</u> <u>sketched</u> a scene of the trees.	has	sketched
2. Have you ever visited the White House?		
3. A senator is elected for a term of six years.		
4. A president can serve for two elected terms.		
5. What will be needed for the experiment?		
6. The farmer has planted three acres of corn.		
7. The children were dressed in costumes.		
8. The pool has been closed all week.		
9. The beaches will reopen on Saturday.		
10. The planes are circling the airport now.		
11. The criminal could not control his temper.		
12. Have you ever collected dolls?		
13. Valerie will be going to the zoo tomorrow.		
14. The Tigers have won the tournament.		

Verb Tenses

Tense is time expressed by a verb. The tense tells whether the action or state of being takes place in the present, past, or future.

The present tense tells about action or state of being happening now. Sometimes *s* or *es* is added to the base word when the subject is singular.

> *Example:*   I play the flute. I am on vacation. She likes Jello.

The past tense tells about action or state of being that has been completed. Most past-tense regular verbs end in *d* or *ed*. Others change their spelling.

> *Example:*   The boy climbed the tree. He was in the park. She sang a song.

The future tense tells about action or state of being that will take place at some time in the future. The helping verbs *will* or *shall* are used with the main verb.

> *Example:*   The bus will arrive in one hour. I shall be on it.

Directions: Underline the verb in each sentence. Label the verb tense *present, past,* or *future.*

_____   1. Will the airplane take off on time?

_____   2. The flight left Kennedy Airport at 11:00 A.M.

_____   3. Jordan landed at 2:00 P.M. in Fort Lauderdale.

_____   4. The plane ride was bumpy and uncomfortable.

_____   5. The pilot steers the plane to the terminal.

_____   6. Now Jordan waits for his baggage.

_____   7. Jordan meets his grandparents and drives home.

_____   8. The rain beats heavily on the windshield.

_____   9. According to the forecast, the sun will shine in the morning.

_____   10. Jordan and his grandfather played golf every morning.

Directions: Complete the sentences with the correct indicated tense of each italicized verb in parentheses.

11. The sun _____ in the east every morning. (*rise*, present)

12. The astronauts' spacesuits _____ them from the cold and heat. (*protect*, past)

13. NASA _____ a new weather satellite. (*launch*, past)

14. The next space shuttle _____ Earth for many years. (*circle*, future)

15. Once many herds of buffalo _____ this country. (*roam*, past)

Verbs with Direct and Indirect Objects

A *direct object* is the word in the sentence that receives any action from the verb.

> *Example:*   *The dog caught the ball.*
> The verb is *caught.*
> What was caught? (*ball*)

Ball is the direct object because it receives the action of the verb. You may find it helpful to first find the verb and then ask "what?"

Directions: Put two lines under the verb and one line under the direct object.

1. Mom drove us to the mall.
2. John asked for the book, and the librarian brought it.
3. Dad read the newspaper before dinner.
4. We picked apples from the tree.
5. The teacher collected the papers.
6. They found us asleep in front of the television.

An *indirect object* tells if something was done for someone or to someone. This is the indirect object of the sentence.

> *Example:*   *Martha brought him a book.*
> The verb is *brought.*
> The direct object is *book.* (Brought what?)

The indirect object answers the question *for whom?* (him) *Him* is the indirect object. Indirect objects always come before the direct object.

Directions: Answer the questions to find the direct and indirect objects in the following sentences.

1. Mom bought us a new CD.

A. What is the verb? _____

B. What is the direct object? _____

C. For whom or to whom is something being done? _____ is the indirect object.

2. Please send him this letter.

A. What is the verb? _____

B. What is the direct object? _____

C. For whom or to whom is something being done? _____ is the indirect object.

Verbs and Predicate Adjectives

Every sentence has two parts. One part is the complete subject, and the other part is the complete predicate. The predicate of the sentence contains the verb, also known as the simple predicate. Two types of verbs can be used. One is an action verb, and the other is a linking verb, also known as the state-of-being verb. An adjective that comes after a state-of-being verb and modifies the subject is called a *predicate adjective.*

> *Example:*   The child was tired.
> *Child* is the subject.
> *Tired* describes the child and comes after the predicate *was.*

Directions: After each sentence, write the *subject, predicate* and *predicate adjective* on the lines provided. Be alert that some of these sentences are inverted, so the predicates (and predicate adjectives) will come before the subjects rather than after.

Sentence	Subject	Predicate	Predicate Adjective(s)
1. The soup was hot and delicious.			
2. The room was dark and cool.			
3. Famous throughout the world is the Statue of Liberty.			
4. Fierce and cold was the wind.			
5. We felt happy after getting our gifts.			
6. Jodi felt relaxed after reading her book.			
7. The lights in the store windows are colorful.			
8. The game was unbelievable.			
9. The train whistle sounds low.			
10. Cool and chilling was the rain.			

Directions: Complete the following sentences.

1. The cake was _____ .

2. The sky seemed _____ .

3. Old and worn was _____ .

4. Loud and noisy is _____ .

5. The song is _____ .

Principal Parts of Regular Verbs

The three main forms of a verb are its *principal parts*. The principal parts are the *present*, the *past*, and the *past participle*.

The **present part** of the verb is its present tense. To form the future tense, just add *will* or *shall* to the present part.

The **past part** of the verb is its past tense. Add *d, ed,* or change a *y* to an *i* if preceded by a consonant.

The **past participle** is always used with a helping verb such as *have, has, had, was, has been, had been, will have, should have been, could have been.*

Present	Past	Past Participle
walk(s)	walked	(have, has, had) walked
study(s)	studied	(have, has, had) studied
rub(s)	rubbed	(have, has, had) rubbed

Directions: Write the past and past participle for each of the following verbs.

	Present	Past	Past Participle
1. rush	_____	_____	_____
2. ruin	_____	_____	_____
3. pass	_____	_____	_____
4. try	_____	_____	_____
5. grade	_____	_____	_____
6. provide	_____	_____	_____
7. slip	_____	_____	_____

Directions: Complete each sentence with a correct form of the verb in parentheses. Then write the name of the principal part used.

8. Many kinds of animals _____ Africa's plains. (roam)   _____

9. Monkeys have always _____ trees in the jungle. (climb)   _____

10. Crocodiles _____ in Africa's rivers. (live)   _____

11. Elephants have been _____ for their tusks. (kill)   _____

12. Last year the children _____ gazelles. (study)   _____

Irregular Verbs

Irregular verbs are verbs that do not add *d* or *ed* to the past or past participle forms. Changes are made to the spelling of the present tense to form the past or past participle.

Present	Past	Past Participle (have, has, had)	Present	Past	Past Participle (have, has, had)
come(s)	came	come	begin(s)	began	begun
run(s)	ran	run	ring(s)	rang	rung
go(es)	went	gone	drink(s)	drank	drunk
do(es)	did	done	swim(s)	swam	swum
see(s)	saw	seen	fall(s)	fell	fallen
say(s)	said	said	eat(s)	ate	eaten
bring(s)	brought	brought	fly(ies)	flew	flown
think(s)	thought	thought	know(s)	knew	known
sell(s)	sold	sold	ride(s)	rode	ridden
catch(es)	caught	caught	write(s)	wrote	written
tear(s)	torn	torn	take(s)	took	taken
freeze(s)	froze	frozen	grow(s)	grew	grown
break(s)	broke	broken	give(s)	gave	given
choose(s)	chose	chosen	wear(s)	wore	worn
speak(s)	spoke	spoken	steal(s)	stole	stolen
throw(s)	threw	thrown	teach(es)	taught	taught

Irregular Verbs *(cont.)*

Directions: Circle the correct form of the irregular verb in the parentheses.

1. John F. Kennedy (say, said) in a speech, "Ask not what your country can do for you; ask what you can do for your country."

2. The tortoise and the hare (ran, run) in a race.

3. The teacher has (chose, chosen) a new book for the class to read.

4. How many bases were (stole, stolen) last year?

5. Redwood trees (grow, grown) to great heights.

6. R. L. Stine has (wrote, written) many thrillers and mystery stories for young adults.

7. Who (took, taken) a trip in a time machine?

8. The hailstones have (fell, fallen) from the sky for 60 minutes.

9. The flock of birds (flown, flew) south for the winter.

10. The explorers nearly (froze, frozen) to death in Antarctica.

Directions: Complete each sentence with the correct form of the verb in parentheses.

11. Last week the children _____ a rainbow after the rain stopped. (see)

12. Have you ever _____ a horse in a rodeo? (ride)

13. Babe Ruth's home run record was _____ in 1998. (break)

14. The pond _____ last week during the storm. (freeze)

15. Has the dog _____ yet today? (eat)

16. The guidance counselor _____ good advice to the students. (give)

17. Many cities _____ tremendously during the nineteenth century. (grow)

18. The outfielder _____ the ball to win the game. (catch)

Irregular Verbs *(cont.)*

Directions: Write the correct form of the verb in parentheses.

1. The winning team was _____ a trophy and a cash prize. (give)

2. Mozart had _____ how to compose music at the age of five. (know)

3. Which languages are _____ in Canada? (speak)

4. The fabric on the couch was _____ by the movers. (tear)

5. My uncle _____ the New York Marathon in three hours. (run)

6. *The Wizard of Oz* was _____ by L. Frank Baum after telling stories to his children. (write)

7. John Glenn has _____ on two space missions during his lifetime. (go)

Directions: Write the principal parts of these verbs.

Present	Past	Past Participle
1. go		
2. come		
3. throw		
4. eat		
5. fly		
6. forget		
7. begin		
8. buy		
9. hear		

Directions: Circle the sets of principal parts that are correct.

1. go(es), went, went
2. come(s), came, come
3. bring(s), brang, brought
4. drink(s), drank, drunken
5. take(s), taked, took
6. grow(s), grew, grown
7. steal(s), stealed, stole
8. see(s), saw, saw
9. say(s), said, said
10. run(s), ran, run
11. teach(es), teached, taught
12. forget(s), forgot, forgot
13. sing(s), sang, sung
14. know(s), knew, known
15. ride(s), road, rode
16. throw(s), threw, thrown
17. choose(s), chose, chosed
18. fly(s), flew, flew
19. do(es), did, done
20. eat(s), ate, ate

Confusing Verbs

Some verbs tend to be confusing. It is important to recognize the differences in meanings between the confusing sets of verbs.

Lay/Lie: Lay means "to put" or "to place." Principal parts: *lay, laid,* (have or has) *laid*

Lie means "to rest" or "to recline." Principal parts: *lie, lay,* (have or has) *lain*

Leave/Let: Leave means "to depart" or "let be." Principal parts: *leave, left,* (have or has) *left*

Let means "to permit." Principal parts: *let, let,* (have or has) *let*

Learn/Teach: Learn means "to understand." Principal parts: *learn, learned,* (have or has) *learned*

Teach means "to explain." Principal parts: *teach, taught,* (have or has) *taught*

Raise/Rise: Raise means "to hoist or lift." Principal parts: *raise, raised,* (have or has) *raised*

Rise means "to get or go up." Principal parts: *rise, rose,* (have or has) *risen*

Set/Sit: Set means "to place or put down." Principal parts: *set, set,* (have or has) *set*

Sit means "to rest." Principal parts: *sit, sat,* (have or has) *sat*

May/Can: May means "to have permission."

Can means "to be able to."

Directions: Circle the correct verb in parentheses.

1. (Can, May) I bring a camera into the museum?
2. The body builder (may, can) press two hundred pounds.
3. The foundation of the new stadium was (lay, laid) by the workers.
4. I (lie, lay) in bed at night, dreaming of becoming a move star.
5. The trains (left, let) on time this morning.
6. (Let, Leave) the boys carry the books to the car.
7. (Leave, Let) the keys to the car on the table by the door.
8. Please (set, sat) the chairs around the table.
9. Michael Jordan (sat, set) with the championship basketball team at the awards dinner.
10. The flag is (raised, risen) at school each morning by the custodians.
11. The sun (raises, rises) later in the winter.
12. The students (raised, rose) important issues at the meeting.
13. The price of theater tickets has (risen, rose) in recent years.
14. You can (learn, teach) to play tennis if you practice.
15. Girls were (learned, taught) how to spin and weave during the colonial period.
16. Animal trainers (learn, teach) the dolphins to do tricks.
17. Helen Keller (learned, taught) how to read, speak, and write from Ann Sullivan.
18. Merlin (taught, learned) King Arthur about the magical powers of the sword.
19. (Let, Leave) the meat marinate in the refrigerator overnight.
20. (May, Can) a laser beam repair eye damage?

Subject-Verb Agreement

A subject and a verb in a sentence must agree in *number*. If the subject is singular, the verb must be singular. If a subject is plural, the verb must be plural. This is called *agreement in number*.

The letter *s* is usually added to a verb when a subject is singular. (Notice that this reverses the usual practice for nouns.)

> *Example:*   The teacher defines the words for the class.
> *Teacher* is singular, and *defines* is singular.

The letter *s* is usually dropped from a verb when a subject is plural.

> *Example:*   The teachers define the words for the class.
> *Teachers* is plural, and *define* is plural.

Directions: Decide if the subject is singular or plural and then choose the verb that agrees in number.

1. The boy (hold, holds) the bat tightly.

2. Policemen (protect, protects) citizens.

3. The librarian (place, places) the books on shelves.

4. They always (cross, crosses) the street at the corner.

5. When he (give, gives) me the book, I will lend it to you.

Certain verbs are used differently in sentences.

Singular Form	**Plural Form**
is	are
was	were
has	have
does	do

> *Examples:*   There is (There's) the parade. (one parade)
> There are (There're) several parades. (more than one parade)
> Here is (Here's) the book for the report. (one book)
> Here are (Here're) the books for the report. (more than one book)

Directions: Underline the correct verb.

1. Billy (is, are) near home.

2. There (is, are) three cars in the driveway.

3. My socks (have, has) holes.

4. (Was, Were) the girls on time for the movie?

5. No two snowflakes (has, have) the same pattern.

Compound Subject-Verb Agreement

Compound subjects are plural if they are united by the word *and*. If two subjects are linked by the words *neither . . . nor* or by the words *either . . . or*, they use the singular verb form.

Examples

1. Lisa and Judy are going to the school dance.
   (Lisa is linked to Judy with the word *and*. The subject is plural.)

2. Neither Lisa nor Judy is going to the school dance.
   (*Neither* and *nor* mean that each girl is singular.)

3. Either Lisa or Judy is going to the school dance.
   (*Either* and *or* mean each girl is singular.)

Directions: Write the subject and the verb from each sentence under the proper heading.

Sentence	Subject	Verb
1. One of my feet hurts.	_____	_____
2. Neither the chicken nor the fish tasted good.	_____	_____
3. Jim and Steve play hockey.	_____	_____
4. The dog in the window of the pet store seems tired.	_____	_____
5. The people on the bus are going home.	_____	_____
6. You are my best friend.	_____	_____
7. Have you heard the news?	_____	_____
8. Everyone loves the new dresses.	_____	_____
9. Jane and Carla have new dresses.	_____	_____
10. All the television programs were good.	_____	_____
11. Someone took my coat by mistake.	_____	_____
12. English and science are my two best subjects.	_____	_____
13. No one knows the combination to the locker.	_____	_____
14. Either Lisa or I will call you later.	_____	_____
15. In from the rain ran Aunt Maggie and Uncle Fred.	_____	_____

Adjectives

Adjectives are used to give added meaning to a noun or pronoun.

A. An adjective can tell what kind.
    Example: The *large* bus passed us.
                 Bus is the noun, and *large* describes what kind of bus.

B. An adjective can tell which one.
    Example: This bus is mine.
                 Bus is the noun, and *this* describes which one.

C. An adjective can tell how many.
    Example: One bus came by.
                 Bus is the noun, and *one* tells how many.

Directions: Underline the adjective or adjectives in each sentence. On the lines, write whether the adjective tells *what kind, which one,* or *how many.*

1. My favorite doll is on the dresser._____

2. The tree in the front yard loses its leaves in autumn. _____

3. Eight boys went to the movies after lunch._____

4. It is difficult to see on cloudy, rainy nights. _____

5. I put chocolate sauce on the ice cream._____

6. I like well-baked, cheese-covered pizza. _____

7. Nine players are needed to complete the team._____

8. The cute little Dalmatian puppies licked my face. _____

9. The boy in the front of the line wore a red hat. _____

10. We saw the flashing lights as the two ships passed. _____

11. The Empire State Building is a tourist attraction._____

12. Children love to learn about long, winding rivers. _____

13. Many large and small countries belong to the U.N. _____

14. Five hot, tired, happy children finished the race. _____

15. Several balloons needed to be inflated for the parade. _____

Directions: Choose a word from the word box that will describe the noun.

• big	• hairy	• wet	• six	• the	• this

1. A (what kind?) dog came around the corner. (three words)   _____

2. He was (how many?) years old.   _____

3. He was carrying a (what kind?) boot in his mouth.   _____

4. He looked like (which one?) was the best thing he ever found. _____

Demonstrative Adjectives

Demonstrative adjectives are words that point out specific things.

A. **Articles** are words that describe a noun. They point out that a noun is the next word in the sentence.

a and the

Example: The dog ran to his owner.
                  (*The* is the article and is followed by the noun *dog*.)

B. **Singular demonstrative adjectives** are used with singular nouns and the word *kind*.

this that

Examples: This book is what I need for my report.
                  (*This* is the demonstrative adjective followed by the word *book*.)
                  This kind of apple is my favorite.
                  (*This* is the demonstrative adjective followed by the word *kind*.)

C. **Plural demonstrative adjectives** are used with plural nouns. They are also used with the word *kinds*.

these those

Examples: These toys belong to Neil.
                  (*These* is the demonstrative adjective and *toys* is the noun.)
                  Those kinds of balloons are on the left side of the truck.
                  (*Those* is the demonstrative adjective and *kinds* is the noun.)

Directions: Underline the correct word in each sentence.

1. Look at (this, these) flowers and tell me which to buy.

2. (Those, This) kinds of roses are the prettiest I've ever seen.

3. (This, These) ice cream is cool and creamy.

4. I think (this, these) kind of coat is the one I will buy.

5. I've never seen (this, these) fabric used before.

6. (This, These) songs were the same ones we played at my cousins' party.

7. Would you ever pick (that, those) colors?

8. Please place (those, them) books on the back shelf.

9. (The, A) girls are reading the story now.

10. Tom's newspaper covered (these, the) entire kitchen table.

11. (These, Them) trees lose their leaves in the fall.

12. When the knives become dull, we sharpen (these, them).

13. Don't let the baby go down (those, them) aisles in the store.

14. (Those, That) kinds of fruits are best in this recipe.

Degrees of Comparison

Degrees of comparison are ways in which adjectives show levels of quality, quantity, or intensity.

A. The **positive degree** is used to describe only one thing.
   Examples: This pie is sweet.
   This pie is delicious.
   (There is only one pie being described.)

B. The **comparative degree** is used to compare only two things. To form the comparative degree, *er* is added at the end of most adjectives. Sometimes the word *more* comes before the adjective.
   Examples: The cherry pie is sweeter than the apple pie.
   The cherry pie is more delicious than the apple pie.
   (There are two different kinds of pie that are compared.)

C. The **superlative degree** is used to compare three or more things. Usually *est* is added at the end of most adjectives. Sometimes the word *most* comes before the adjective.
   Examples: The peach pie was the sweetest of all.
   The peach pie was the most delicious of all.

D. A few adjectives form *irregular degrees of comparison,* such as *good, better,* and *best* or *many, more,* and *most.*

Directions: Pick the correct form of comparison in each of the following sentences.

1. The boy was (small, smaller, smallest) for his age.
2. That joke was even (funny, funnier, funniest) than the first one.
3. I liked the (big, bigger, biggest) of the two stuffed animals.
4. Do you want to be the (tall, taller, tallest) in your family?
5. That was (thrilling, more thrilling, the most thrilling) than the last movie I saw.
6. Doing that skating trick was the (difficult, more difficult, most difficult) thing I have ever done.
7. I know that I can do (good, better, best) than I did last time.
8. I counted the (few, fewer, fewest) marbles of all.

Directions: Fill in the correct form of the adjective on the chart below.

Positive	Comparative	Superlative
1. good	_____	best
2. _____	more happy	most happy
3. big	bigger	_____
4. lonely	_____	loneliest
5. enjoyable	_____	most enjoyable
6. many	more	_____
7. _____	nicer	nicest

Adverbs

Adverbs are words that modify or describe verbs, adjectives, or other adverbs. They answer the questions *how, when, where,* and *to what extent.* Many adverbs are formed by adding *ly* to adjectives: loud + *ly* = loudly. Other common adverbs include such words as *now, later, tomorrow, first, here, there, away, nearby, very, mostly, quite, ever, never, too, not, well, worse, worst, much, more, little, less, least.*

Directions: In each sentence below draw a line under each adverb. Then circle the word that it modifies or describes.

    Example: The bird (flew) swiftly across the sky.

1. Penicillin was discovered accidentally by Alexander Fleming.

2. This medicine is usually prescribed to treat illnesses caused by bacteria.

3. During the seventh century the Quakers were treated badly in England.

4. William Penn, the founder of Pennsylvania, was a very famous Quaker.

5. Porcupine quills are really slender bunches of hair that have grown together.

6. Poplar trees grow best in moist places.

7. Alexander Pope was one of the greatest English poets.

8. Young pony express riders rode swiftly from Missouri to California.

9. These riders always delivered the mail, rain or snow.

10. The promoters of the pony express were ruined financially when the telegraph connections were completed from coast to coast.

Directions: Draw a line under each adverb in the sentence. On the line to the right, write whether the adverb tells *how, when, where,* or *to what extent.*

11. The pagodas of India are elaborately designed houses of worship.   _____

12. Japanese pagodas are usually built of wood.   _____

13. The paint was applied thickly to the canvas.   _____

14. Often, parsley is used to decorate meat dishes.   _____

15. Please place the turkey platter here.   _____

Adverb Comparisons

Like adjectives, *adverbs* also have degrees of comparison. The *positive degree* is used when only one thing is being described. The *comparative degree* is used when two actions are being compared. The *superlative degree* is used when comparing three or more things.

The comparative and superlative are formed in three ways. Most one-syllable and a few two-syllable words add *er* and *est* to the positive form. Most adverbs that end in *ly* or have two or more syllables usually add *more* or *most, less* or *least*. A few adverbs change completely.

Positive	Comparative	Superlative
soon	sooner	soonest
fast	faster	fastest
early	earlier	earliest
quickly	more quickly	most quickly
carefully	more carefully	most carefully
swiftly	less swiftly	least swiftly
little	less	least
much	more	most
well	better	best
badly	worse	worst

Directions: In each sentence below, underline the adverb that is being used in the comparison. On the line identify the form by writing **P** for *positive,* **C** for *comparative,* or **S** for *superlative.*

_____ 1. The front tires are firmer than the rear tires.

_____ 2. Which type of fish swims the fastest?

_____ 3. Hurricanes usually form over warm, tropical waters.

_____ 4. In the eye of the hurricane, the winds are less severe.

_____ 5. Hurricanes develop most often in the summer or early fall.

Directions: In the sentences below underline the correct form of the adverb in parentheses.

6. The rain fell (steadily, more steadily, most steadily) for the entire day.

7. The Jets quarterback throws (far, farther, farthest) than the Giants quarterback.

8. Our basketball team ranks (high, higher, highest) than any other team in the league.

9. Which tennis player hits the ball the (hard, hardest, most hard)?

10. The New York Rangers hockey team plays the (skillfulliest, more skillfully, most skillfully) of all the American teams.

Reviewing Adjective and Adverb Usage

Knowing whether to use an adjective or an adverb can be very confusing since at times the words look very much alike. In addition, some words can be used as adjectives or as adverbs, depending upon their placement in a sentence. To know when to use an adjective or an adverb, decide which word is being modified.

An **adjective** *modifies a noun or pronoun.* It tells which one, what kind, or how many. An **adverb** *modifies a verb, adjective, or another adverb* (or sometimes an entire sentence). It tells *how, when, where,* or *to what extent.*

Directions: In the sentences below, identify the underlined words as adjectives or adverbs. Circle the word that is being modified.

_____ 1. The <u>patient</u> teacher explained the lesson again.

_____ 2. The conductor waited <u>patiently</u> to begin the concert.

_____ 3. The department store sale ended <u>today</u>.

_____ 4. In the restaurants, the customers ordered their <u>favorite</u> desserts.

_____ 5. The young artist paints <u>beautifully</u> in oils and watercolors.

Directions: In the sentences below, circle the correct modifiers in parentheses.

6. The first airplane flew (slow, slowly) and (steady, steadily) across the sky.

7. Today jets speed (smoothly, smooth) and (quick, quickly) through the air.

8. The sheep were (terrible, terribly) frightened during the (fierce, fiercely) hurricane.

9. The dog turned (sudden, suddenly) and growled (ferociously, ferocious) at the cat.

10. Harry Houdini became (famous, famously) for his (amazing, amazingly) escapes.

Directions: In the sentences below, underline the errors in the use of modifiers. Write the correct modifier on the line.

_____ 11. The colors in a rainbow look so beautifully.

_____ 12. Babe Ruth is sure remembered as an outstanding baseball player.

_____ 13. The audience listened attentive to the guest speaker.

_____ 14. The Boston Marathon was a real close race this year.

Reviewing Confusing Adverbs and Adjectives

The words *good* and *well, bad* and *badly* are used incorrectly many times. *Good* and *bad* are adjectives that tell what kind. They follow linking verbs. The words *well* and *badly* are adverbs that tell how something is done. They follow action words. *Well* is also an adjective when it modifies a noun or pronoun meaning "healthy."

Examples: The cake looks *good*. (adjective)
Joe skates *well*. (adverb)
Joan does not feel *well* today. (adjective)
I feel *bad* about the accident. (adjective)
Dan acted *badly* at the show. (adverb)

Directions: In the sentences below circle the correct word in parentheses.

1. James looked (good, well) in the Halloween costume.

2. My tennis instructor serves really (good, well).

3. Homeless children need food and clothing (bad, badly).

4. Everyone at the party had a (good, well) time.

5. The patient feels (good, well) today.

6. Characters in fairy tales are either (good, well) or evil.

Negatives are words that are used to say "not." The appearance of two negatives in one sentence is called a *double negative*. Double negatives should be avoided when speaking or writing. Examples of negatives include *no, no one, none, nobody, not, nowhere, never, nothing,* and contractions with *n't.*

• The lost puppy didn't have no food to eat.	*Incorrect*
• The lost puppy didn't have any food to eat.	*Correct*
• The lost puppy had no food to eat.	*Correct*

Directions: In the sentences below circle the correct word in parentheses.

7. The thieves searched the house for the jewelry, but couldn't find (any, none).

8. I have not (ever, never) traveled to Europe.

9. The owner of the pet store doesn't know (anything, nothing) about turtles.

10. Never go (anywhere, nowhere) without telling your parents.

11. Nobody has ever seen (no, any) UFOs in New York City.

12. The fire engines arrived, even though there wasn't (no, any) fire.

Conjunctions and Interjections

Conjunctions are words that are used to join parts of sentences or whole sentences.

Following are frequently used conjunctions:
>　*and*　　　*for*　　　*or*　　　*but*　　　*nor*　　　*yet*　　　*so*

> *Examples:*　Tina and Toni went to the store.
> (The word *and* connects two subjects.)
> Tina can talk on the phone. Tina can glance at the newspaper.
> Tina can talk on the phone and glance at the newspaper.
> (The word *and* connects the two sentences by joining the predicates with the word *and*.)

Directions: Use a conjunction to join each of the following sentences. Write the new sentence on the line below.

1. I enjoy going to the theater. I enjoy going ice skating.

   _____

2. I eat lunch with Mary in the school cafeteria. I eat lunch with Brian in school.

   _____

3. Debra can swim faster than Henry. Henry won the race.

   _____

4. I don't like to go mountain climbing. I don't enjoy building things.

   _____

Interjections are words that express surprise or strong emotions. If strong emotion is expressed, an exclamation point usually follows it, but mild emotion is usually followed be a comma. Some commonly used interjections are these:
>　*oh*　　　*my*　　　*wow*　　　*hey*　　　*gosh*　　　*yeah*　　　*yes*

> *Examples:*　Oh! This is an unexpected surprise.
> Yes, it was wonderful.

Directions: Underline each interjection and punctuate each sentence.

1. oh said Sylvia as she suddenly fell forward
2. ouch the hammer hit my finger
3. hey wait for me
4. oh no what did I do with my homework
5. well that might just work
6. ah I see what you mean
7. ssh be quiet so he doesn't hear you
8. ugh what an ugly shirt
9. wow I've never seen a bug like that before

Prepositions

Prepositions are words that relate a noun or pronoun to other words in a sentence. Some commonly used prepositions are these:

into	over	beneath	above	around	under	alongside	by
from	onto	of	upon	between	through	during	in
on	for	among	across	toward	against	besides	about

Directions: Underline the preposition in each of the following sentences.

1. The green car pulled alongside the tan truck.
2. Billy climbed into the upper bunk bed first.
3. We looked around the corner to see if they were coming.
4. Over the cloud flew the airplane.
5. Harry and Frank stood in front of the line.
6. We found the reddest apple among the bunch.
7. The little girl crossed the street against the crowd.
8. The dog looked beneath the couch.
9. To get to his house, you must drive through the Holland Tunnel.
10. We had to go across the George Washington Bridge.

A *prepositional phrase* is a group of words that begin with a preposition.

> *Example:*   The tiger ran into the cage.

Into is the preposition that begins the phrase *into the cage*.

Directions: Match the sentence in column A with the correct prepositional phrase in column B to form a complete sentence.

Column A	**Match**	**Column B**
1. All the people handed their tickets	_____	A. against the wall.
2. She was laughing so loudly that people	_____	B. into the clouds.
3. We decided to take the train	_____	C. to the attendant at the entrance.
4. The booklet was buried	_____	D. under all the papers.
5. Did you receive a letter	_____	E. from Aunt Millie?
6. The plane rose	_____	F. during the movie.
7. The baby dropped the rattle	_____	G. onto the floor.
8. They told funny stories	_____	H. into the city.
9. We decided to move the couch	_____	I. across the way turned to look.
10. Everyone told him not to talk	_____	J. about our vacation.

Prepositions (cont.)

The *object* in a prepositional phrase is a noun or a pronoun. Sometimes other words may separate the preposition and the object of the preposition.

> *Example:*   Tom works at the local supermarket.
>
> *At* is the preposition.
>
> *At the supermarket* is the prepositional phrase.
>
> *Supermarket* is the noun in the prepositional phrase, otherwise known as the object of the preposition.

Directions: In each of the following sentences, underline the prepositional phrase and circle the object of the preposition.

1. The children were running around the playground.

2. The house was located on the next block.

3. The little boy ate everything except the broccoli.

4. Out of the front door ran the barking dog.

5. The baseball was hit over the foul line.

6. Like me, he wanted to see that television show.

7. I haven't eaten since breakfast.

8. With a shout of hello, she entered the quiet room.

9. This letter from Aunt Rose arrived today.

10. Into the mailbox we placed the party invitations.

11. The red car was parked near the road.

12. Alongside the stable were the horses.

Prefixes, Suffixes, and Roots

A *prefix* is a syllable or syllables attached to the beginning of a word that changes the meaning of the word.

A *suffix* is a syllable or syllables attached to the end of a base word. A suffix changes a word's meaning or its part of speech.

A *root* is a word part that can combine with prefixes, suffixes, base words, or other roots to create new words.

Prefixes, suffixes, and roots have predetermined meanings.

Directions: Match the prefix to its meaning.

_____	1. bi	A. ahead, in front of
_____	2. ex	B. above, too much
_____	3. extra	C. two, twice
_____	4. fore	D. former
_____	5. over	E. three
_____	6. post	F. half, partly
_____	7. pre	G. after
_____	8. re	H. before
_____	9. semi	I. again
_____	10. tri	J. beyond, outside of

Directions: Use one of the prefixes meaning *not* to complete the words below. The following prefixes mean *not*: *dis, il, im, in, ir, mis, non, un.*

_____ cooperative	_____ logical	_____ regular
_____ approve	_____ correct	_____ understand
_____ proper	_____ sense	_____ balance

Directions: Circle the suffix in the following words. Underline the base word.

powerful	dangerous	foolish	countless
softness	humidity	artist	production
responsible	farmer	acceptance	applicant
government	Swedish	gently	tighten

Directions: Draw a line between each root or word part. Write the correct root next to its meaning.

automatic	geography	thermometer	telescope	photograph
microsurgery	telephone	periscope	kilowatt	autograph
geology	multimedia	photogenic	television	tripod

heat_____	see _____	far_____	study of _____
measure _____	self _____	hear _____	small_____
earth_____	light _____	many _____	thousand_____

Homophones

Homophones are words that sound the same but have different meanings and spellings. *Homographs* are words that are spelled alike but have different meanings and sometimes different pronunciations.

Directions: Circle the correct word in each sentence.

1. (Two, Too) uninvited guests came (to, too) the party.

2. The children (road, rode) in the bus down the bumpy (rode, road).

3. The (nights, knights) wore their armor for many (knights, nights).

4. Do you (know, no) how to slide into a base?

5. I could not (wear, where) my (new, knew) coat to play.

6. John (won, one) a Tony for his (role, roll) in the Broadway show.

7. The glistening (sun, son) was shining on the (pier, peer).

8. Do you order your (steak, stake) rare or well done?

9. The (steel, steal) bridge was swaying during the storm.

10. Michael Jordan has designed a new (pair, pear) of sneakers.

11. The (clothes, close) closet is packed with winter items.

12. Do you like to fly in a (plane, plain)?

13. The collie gave (birth, berth) to five puppies.

14. During the avalanche, the mountain climber's (toes, tows) became frostbitten.

15. Ten (guests, guessed) arrived at the party late.

Using the Encyclopedia

An *encyclopedia* is a set of books that can be used to find general information on a subject. There are many books that make up the complete set. Each one is called a volume. Topics in each volume are arranged in alphabetical order. There is also an *index* which can be used to find information about your topic. The index will note if there is information on the topic in more than one volume and on what pages the information can be found. Topics can also be cross referenced. This means that other places are suggested at the end of each article where a reader can look to find more information. Maps, photographs and art are also included to help the reader gain a greater understanding of the subject.

There are many people who write the articles that are included in any encyclopedia. That is why the set is known by a publisher rather than by an author. You can find encyclopedias in school libraries, public libraries, CDs, and online on the computer.

Directions: Use the set of encyclopedias pictured on this page. Write the number of the volume you would use to locate information for the topics below.

A	B	C	D	E	F-G	H	I-J	K	L
1	2	3	4	5	6	7	8	9	10

M	N-O	P-Q	R	S	T	U	V	W	XYZ
11	12	13	14	15	16	17	18	19	20

1. plants _____

2. France_____

3. atoms _____

4. baseball_____

5. the Tropic of Cancer_____

6. the Aztec Indians _____

7. planets_____

8. Mozart _____

9. Zeus _____

10. light _____

11. sharks _____

12. pharaohs _____

An Atlas and an Almanac

An *atlas* and an *almanac* are two excellent references. An atlas is a book of maps and charts. It contains information about land features and the climatic conditions of places all around the world. In addition, facts about natural resources, farming areas, and industrial areas are included.

An almanac is a reference book that is updated and printed every year. Topics of general interest such as sports, current events, entertainment, state, national, and international facts are included. Information about past happenings can also be found.

Directions: Choose either an atlas or an almanac as the best reference book to answer these questions.

1. What is the state flower of New York? _____

2. What is the largest city in China? _____

3. What is the height of Mount Everest? _____

4. Who won the World Series in 1968? _____

5. What is the name of your state senator? _____

6. What are the names of the oceans of the world? _____

7. What is the name of the time zone in which Alaska is located? _____

8. What is the name of an endangered species? _____

9. What is the longest river in the world? _____

10. Who was the most recent past governor in Montana? _____

11. What countries border India? _____

12. What does Germany import? _____

13. What is the capital of Denmark? _____

14. What is the state bird of Georgia? _____

15. Who were the winners of the 1997 Academy Awards? _____

Writing a Friendly Letter

There are many times when you may have to write a friendly letter. Sending news about family and friends, sending invitations, and writing letters of thanks are examples of when friendly letters can be written.

The friendly letter has different parts. The address of the person writing the letter is in the upper right corner and is followed by the date. This is called the *heading*.

On the left is a *greeting* or opening. Most people start letters by using the word *Dear* and the name of the person to whom they are writing. This is followed by a comma.

Next comes the *body,* or main part, of the letter. It usually has at least three paragraphs. The first paragraph updates the reader as to any interesting news the sender of the letter wants to share. The second paragraph may ask questions and include an invitation from the writer. The final paragraph has concluding remarks and instructions.

The *closing* is the way the writer signs off. If two words such as "Your friend" are used, the first letter of the first word is capitalized while the second word is written with a lowercase letter. Start the closing in the middle of a new line directly under the body. The final step is to add the signature of the writer on the line below and directly under the closing.

> 475 Homedale Avenue
> Lakewood, New York 12755
> May 27, 2000

Dear Pete,

I have wanted to write to you for a long time, but I've really been busy. School, of course, takes up most of my time, but I have also been involved with other things. I joined a baseball team. We practice two or three times a week and play a game against another team every Thursday. It is so much fun, and we're in second place right now.

Do you still play ball? How is your team doing? I talked to my parents, and they said that I could invite you to spend the second weekend in June at my house. It will be so great! We can play video games, go to a movie, and even go to Yankee Stadium to see a real baseball game.

Please write back to me and let me know if your parents will let you come. Also, let me know all the news about your team. I hope I'll hear from you soon.

> Your friend,
> Bert

Directions: Answer the following questions about the letter.

1. Who wrote the letter? _____

2. Where does the writer live? _____

3. Why did he write the letter? _____

4. What specific instructions did the writer give? _____

Business Letter

There are many reasons for writing a business letter. You might need to ask for information, make a complaint, write to a government agency or even write to a publication such as a magazine or newspaper. Every business letter should include certain things.

❏ The *heading* is the part of the letter that contains your address and the date the letter was written.

❏ The *inside address* has the address and name of the company or the name and title of the person to whom you are writing the letter.

❏ The *greeting* is most often *"Dear"* plus the title *Mr., Mrs., Miss,* or *Ms.* and the last name of the person receiving the letter. If a name is not known, you may write "Gentlemen" or "Dear Sir" or "Dear Madam." The greeting in a business letter is followed by a colon.

❏ The *body* is the main section of the letter. It states the reason you are writing and the outcome you hope to achieve.

❏ The *closing* ends the letter with "sincerely" or "Yours truly" and comes just before the signature. The closing is followed by a comma.

❏ The *signature* is written by hand and signed, using script.

Directions: Insert the letter parts in the box below into the proper places on the business letter form on page 168.

All About Toy Company, 2471 Game Lane, Happyville, New York 17555

Gentlemen: I have always enjoyed the toys that your company produces and sells. Recently I purchased the Whammer Radio Car and remote control unit. It is not working properly. The toy moves in reverse when it should go forward. The buttons on the remote sometimes stick. I am shipping this toy back to you so that you can either fix it or replace it with a working model.

Thank you for your help. Sincerely, Robert Singleton

Business Letter *(cont.)*

Directions: Insert the parts of the letter written on page 167 in the proper places on the business letter form below.

Heading   _____

_____

_____

_____

Inside Address   _____

_____

_____

Greeting   _____

Body   _____

_____

_____

_____

_____

_____

_____

_____

Closing   _____

Signature   _____

Addressing Envelopes

The envelope that you use should have certain information written on the front.

The *return address* contains the name and address of the person who wrote the letter. It is placed in the upper left corner of the envelope.

The *mailing address* contains the name of the person or company receiving the letter. It is placed in the middle of the envelope. The first line should have the person or company name, while the second line has the street address, and the third line has the city, state, and zip code.

A postage stamp ensures delivery and is placed in the upper right corner of the envelope.

Example:

Martin Murphy
886 Fulton Street
Oakfield, NJ 11144

Andrew Bickney
270 Maplewood Avenue
Pinecrest, CT 24266

Directions: Use the following information to address the envelope below.

From: Susan Hanker, 42 Lightning Street, Bayview, New Hampshire 18923

To: The Fun to Read Book Company, 89 Tulip Blvd., Evans, Maine 90906

Reviewing Capitalization

- **Capitalize proper nouns** (*people, places, and things*):
  Michelle Ohio River

- **Capitalize proper adjectives:**
  Islamic   French   Chinese   Norwegian   French   Spanish rice   Greek myths

- **Capitalize the pronoun *I*.**

- **Capitalize titles when abbreviated or used with names:**
  Dr.   Mrs.   Rev.   Gen.   President Kennedy   Queen Elizabeth

- **Capitalize months, days, holidays, and historical events:**
  January   Tuesday   Labor Day   World War II

- **Capitalize words referring to religions, their scriptures, or God:**
  Bible   Jehovah   Koran   Islam   Judaism   Christianity

- **Capitalize clubs, businesses, and organizations:**
  Boy Scouts of America   IBM   Chamber of Commerce

- **Capitalize abbreviations and parts of addresses:**
  Rd.   St.   Ave.   NY   NJ   Detroit

- **Capitalize the first word of every sentence:**
  The boat sailed around the world.

- **Capitalize the first word, the last word, and all other words except articles, conjunctions, and short prepositions in titles of any written work such as a book or magazine:**
  Number the Stars   *National Geographic*   *The Adventures of Huckleberry Finn*

- **Capitalize *B.C., A.M., P.M.***

Reviewing Capitalization *(cont.)*

Directions: In the following sentences use capital letters where necessary.

1. the eiffel tower is located in paris, france.

2. rhode island, delaware, connecticut, hawaii, and new jersey are the five smallest states by area in the u.s.

3. *the nutcracker,* a famous ballet, is performed during the christmas season.

4. edgar allan poe wrote the thrilling short story "the fall of the house of usher."

5. the flight is scheduled to depart from la guardia airport at 10:30 a.m. and arrive in san francisco at 5:30 p.m.

6. i am going to receive the magazine *car and driver* on the first tuesday of march.

7. the novel the *castle in the attic* is an adventure story based on the middle ages.

8. the statue of liberty, a gift to the united states from france, is visible from new york city.

9. did you see the thanksgiving day parade as it proceeded down fifth avenue?

10. the taj mahal, an indian tomb, is an example of the blending of hindu and muslim architecture.

Directions: Correct these titles and names.

11. dr. erica weiss _____

12. *sports illustrated* _____

13. mr. james frank _____

14. dallas, texas _____

15. park place _____

16. george washington bridge _____

17. 5:40 a.m. _____

18. *the island of the blue dolphins* _____

19. pres. ronald reagan _____

20. the civil war _____

Reviewing Punctuation

(Periods, Question Marks, and Exclamation Points)

- Periods are used at the ends of declarative sentences and most imperative ones.
    The bird flew out of the cage. Please leave a tip.

- Periods are used after an abbreviation or an initial.
    Apr.   Mt.   St.   Mr.   R. L. Stine   Capt. R. B. White

- Periods are used after a number in the main topic and after a letter subtopic of an outline
    I.   Largest cities of the world
        A.   New York
        B.   London
        C.   Paris

- Question marks are placed at the ends of interrogative sentences.
    What time did the train leave the tracks?

- Exclamation points are used at the end of exclamatory sentences and after a strong interjection.
    What a wonderful play that was! Wow! That game was exciting.

Directions: Add periods, question marks, and exclamation points where needed.

1. How do male humpbacks communicate to the female humpback whales
2. What an incredible landing the pilot made
3. Great Your performance on the test was nearly perfect
4. The New York Knicks played the Chicago Bulls in Madison Square Garden
5. The Super Bowl was broadcast at 6:00 P M on Jan 31, 1999
6. Which president was elected first, Franklin D Roosevelt or Rutherford B Hayes
7. Mrs. B B Johnson, Jr was chosen to lead the parade
8. Watch out A deer is crossing the highway
9. Oh, no The elephants are stampeding toward the audience
10. Wow My bedroom will be 20 ft long and 15 ft wide

Directions: Place periods and capital letters where needed.

11. mr james mulligan
12. mt rushmore
13. the year 456 b c
14. p o box 345
15. rev jesse jackson
16. j h thompson and co
17. i museums of new york
        a guggenheim
        b metropolitan museum of art
        c museum of natural history

Reviewing Punctuation *(cont.)*

(Commas, Apostrophes, and Quotation Marks)

- Commas separate three or more items in a series:
  A tiger, lion, and elephant were in the circus ring.

- Commas are placed before *and, but,* or *or* when they are used to combine two sentences:
  Do you want to rent a movie, or shall we go bowling?

- Commas are used to help the reader pause and understand the sentence better:
  After I left the baby started to cry.
  After I left, the baby started to cry.

- Commas are used after mild interjections:
  Well, I guess I missed the train.

- Commas are used to set off an appositive:
  Mr. Jones, the mailman, is new.

- Commas are used to set off the name of a person spoken to:
  Mary, may I borrow your book?
  Please take out your pencil, Johnny.
  I hope, Sue, that you have your keys.

- Commas are used to separate the city from the state or country and in dates:
  Have you ever been to Melbourne, Australia?
  Chicago, Illinois, is known as the Windy City.
  March 15, 1978, is Jordan's birthday.

- Commas are used after the greeting of a friendly letter and the closing of any letter:
  Dear Pam,   *Sincerely,*   *Your pal,*

- Commas are used to set off words in a direct quotation. Quotation marks are placed before and after the words of a direct quotation. Capitalize the first word of a quotation. Place the comma, question mark, or exclamation point inside the quotation marks if it belongs to the quotation itself.
  "How was the gift?" asked Heather.
  Julie answered, "It was perfect!"
  "Don't water the plants," said Joey.

- Apostrophes are used to show possession or in a contraction.
  Gary's   can't

Directions: Add commas, quotation marks, and apostrophes where needed.

1. Please give our guest a warm welcome said the host of the talk show.

2. Governor how will the new tax increase affect the local schools asked the reporter.

3. Be careful driving to work warned the meteorologist Freezing temperatures have caused black ice to form on the roads.

4. Mars Jupiter Venus and Saturn are planets in our solar system.

5. The babys tears wouldnt stop for hours.

6. The *Titanic* sank in the atlantic ocean on April 15 1912.

Test Yourself

Circle the letter for the correct answer in each item that follows.

1. Which type of sentence is this?
   How many children are in this school?
   A. declarative   B. interrogative   C. exclamatory   D. imperative

2. What is the simple subject in this sentence?
   Does John ride a bus to work each day?
   A. does   B. ride   C. John   D. bus

3. Which type of sentence is this?
   The tall oak tree is surrounded by benches.
   A. declarative   B. interrogative   C. imperative   D. exclamatory

4. What is the complete subject in this sentence?
   The white kitten looks like a cotton ball.
   A. white kitten   B. looks   C. The white kitten   D. kitten

5. What type of sentence is this?
   What a wonderful vacation we had!
   A. declarative   B. interrogative   C. imperative   D. exclamatory

6. What is the simple subject in this sentence?
   The police detective arrested the criminal.
   A. the police   B. detective   C. arrested   D. criminal

7. What type of sentence is this?
   Park the car in the garage.
   A. declarative   B. interrogative   C. imperative   D. exclamatory

8. What is the simple subject in this sentence?
   Plant the seeds in the garden.
   A. plant   B. seeds   C. (you) understood   D. garden

9. What is the simple predicate in this sentence?
   The soccer player scored three goals.
   A. player   B. goals   C. scored   D. scored three goals

10. What is the complete predicate in this sentence?
    The passenger train arrived on schedule at the station.
    A. The passenger train   B. arrived on schedule at the station   C. train   D. arrived on schedule

11. What is the simple predicate in this sentence?
    Did the quarterback throw a touchdown?
    A. quarterback   B. did throw   C. touchdown   D. throw

Test Yourself *(cont.)*

12. What is the simple predicate in this sentence?
    Read three chapters in the book.

    A. (you) understood   B. chapters   C. read   D. book

13. What is the singular noun in this sentence?
    The happy toddlers are playing in the park.

    A. are playing   B. toddlers   C. park   D. happy

14. Find the plural noun.

    A. women   B. television   C. man   D. runs

15. Which phrase contains a singular possessive noun?

    A. foxes' tails   B. state's capital   C. children's toys   D. chairs' cushions

16. Which group of nouns does not demonstrate correct singular-plural spellings?

    A. sheep—sheep   B. mouse—mice   C. tail—tails   D. salmon—salmons

17. Which set of nouns does not demonstrate correct singular-plural spellings?

    A. sheep—sheeps   B. beach—beaches   C. table—tables   D. bush—bushes

18. What is the proper noun in this sentence?
    Which bridge is located in San Francisco?

    A. bridge   B. located   C. San Francisco   D. Which

19. Find the common noun in this sentence.
    James thinks the best hamburgers are at McDonald's.

    A. James   B. best   C. McDonald's   D. hamburgers

20. Which word is a linking verb?

    A. swim   B. bounce   C. is   D. drop

21. What is the helping verb in this sentence?
    Mary and Joe are watching the movie.

    A. and   B. are   C. watching   D. are watching

22. Which word is an action verb?

    A. are   B. was   C. appear   D. vote

23. Which sentence has a verb in the future tense?

    A. The basketball game was cancelled.

    B. The stereo broke yesterday.

    C. Will the artist display his work at the gallery?

    D. Palm trees grow best in warm, humid environments.

Test Yourself *(cont.)*

24. Which verb is in the past tense?

    A. carry   B. went   C. do   D. see

25. Which set of principal parts is correct?

    A. know(s), knew, knew   C. throw(s), threw, thrown
    B. go(es), gone, went   D. catch(es), catched, caught

26. Which set of principal parts is correct?

    A. play(s), played, played   C. flip(s), fliped, fliped
    B. teach(es), teached, taught   D. bring(s), brang, brought

27. Which sentence is incorrect?

    A. The king sat on the throne.   C. The reporter rose an important question.
    B. Let the meat marinate overnight.   D. The tiger may run very quickly.

28. Which word is the direct object in this sentence?
    Pioneer children did many chores on the farm.

    A. children   B. did   C. farm   D. chores

29. Which sentence is correct?

    A. The race car gone around the track at 100 miles per hour.
    B. Judy Blume written the book *Freckle Juice*.
    C. Frank had fallen down the well.
    D. The carpenter done a good job on the construction.

30. For which question would an encyclopedia be the best reference?

    A. What is the population of Tokyo?
    B. Who won the Super Bowl in 1985?
    C. Who was Alexander Hamilton?
    D. What were the election results in California in 1960?

31. For which question would an atlas be the best reference?

    A. How does a periscope work?
    B. Where is the Thames River?
    C. What are ultraviolet rays?
    D. What is the meaning of *apparition*?

32. For which question would an almanac be the best reference?

    A. What is the meaning of *subtle*?
    B. How many women were on active duty in the US Army in 1990?
    C. What is phototropism?
    D. How did World War I begin?

Test Yourself *(cont.)*

33. Which sentence is correct?

    A. The movie begins at 2:30 a.m.
    B. Dr Frank T Jones has opened a new office.
    C. Did the Civil War begin on April 12, 1861?
    D. Flour eggs cheese and milk are on the shopping list.

34. Which word is the simple predicate in this sentence?
    The ruins of Pompeii are an impressive sight.

    A. are   B. impressive   C. sight   D. ruins

35. What is the subject pronoun in this sentence?
    They lost their hearing because of loud sounds.

    A. hearing   B. They   C. sounds   D. their

36. What is the object pronoun in this sentence?
    She gave him her cards for his collection.

    A. his   B. her   C. him   D. she

37. Which sentence is not correct?

    A. Your probably afraid of sharks.
    B. Cats take good care of their fur.
    C. What are your views on the strike?
    D. The woodpecker uses its beak to peck.

38. Which pronoun is reflexive?

    A. ourselves   B. him   C. we   D. I

39. Which pronoun correctly completes this sentence?
    Steven and _____ collect baseball cards.

    A. me   B. I   C. us   D. him

40. Complete this sentence correctly.
    The farmers planted _____ corn early this year.

    A. there   B. his   C. they're   D. their

41. Which word in the sentence is used as a proper adjective?
    The American people experienced the warmest winter ever.

    A. warmest   B. ever   C. people   D. American

42. Which sentence is not correct?

    A. Which trees are the oldest trees in the world?
    B. Pluto is the most smallest planet.
    C. Indian elephants have shorter trunks than African elephants.
    D. Superman flies faster than a speeding bullet.

Test Yourself *(cont.)*

43. Find the adverb in this sentence.

    The bride walked slowly down the aisle.

    A. bride   B. walked   C. down   D. slowly

44. Which sentence is correct?

    A. Mark McGuire plays baseball good.

    B. The wolf in "The Three Little Pigs" acted bad.

    C. The teacher read us a good book.

    D. Nobody saw no spaceships at the airport.

45. What is the preposition in this sentence?

    The man with the suitcase is a salesman.

    A. man   B. with   C. the   D. is

46. Which prepositional phrase is used as an adjective in this sentence?

    The girl with the toy went into the park.

    A. girl with the   B. with the toy   C. went into the park   D. into the park

47. Which sentence is correct?

    A. The department store have a sale today.

    B. There are clams in the ocean.

    C. Two computers was broken.

    D. The butterfly do fly south each fall.

48. Which sentence is correct?

    A. R J Johnson, Jr donated money to the hospital.

    B. Sheila lives on hampton ct in chicago illinois.

    C. The Shearson Publishing Co. is located in Boston, Massachusetts.

    D. The Wright Brothers made their first flight near kitty hawk on Dec 17 1903.

49. Which sentence is not correct?

    A. The dog ran to its owner.

    B. They're going to graduate next year.

    C. Do you know which road to take?

    D. For roses were delivered four Stacey.

50. Which prefix means to repeat?

    A. pre-   B. re-   C. ex-   D. over

Mathematics Vocabulary

The mathematics terms listed below are important tools for understanding procedures in computation and problem solving. Check a dictionary or mathematics textbook for the meanings.

- acute angle
- acute triangle
- addend
- angle arc
- area
- average
- base
- capacity
- Celsius
- center
- centimeter
- circle
- circumference
- common denominator
- common factor
- common multiple
- compatible numbers
- composite numbers
- cone
- congruent
- cube
- cubic centimeter
- cup
- cylinder
- data
- decimal
- decimal point
- decimeter
- degree

- degrees Celsius
- degrees Fahrenheit
- denominator
- diagonal
- diameter
- difference
- discount
- dividend
- divisible
- divisor
- edge
- elapsed time
- equation
- equilateral triangle
- equivalent fractions
- estimate
- even number
- expanded form
- exponent
- face
- factor
- Fahrenheit
- flip
- foot
- formula
- fraction
- front-end estimation
- gallon

- gram
- greatest common factor (GCF)
- hexagon
- hypotenuse
- inch
- integers
- intersecting lines
- isosceles triangle
- kilogram
- kilometer
- least common denominator (LCD)
- legs
- line
- line segment
- line of symmetry
- liter
- lowest terms
- mass
- mean
- media
- meter
- mile
- milligram
- milliliter
- millimeter
- mixed number
- mode
- multiple

Mathematics Vocabulary *(cont.)*

- negative number
- numerator
- obtuse angle
- obtuse triangle
- octagon
- odd number
- opposites
- ordered pairs
- ounce
- outcome
- parallel lines
- parallelogram
- pentagon
- percent
- perimeter
- perpendicular
- pint
- plane
- point
- polygon
- positive number
- pound
- power
- prime factorization
- prime number
- prism

- probability
- product
- proportion
- pyramid
- quadrilateral
- quart
- quotient
- radius
- range
- rate
- ratio
- ray
- reciprocals
- rectangle
- regular polygon
- remainder
- repeating decimal
- rhombus
- right angle
- round
- sample
- scale
- scientific notation
- sides
- similar figures
- slide

- solution
- solve
- space figure
- sphere
- square
- square centimeter
- standard form
- sum
- surface area
- symmetrical figure
- temperature
- terms
- ton
- trapezoid
- traversable
- tree diagram
- triangle
- turn
- unit rate
- variable
- Venn diagram
- vertex
- volume
- word form
- yard

Math Terminology

Complete each sentence below with the proper term from the vocabulary listed in the word bank.

Word Bank

• addend	• difference	• discount	• dividend
• denominator	• edge	• estimate	• even number
• divisor	• factors	• fraction	• integers
• exponent	• mean	• median	• mixed number
• mass	• multiple	• numerator	• odd number
• mode	• prime number	• product	• quotient
• range	• sum	• variable	• volume
• average	• capacity	• congruent	

---

1. The segment formed when two faces of a space figure meet is called the _____ .

2. In division the number that divides the dividend is called the _____ .

3. In division the _____ is the answer.

4. In multiplication the _____ is the answer.

5. The _____ is the answer in addition.

6. The _____ is the answer in subtraction.

7. In division the number being divided is called the _____ .

8. The _____ are the numbers being added together in an addition problem.

9. Any number that can be divided by 2 without having a remainder is considered an _____ number.

10. An _____ number is any number that cannot be divided by 2 without a remainder.

11. A _____ is a number that compares part of an object or a set with the whole object or set.

12. The top number in a fraction is called the _____ ; the bottom number of any fraction is called the _____ .

13. Any answer that is not exact is an _____ .

Reviewing Math Terminology

14. The numbers being multiplied together to obtain a product are the _____ .

15. A _____ number is a whole number and a fraction (2³/₄).

16. If a number has only two factors, itself and 1, it is called a _____ number.

17. Any number greater than zero is a _____ number, while any number less than zero is a _____ number.

18. The _____ is the quotient found by dividing the sum of a set of data by the number of items of data.

19. The middle number in a set of data after the data is arranged in order from the least to the greatest is the _____ .

20. A _____ is the difference between the greatest number and the least number..

21. The amount of fluid a container can hold is its _____ measured in milliliters/liters or cups/quarts/gallons.

22. The _____ of an object is the amount of matter in it as determined by its weight in grams/kilograms or ounces/pounds.

23. When buying an object on sale, the _____ is the decrease in the price of the item.

24. The _____ is the number that appears most often in a set of data.

25. The _____ is the amount of space an object contains measured in cubic units.

26. A _____ is a letter that takes the place of a number. *Ex:* 5 + n = 9, n=4.

27. Two objects are _____ when they have the same size and shape.

28. The _____ tells the number of times a factor is used.

29. Whole numbers and their opposites are called _____ ; any positive number, any negative number, and zero.

30. The numeral 16 is a _____ of 4 because it is the product of a given number and any whole number.

Mathematical Properties

In order to add, subtract, multiply, and divide, it is important to know the basic principles associated with these procedures.

A. **Commutative Property of Addition:** Changing the order of the addends does not change the sum.

B. **Associative Property of Addition:** Changing the grouping of the addends does not change the sum. To know what to do first, look at the parentheses.

C. **Opposites Property of Addition and Subtraction:** Addition and subtraction are opposite operations. One undoes the other.

D. **Zero Property of Addition:** The sum of any number and zero is the number.

Mathematical Properties *(cont.)*

E. **Zero Properties of Subtraction:** The difference between any number and zero is that number. The difference between any number and itself is zero.

F. **Commutative Property of Multiplication:** Changing the order of factors does not change the product.

G. **Associative Property of Multiplication:** Changing the grouping of factors does not change the product.

H. **Zero Property of Multiplication:** The product of zero and any number is zero.

I. **Property of One in Multiplication:** The product of one and any number is that number.

J. **Distributive Property of Multiplication:** When two or more numbers are being multiplied by the same factor, you can multiply and then add or add and then multiply.

K. **Opposites Property of Multiplication and Division:** Multiplying by a number is the opposite of dividing by that number.

Mathematical Properties *(cont.)*

Match the Mathematical Properties (A–K) on pages 183 and 184 to the associated equations:

_____   1. $9 - 0 = 9, 9 - 9 = 0$

_____   2. $4 + 2 = 4, 6 - 4 = 2$

_____   3. $5 + 0 = 5, 0 + 5 = 5$

_____   4. $(3 + 2) + 4 = 9$ and $3 + (2 + 4) = 9$, so $(3 + 2) + 4 = 3 + (2 + 4)$

_____   5. $5 + 3 = 8, 3 + 5 = 8$

_____   6. $7 \times 1 = 7, 1 \times 7 = 7$

_____   7. $3 \times 0 = 0, 0 \times 3 = 0$

_____   8. $(3 \times 2) \times 5 = 3 \times (2 \times 5)$

_____   9. $3 \times (2 + 3) = (3 \times 2) + (3 \times 3)$

_____   10. $3 \times 5 = 15$, so $15 \div 3 = 5$

_____   11. $7 \times 4 = 4 \times 7$

Practice: Use one of the properties to complete the equations.

12. $7 + 8 = 8 +$ _____

13. $3 \times 8 = 8 \times$ _____

14. $6 \times 8 = 8 \times$ _____

15. _____ $\times$ _____ $= 0$

16. $(4 + 8) + 5 = 4 + ($ _____ $+ 5)$

17. $0 + 6 =$ _____ , so _____ $-$ _____ $= 0$

18. $(6 \times 4) \times 3 = 6 \times ($ _____ $\times 3)$

19. $2 \times ($ _____ $\times 4) = (2 \times 3) \times 4$

20. _____ $\times (3 + 5) = (7 \times 3) + (7 \times 5)$

21. _____ $\times ($ _____ $+$ _____ $) = (8 \times 4) + (8 \times 6)$

22. $4 \times ($ _____ $+$ _____ $) = (4 \times 5) + (4 \times 9)$

23. $n \times 5 = 40 \quad n =$ _____

24. $7 \times n = 56 \quad n =$ _____

25. $72 - n = 8 \quad n =$ _____

Estimation

Estimate by rounding to the place value indicated.

1. 56
   tens _____

2. 3,653
   hundreds _____

3. 457,830
   thousands _____

4. $2.96
   dollar_____

5. $17.75
   10 cents_____

6. $351.72
   10 cents_____

7. 36,245
   hundreds

8. 463,781
   ten thousands

9. $57.68
   dollar

   _____   _____   _____

The number has been rounded to the place value indicated. Write the least whole number that rounds to the given number.

10. 75,000
    thousand_____

11. 20,000
    ten thousand_____

12. 53,000,000
    million _____

13. 900,000
    hundred thousand_____

Write the greatest whole number that rounds to the given number.

14. 36,000
    thousand_____

15. 80,000
    ten thousand_____

16. 37,000,000
    million _____

17. 600,000
    hundred thousand_____

Applying Estimation:

18. A restaurant chain earned $73,853,361 last year after paying expenses. The owners expect to earn approximately the same amount next year, rounded to the nearest hundred thousand dollars. What is their projected profit?

_____

Addition and Subtraction

Calculate the difference or the sum. Use the inverse operation (addition or subtraction) to check your answer.

1.   748   _____
   − 359   + _____

2.   456   _____
   + 789   − _____

3.   8,675   _____
   + 3,489   − _____

4.   8,974   _____
   − 6,975   + _____

5.   15,908   _____
   − 13,989   + _____

6.   36,371   _____
   − 16,565   + _____

Round to estimate the sum or difference, using the adjusted front-end method.

Reminder: Adjusted front-end estimation means to estimate to the value on the left.

7.   39,735
   + 91,306

8.   77,431
   − 16,356

9.   35,251
   + 43,300

10.   73,086
   − 29,731

11.   88,880
   + 25,365

12.   3456
   + 5730

13.   5561
   − 2453

14.   4783
   + 2936

15.   6482
   − 3509

Problem Solving: Estimation in Addition and Subtraction

Solve the following word problems involving estimation, rounding, and actual computation in addition and subtraction.

1. George collected 365 coins last year. This year he has collected an additional 256 different coins. About how many coins has he collected altogether in these two years? Exactly how many were collected?

   Estimated Answer   _____

   Actual Answer   _____

2. The Browns and the Beimals bought new cars. The Browns paid $27,328, and the Beimals paid $32,751. Approximately what is the difference between the buying prices of the two cars rounded to the nearest thousand? How much more did the Beimals actually pay?

   Estimated Difference   _____

   Actual Difference   _____

3. The local Boy Scout troop is planning a family picnic. They ordered 156 hot dogs and 275 hamburgers. If each person eats one item, approximately how many people does the troop plan to feed? (Use front end-adjustment.) Exactly how many people will be attending?

   Estimated Attendance   _____

   Actual Attendance   _____

4. Juan hiked 404 miles during August and biked 824 miles during July. About how many miles has he covered during the summer? Calculate the actual mileage.

   Estimated Mileage   _____

   Actual Mileage   _____

5. Mrs. Ballin owns a candy shop. Last year her costs were $66,350. She sold $115,849 worth of candy. Approximately what was her profit, rounded to the nearest thousand? What was her precise profit?

   Approximate Profit   _____

   Exact Profit   _____

Estimating Decimals

Estimate the sum or difference using the adjusted front-end estimation. Then calculate the actual sum or difference.

1. 2.7   estimate
    + 6.93   _____

2. 4.75   estimate
    − 1.76   _____

3. 9.57   estimate
    + 0.44   _____

4. 0.58   estimate
    − 0.435   _____

5. 6.77   estimate
    + 2.8   _____

6. 15.3   estimate
    − 7.5   _____

7. 19.2   estimate
    + 36.5   _____

8. 4.2   estimate
    − 0.723   _____

9. 27.3   estimate
    − 22.9   _____

Estimate to compare the sum or difference. Use > for greater than and < for lesser than.

10. 16.3 + 2.33 ◯ 18

11. 26.75 − 12.09 ◯ 19

Tell whether the estimate is an overestimate or underestimate

12. 7.3 + 9.6 ≈ 20

13. 10.7 + 9.9 ≈ 30

On Your Own!

14. Cindy needs to cut ribbon for gift wrapping. She needs ribbons 2.6 meters, 1.5 meters, 0.75 meters, and 1.8 meters long. Her roll of ribbon has 5 meters. Will she have enough ribbon to wrap the gifts?

_____

_____

_____

_____

Adding and Subtracting Decimals

Place the decimal point in the sum.

1. $7.5 + 0.33 + 12.654$ _____

2. $6.053 + 2.271 + 12.6$ _____

Find the sum.

3. $5.6 + 4.7$ _____

4. $22.75 + 16.1$ _____

5. $\$66.21 + \$6.93$ _____

6. $12.306 + 0.19$ _____

7.
```
    3.82
   14.254
 +  6.75
 _____
```

8.
```
    4.3
   31.72
 + 5.246
 _____
```

9.
```
   0.1437
   50.22
 +  7.34
 _____
```

10.
```
    6.7
   52.43
 + 1.625
 _____
```

11. $\$0.55 + \$37.81 + \$55.00 =$ _____

12. $60.1 + 352.33 + 5,075 + 0.88 =$ _____

Place the decimal point in the difference.

13. $6.75 - 3.25 =$ _____

14. $36.005 - 0.35 =$ _____

Find the difference.

15. $10.6 - 4.35 =$ _____

16. $245.8 - 83.19 =$ _____

17. $77.112 - 6.03 =$ _____

18. $8.045 - 3.72 =$ _____

19.
```
   60.44
 -  2.755
 _____
```

20.
```
    5.6
 - 0.89
 _____
```

21.
```
   72.8
 - 0.654
 _____
```

22.
```
   67.03
 - 0.0058
 _____
```

23. $\$37.82 - \$8.46 =$

24. $456.08 - 93.95 =$ _____

Problem Solving: Adding and Subtracting Decimals

1. The monthly rainfall during the spring was 3.4 inches, 8.6 inches, and 10.2 inches over three months. What was the total rainfall?

   _____

2. Sheila is redecorating the guest room. She needs 8.25 yards for the curtains and 16.25 yards for the bedspread and to recover the chair. How many yards must be bought to assure Sheila that she will have enough material?

   _____

3. The tennis player served the tennis ball at a top speed of 111.35 miles per hour. His opponent serves at a top speed of 106.85 miles per hour. What is the difference between the two speeds?

   _____

4. Deacon and Gary had lunch together at a restaurant. Deacon's entree cost $13.75, while Gary's entree was $12.55. Both men had dessert for $1.95 each. How much was the total bill?

   _____

5. Mr. James has 3 deposits of $1,242.30, $653.21, and $125.89 to make in his checking account. How much is his total deposit?

   _____

6. Mr. Lee has a balance of $2,563.37 in his checking account. He needs to write two checks: one for $833.25 and the other for $475.66. How much will be left in his checking account?

   _____

7. Stacey scored a 5.75 in the technical merit category in the ice skating championship. In the artistic interpretation category, she scored a 5.9. Meredith outscored Stacey by 0.32. What was Meredith's overall score?

   _____

8. When John went shopping, he bought sneakers for $65.75, a pair of shorts for $18.50, and a T-shirt for $12.95. How much money did he have left for lunch if he started out with $100.00?

   _____

9. Heather wants to buy a new video game that costs $74.99. She only has $33.50. How much more does she need?

   _____

Factors

- *Factors* are numbers that can be equally divided with no remainder.

- A *prime number* has itself and one as a factor.

- A *composite number* has more than two factors.

Example: Find the factors of 15.

The factors of 15 are 1, 3, 5.

15 is a composite number because it has more than two factors.

1 x 15   or

                                        3 x 5

Directions: Factor each number and then identify it as being a prime or a composite number.

1. Factor 6   6

    or   / \

   __ x __   __ x __

   The factors of 6 are _____ .
   6 is a (prime, composite) number.

2. Factor 8

   / \   or   8

   __ x __

                           __ x __

   The factors of 8 are _____ .
   8 is a (prime, composite) number.

3. Factor 7

   / \

   __ x __

   The factors of 7 are _____ .
   7 is a (prime, composite) number.

4. Factor 18

   / \   or   18

   __ x __   or   18

                          __ x __

                                                      __ x __

   The factors of 18 are _____ .
   18 is a (prime, composite) number.

Factors *(cont.)*

Factors can be written in exponent form.

> *Example:*   Find the factors of 20 and write them in exponent form.

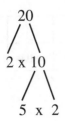

20

2 x 10

5 x 2

The factors of 20 are

2 x 2 x 5 =

2^2 x 5

Directions: Find the factors of each number and then write the factors in exponent form.

1. 18 _____

2. 16 _____

3. 20 _____

4. 24 _____

5. 9 _____

6. 32 _____

7. 75 _____

8. 12 _____

9. 36 _____

The *greatest common factor* (GCF) is the largest factor that a set of numbers has in common.

> *Example:*   Find the GCF of 6 and 12.
> > A. Find the factors of both numbers.
> >   6 = 1, 2, 3
> >   12 = 1, 2, 3, 4, 6
> > B. Find the common factors.
> >   2 and 3 are factors of 6 and 12.
> > C. The GCF of 6 and 12 is 3 (excluding 6 itself).

Directions: Find the GCF for each set of numbers.

10. 4 _____

    12 _____

11. 10 _____

    30 _____

12. 20 _____

    30 _____

13. 12 _____

    18 _____

14. 15 _____

    50 _____

15. 18 _____

    20 _____

Multiples

Any whole number can be multiplied by another. When we do this, the resulting number is a *multiple*.

Directions: Fill in the chart with the missing multiples. To find the multiples of 4, multiply by 4.

4 x

1	2	3	4	5	6	7	8	9	10
	8								40

multiple

Find the multiples of 2.

2 x

1	2	3	4	5	6	7	8	9	10

multiple

As we look across the chart, we can see that (excluding the number itself and 1) 8, 12, 16, and 20 appear as multiples of both 2 and 4. These are called *common multiples*.

The least common multiple (excluding itself and 1) is the lowest common number that both numbers have in common. For 2 and 4, the least common multiple (LCM) is 8.

Exercise: Find the multiples of 3 and 5.

3 multiples   0 __ __ __ __ __ __ __ 24

5 multiples   0 __ __ __ __ __ __ 35 __

Circle the least common multiple of 3 and 5.

What are the first two LCM for the following numbers?

a. 3 and 6 _____

b. 6 and 9 _____

c. 8 and 10 _____

d. 10 and 20 _____

e. 3 and 8 _____

f. 4 and 7 _____

g. Tom and Karen are planning a party. They want to buy bags of blue and yellow balloons. The blue balloons have 4 in a package and the yellow balloons have 5 in each package. In order to have an equal number of blue and yellow balloons, what is the least number of packages of each color they will have to buy?

_____

Multiplication Practice

Estimate the product and compare. Use > or <.

1. 47 x 23 ◯ 2000

2. 9 x 58 ◯ 700

3. 196 x 36 ◯ 3000

Use mental math to choose the best estimate.

4. 653 x 345 =   a. 100,000   b. 210,000   c. 400,000

5. 2,860 x 9 =   a. 7,000   b. 27,000   c. 18,000

6. 6,957 x 520 =   a. 3,500,000   b. 350,000   c. 35,000

Estimate the product.

7.   78   8.   4,630   9.   247   10.   419
    x 8   x 5   x 7   x 6
   _____   _____   _____   _____

Find the product in the following multiplication problems with two- and three-digit factors.

11.   71   12.   89   13.   436   14.   2,306
     x 38   x 56   x 84   x 275
    _____   _____   _____   _____

15.   436   16.   2,657   17.   82,467   18.   367,478
     x 805   x 838   x 247   x 658
    _____   _____   _____   _____

19. 735,669 x 302 = _____   20. 23,509 x 1,017 = _____

Multiplying Decimals

Place the decimal point in the product by estimating first.

1. 7.6 x 8.3 = _____

2. 4.65 x 6.8 = _____

3. 0.84 x 5.3 = _____

4. 0.45 x 0.93 = _____

Estimate the product. Then calculate the exact product.

5.   26.73
     x 6.8

6.   78
     x 2.9

7.   6.245
     x 0.7

8.   65.8
     x 337

Calculate the product. Round money problems to the nearest cent.

9.   7.356
     x 6.8

10. $17.93
     x 0.6

11. $683.25
     x 0.27

12. $43.78
     x 0.5

13.   0.035
     x 8

14.   25.89
     x 30.5

15.   0.0057
     x 778

16.   7.206
     x 18

17. $365.27 x 2.8 = _____

18. 6,983 x 6.217 = _____

19. 15.3 x 1,000 = _____

20. 536 x 100 = _____

21. 0.25 x 10 = _____

22. 0.884 x 100 = _____

23. 928.75 x 10 = _____

24. 8.6 x 1000 = _____

Problem Solving: Multiplication

Solve the following word problems involving multiplication.

1. Turkey costs $7.99 a pound. How much will 3.125 pounds cost, rounded to the nearest cent?

_____

2. Sheets of foam board are 0.50 cm thick. How thick is a pile of two dozen foam boards?

_____

3. The ferry makes 8 round trips across the river each day. A one-way excursion is 3.5 miles. How many miles are traveled in a week?

_____

4. Mrs. Ruby drove 152 miles. Her husband drove the next 273 miles. The next day they drove twice as far. How many miles were traveled in the two-day trip?

_____

5. A plane travels a distance of 1,637 miles in three hours. How many miles will the plane travel in 12 hours?

_____

6. Andrew earns $6.50 per hour working the night shift at McDonald's. Last week he worked 39.75 hours How much did he earn?

_____

7. Sherry went shopping at the neighborhood drugstore. She bought three bottles of nail polish at $2.19 each, two new lipsticks at $4.66 each, and four shampoos at $3.25 each. How much did she spend in the drugstore?

_____

8. Mrs. Miller bought 16 rolls of film for her photography class. There were 36 exposures on each roll of film. All the pictures were developed except for two rolls. How many pictures were developed? Each print cost $0.28 to develop. How much did Mrs. Miller spend on developing?

_____

Estimation in Division

Estimate to find the best quotient. Circle the answer.

1. 6$\overline{)487}$ a. 60   b. 70   c. 80   d. 50

2. 5$\overline{)14,482}$ a. 300   b. 30   c. 2,500   d. 3,000

3. 4,627 ÷ 23   a. 100   b. 2,000   c. 200   d. 3,000

4. 8$\overline{)688}$ a. 100   b. 10   c. 80   d. 800

Write the best estimated quotient.

5. 7$\overline{)65}$ 6. 6$\overline{)358}$ 7. 5$\overline{)3889}$

Divide to find the quotient.

8. 4$\overline{)316}$ 9. 6$\overline{)2,586}$ 10. 7$\overline{)5,103}$

11. 9$\overline{)73,463}$ 12. 8$\overline{)46,065}$ 13. 3$\overline{)14,053}$

14. 16,084 ÷ 4 =   15. 37,398 ÷ 7 =   16. 5$\overline{)26,009}$

Division with Decimals

Find the quotient.

1. $6.6 \div 3.3 =$ _____

2. $8.8 \div 11 =$ _____

3. $8.4 \div 2.1 =$ _____

4. $19.8 \div 9.9 =$ _____

5. $18.6 \div 6.2 =$ _____

6. $14.8 \div 3.7 =$ _____

7. $0.34\overline{)266.56}$

8. $0.134\overline{)3.39824}$

9. $6.5\overline{)300.3}$

10. $2.6\overline{)9.1}$

11. $0.035\overline{)2.5249}$

12. $0.12\overline{)2.832}$

13. $2.36\overline{)107.852}$

14. $0.57\overline{)0.3249}$

15. $27\overline{)0.96768}$

Divide. Then round the quotient to the place value shown.

16. $\$3.76 \div 5 =$ _____
    (cents)

17. $643.2 \div 2.8 =$ _____
    (hundredths)

18. $97 \div 13 =$ _____
    (tenths)

More Division Practice

Estimate the quotient.

1. $41\overline{)248}$

2. $32\overline{)155}$

3. $17\overline{)3,605}$

4. $15,689 \div 31 =$

5. $1,856 \div 29 =$

6. $57,352 \div 82 =$

Divide to find the quotient.

7. $75\overline{)66,389}$

8. $66\overline{)135,472}$

9. $84\overline{)589}$

10. $7\overline{)8,400}$

11. $34\overline{)5,900}$

12. $33\overline{)2,860}$

13. $5\overline{)18}$

14. $6\overline{)25.62}$

15. $28\overline{)165.088}$

16. $6.540 \div 30 =$

17. $15.15 \div 25 =$

18. $32.550 \div 70 =$

Division Word Problems

Solve each of the word problems.

1. An SST travels at an average rate of 1,200 miles per hour. About how many miles does it travel in one minute?

    _____

2. Ms. Gray is baking cookies for the school fair. She plans on baking 450 cookies. Each tray of cookies holds about 16 cookies. About how many trays will she need to prepare?

    _____

3. A school in Detroit receives a delivery of 1,185 magazines each month in packages of 30. About how many classes are getting class sets of this magazine?

    _____

    If there are five grades in the school, how many classes are on each grade level?

    _____

4. There are 4,556 chickens on the farm. If 34 chickens are kept in each room in the coop, how many rooms are needed?

    _____

5. Jackie counted 2,100 pennies. If she places 50 pennies in each roll, how many rolls will she have?

    _____

6. Samantha earns $318.75 a week in salary. She worked 37.5 hours last week. How much does she earn an hour as a bookkeeper?

    _____

7. Jimmy jogs y miles each day, regardless of the weather. How many miles does Jimmy jog each year? Use y = 6 for the expression.

    _____

8. Christina receives d dollars a week for school lunches from her mother. Christina attended school all five days last week. If she spends the same amount each day, how much is the school lunch? Estimate the expression for $12.75.

    _____

Range, Mean, Median, and Mode

Tom picked these five numbers: 92, 36, 40, 52, 40. He knew that the difference between the greatest number and the least number is called the **range.**

    Example: The range between 92 and 36 is
                         $92 - 36 = 56$

Tom knew that he had five numbers and their sum was equal to 260. If he divided the sum by the total numbers he had, he could find the **mean.**

    Example: $\dfrac{36 + 40 + 52 + 40 + 92}{5} = \dfrac{260}{5} = 52$

When Tom looked at the numbers after he listed them in order from least to greatest, he was able to find the **median.** The median is the number in the middle of the sequence (or the mean of the two middle numbers if there are an even number of items in the sequence).

    Example: 36   40   (40)   52   92

The **mode** is the number that appears most often.

    Example: 36   (40)   52   (40)   92

            The number 40 appears twice, so it is the mode.

Directions: Find the *range, mean, median* and *mode* for each set of numbers.

1. 25, 73, 12, 25, 35

     A.   Order: ____   ____   ____   ____   ____

     B.   Range: ___ – ___ = ___

     C.   Mean: $\dfrac{\_\_\_ + \_\_\_ + \_\_\_ + \_\_\_ + \_\_\_}{5} = \dfrac{\_\_\_}{5} = \_\_\_$

     D.   Median: _____

     E.   Mode: _____

2. 100, 23, 49, 88, 30, 23, 51

     A.   Order: ____   ____   ____   ____   ____   ____   ____

     B.   Range: _____

     C.   Mean: _____

     D.   Median: _____

     E.   Mode: _____

Range, Mean, Median, and Mode *(cont.)*

3. 18, 36, 24, 18

    A. Order: _____

    B. Range: _____

    C. Mean: _____

    D. Median: _____

    E. Mode: _____

4. 22, 70, 22, 84, 36, 42

    A. Order: _____

    B. Range: _____

    C. Mean: _____

    D. Median: _____

    E. Mode: _____

5. 170, 200, 305

    A. Order: _____

    B. Range: _____

    C. Mean: _____

    D. Median: _____

    E. Mode: _____

6. 45, 66, 89, 69, 77, 22, 66

    A. Order: _____

    B. Range: _____

    C. Mean: _____

    D. Median: _____

    E. Mode: _____

Solving Equations

Use the values below to solve the expression 4.8 x a = _____ .

1. a = 25 _____
2. a = 55 _____
3. a = 362 _____
4. a = 13.8 _____

Use the values below to solve the expression $\dfrac{x}{6}$ = _____ .

5. x = 54 _____
6. x = 222 _____
7. x = 4659 _____
8. x = 93 _____

Evaluate the expressions.

9. 26 b, when b = 7
10. $\dfrac{s}{5}$, when s = 155
11. 74 m, when m = 6

12. 5.3 s, when s = 2.6
13. $\dfrac{n}{4.6}$, when n = 35.88
14. $\dfrac{y}{1.8}$, when y = 6.3

Tell how to solve each equation (multiply or divide). Then solve the problem.

Reminder: The inverse of multiplication is division.
The inverse of division is multiplication.

Example: 2 x = 10 divide by 2
$\dfrac{c}{3}$ = 15 multiply by 3

15. 45a = 135
16. 35t = 1,050
17. $\dfrac{m}{16}$ = 100

_____
_____
_____

18. $\dfrac{s}{215}$ = 1
19. 81f = 729
20. 15p = 360

_____
_____
_____

204

Fractions

A *fraction* represents a part of a whole. It compares part of an object or set with the whole object or set. The *numerator* is the top number in the fraction. The *denominator*, or the bottom number, represents into how many parts the whole item is divided. The line separating the numerator and the denominator actually means "divide by."

Write the fraction stated in words.

1. three-sevenths   _____

2. six-eighths   _____

3. three-fourths   _____

4. seven-tenths   _____

5. eight-twelfths   _____

6. fifty-two hundredths   _____

Equivalent fractions are those that are equal to one another. The terms of the fraction, the numerator and the denominator, can be multiplied by the same number (other than zero) to write an equivalent fraction.

$$\text{Example: } \frac{3}{5} = \frac{3 \times 2}{5 \times 2} = \frac{6}{10}$$

What is the equivalent fraction?

7. $\frac{1}{2} = \frac{1 \times 4}{2 \times 4} = $ _____

8. $\frac{1}{3} = \frac{1 \times 3}{3 \times 3} = $ _____

9. $\frac{6}{10} = \frac{6 \times 3}{10 \times 3} = $ _____

Complete the following, using mental math.

10. $\frac{1}{2} = \frac{5}{}$

11. $\frac{3}{7} = \frac{15}{}$

12. $\frac{7}{12} = \frac{}{36}$

13. $\frac{2}{9} = \frac{}{27}$

14. $\frac{2}{3} = \frac{16}{}$

15. $\frac{4}{6} = \frac{2}{}$

16. $\frac{8}{20} = \frac{}{100}$

17. $\frac{5}{21} = \frac{}{105}$

You can write an equivalent fraction that is lower than the original fraction. To write a fraction in lowest terms, divide both terms (the numerator and denominator) by their greatest common factor (GCF). This is called "reducing the fraction."

Reduce the fraction to its lowest terms.

18. $\frac{7}{21} = $

19. $\frac{10}{25} = $

20. $\frac{12}{36} = $

21. $\frac{8}{12} = $

22. $\frac{8}{28} = $

23. $\frac{25}{100} = $

24. $\frac{90}{100} = $

25. $\frac{174}{1,000} = $

Fractions and Decimals

A *mixed number* is a fraction greater than 1, written as a whole number and a fraction. A fraction written with the numerator larger than the denominator is called an *improper fraction*. Improper fractions should be changed into proper fractions or mixed fractions. To change an improper fraction into a mixed fraction, divide the numerator by the denominator.

Example: $\dfrac{16}{5} = 3\dfrac{1}{5}$ $\begin{array}{r} 3\text{ r}1 \\ 5\overline{)16} \\ -15 \\ \hline 1 \end{array}$ or $3\dfrac{1\ \text{(remainder)}}{5\ \text{(divisor)}}$

Write the fraction as a mixed number or a whole number.

1. $\dfrac{25}{6}$ 2. $\dfrac{13}{4}$ 3. $\dfrac{40}{5}$ 4. $\dfrac{38}{7}$ 5. $\dfrac{27}{9}$

Write the mixed number as a fraction.

6. $3\dfrac{2}{7}$ 7. $5\dfrac{3}{5}$ 8. $7\dfrac{2}{9}$ 9. $4\dfrac{3}{8}$ 10. $2\dfrac{9}{10}$

Write the quotient as a mixed number. Write the fraction in lowest terms.

11. $5\overline{)11}$ 12. $8\overline{)38}$ 13. $5\overline{)48}$ 14. $8\overline{)74}$

Mixed numbers may be written as decimals. To write a mixed number as a decimal, first write the fraction as a decimal by dividing the numerator by the denominator. Then add the whole number and the decimal.

Example: $2\dfrac{3}{5}$ $\dfrac{3}{5} = $ $\begin{array}{r} 0.6 \\ 5\overline{)3.0} \end{array}$ $2 + 0.6 = 2.6$

Write the fraction or the mixed number as a decimal.

15. $\dfrac{2}{8}$ $8\overline{)2.0}$ 16. $\dfrac{3}{4}$ $4\overline{)3.0}$ 17. $6\dfrac{4}{20}$ $20\overline{)4.00}$

18. $\dfrac{1}{2}$ 19. $\dfrac{2}{8}$ 20. $\dfrac{15}{25}$ 21. $3\dfrac{6}{10}$

Comparing and Ordering Fractions

Comparing fractions and ordering them from least to greatest is simple when the denominator is the same.

Example: $\dfrac{2}{7} < \dfrac{5}{7}$ because $2 < 5$

In order to compare fractions with different denominators, find the least common multiple (LCM) of the denominators. That is the least common denominator (LCD).

Example: Compare the fractions $\dfrac{2}{4}$ and $\dfrac{3}{4}$ (think 3 x 4 = 12).

$$\frac{2}{3} = \frac{8}{12} \qquad \frac{3}{4} = \frac{9}{12} \qquad \frac{8}{12} < \frac{9}{12} \quad \text{so} \quad \frac{2}{3} < \frac{3}{4}$$

Example: Order the fractions $\dfrac{5}{9}$, $\dfrac{2}{3}$, $\dfrac{3}{4}$ (think 36 9, 3, & 4).

$$\frac{5}{9} = \frac{20}{36} \qquad \frac{2}{3} = \frac{24}{36} \qquad \frac{3}{4} = \frac{27}{36} \quad \text{so} \quad \frac{5}{9} < \frac{2}{3} < \frac{3}{4}$$

Write < or > to compare the fractions.

1. $\dfrac{4}{9} \bigcirc \dfrac{3}{9}$ 2. $\dfrac{2}{3} \bigcirc \dfrac{5}{9}$ 3. $\dfrac{3}{7} \bigcirc \dfrac{15}{21}$ 4. $\dfrac{3}{5} \bigcirc \dfrac{2}{3}$

Arrange the fractions in order from least to greatest.

5. $\dfrac{2}{8}$, $\dfrac{3}{6}$, $\dfrac{5}{12}$ _____ , _____ , _____

6. $\dfrac{3}{15}$, $\dfrac{2}{3}$, $\dfrac{7}{10}$ _____ , _____ , _____

7. $\dfrac{7}{18}$, $\dfrac{2}{9}$, $\dfrac{4}{6}$ _____ , _____ , _____

8. $\dfrac{10}{25}$, $\dfrac{3}{5}$, $\dfrac{16}{50}$ _____ , _____ , _____

9. $\dfrac{2}{4}$, $\dfrac{5}{16}$, $\dfrac{5}{8}$ _____ , _____ , _____

Adding and Subtracting Fractions

To add fractions with the same denominator, add the numerators and write the sum over the same denominator. To subtract fractions with the same denominator, subtract the numerators and write the difference over the same denominator. Always write the sum or difference in lowest terms.

1. $\dfrac{5}{6} - \dfrac{3}{6}$ 　　　2. $\dfrac{4}{7} + \dfrac{2}{7}$ 　　　3. $\dfrac{7}{12} - \dfrac{4}{12}$ 　　　4. $\dfrac{5}{16} + \dfrac{3}{16}$

To add or subtract fractions with different denominators, first write equivalent fractions with a common denominator. Then add or subtract. Write the sum or difference in lowest terms.

5. $\dfrac{3}{5} + \dfrac{2}{8}$ 　　　6. $\dfrac{3}{5} + \dfrac{5}{7}$ 　　　7. $\dfrac{7}{9} - \dfrac{1}{2}$ 　　　8. $\dfrac{4}{5} - \dfrac{3}{4}$

To add or subtract mixed numbers, determine if the fractions have to be changed to equivalent fractions. First change the fractions to equivalent fractions and then proceed with the addition or subtraction.

Sometimes the mixed number will have to be renamed. Change the whole number to a fraction equal to one and add it to the fraction portion, resulting in an improper fraction.

Proceed with the addition or subtraction. Write the sum or difference in lowest terms.

Add or subtract. Then write the answer in lowest terms.

9. $\dfrac{7}{10}$ $-\dfrac{5}{10}$ 　　10. $\dfrac{3}{8}$ $+\dfrac{5}{12}$ 　　11. $\dfrac{3}{4}$ $-\dfrac{1}{5}$ 　　12. $\dfrac{5}{16}$ $+\dfrac{3}{8}$

13. $4\,^3/_4 + 5\,^5/_6$ = _____

14. $9\,^7/_8 - 6\,^2/_4$ = _____

15. $5\,^2/_3 - 2\,^4/_9$ = _____

Multiplying and Dividing Fractions

To multiply a fraction and a whole number, first multiply the numerator of the fraction by the whole number. Then write the product above the denominator.

Example: $4 \times \frac{1}{2} = 4 \times 1 = 4$, then $\frac{4}{2}$ which $= 2$

To multiply fractions, multiply the numerators and then multiply the denominators.

Example: $\frac{1}{2} \times \frac{3}{4} = \frac{1}{2} \times \frac{3}{4} = \frac{3}{8}$

To multiply mixed numbers as fractions, first write the mixed numbers as fractions. Simplify if possible. Then multiply.

Example: $4\frac{1}{2} \times 6\frac{3}{4} = \frac{9}{2} \times \frac{27}{4} = \frac{243}{8} = 30\frac{3}{8}$

Example: $5\frac{1}{3} \times 3\frac{1}{4} = \frac{\overset{4}{\cancel{16}}}{3} \times \frac{13}{\underset{1}{\cancel{4}}} = \frac{4 \times 13}{3 \times 1} = \frac{52}{3} = 17\frac{1}{3}$

To divide a whole number by a fraction, first convert the fraction into its reciprocal (its reverse), and then multiply.

Example: $6 \div \frac{1}{2} = \frac{6}{1} \times \frac{2}{1} = 12$

To divide a fraction by a whole number, first write the reciprocal of the whole number divisor and then multiply.

Example: $\frac{3}{4} \div 3 = \frac{3}{4} \times \frac{1}{3} = \frac{3}{12} = \frac{1}{4}$

To divide a fraction by a fraction, multiply the fraction by the reciprocal of the divisor.

Example: $\frac{3}{4} \div \frac{1}{2} = \frac{3}{4} \times \frac{2}{1} = \frac{6}{4} = 1\frac{2}{4} = 1\frac{1}{2}$

To divide mixed numbers, first write the mixed numbers as fractions. Then multiply by the reciprocal of the divisor.

Example: $5\frac{1}{2} \div 2\frac{1}{4} = \frac{11}{2} \div \frac{9}{4} = \frac{11}{\underset{1}{\cancel{2}}} \times \frac{\overset{2}{\cancel{4}}}{9} = \frac{11 \times 2}{1 \times 9} = \frac{22}{9} = 2\frac{4}{9}$

Practice Multiplying and Dividing Fractions and Mixed Numbers

Multiply and reduce to lowest terms.

1. $5 \times \dfrac{6}{8}$

2. $\dfrac{4}{10} \times 34$

3. $\dfrac{6}{12} \times \dfrac{8}{9}$

4. $\dfrac{5}{11} \times \dfrac{4}{7}$

5. $\dfrac{15}{6} \times \dfrac{3}{8}$

6. $8 \times 3\dfrac{1}{5}$

7. $3\dfrac{3}{7} \times \dfrac{7}{8}$

8. $4\dfrac{1}{4} \times 6\dfrac{2}{5}$

9. $\dfrac{3}{15} \times 60$

10. $\dfrac{13}{15} \times \dfrac{3}{36}$

11. $5\dfrac{5}{7} \times 2\dfrac{3}{5}$

12. $4\dfrac{1}{4} \times 2\dfrac{7}{9}$

Divide and reduce to lowest terms.

13. $4 \div \dfrac{7}{10}$

14. $16 \div \dfrac{3}{8}$

15. $\dfrac{1}{3} \div 5$

16. $\dfrac{4}{9} \div 18$

17. $\dfrac{5}{8} \div \dfrac{3}{5}$

18. $\dfrac{3}{10} \div \dfrac{16}{20}$

19. $4\dfrac{5}{6} \div \dfrac{8}{7}$

20. $2\dfrac{2}{7} \div 3\dfrac{4}{7}$

21. $3\dfrac{1}{12} \div 9\dfrac{2}{3}$

22. $\dfrac{9}{11} \div 36$

23. $5\dfrac{4}{5} \div 6\dfrac{2}{5}$

24. $28 \div \dfrac{1}{2}$

25. Mary made cupcakes. She gave half of them to Joan. Joan shared the cupcakes equally with two friends. How many cupcakes did Mary make if Joan and her friends each got 12 cupcakes?

26. Jerry found three dozen fireflies one summer evening. He gave half of them to his friend Joe, one fourth of them to his friend Larry, and one third of his share to his sister. How many fireflies did he have left?

Customary Measurement

Liquid Measures

Ounces		Cups		Pints		Quarts		Gallons
8	=	1						
16	=	2						
32	=	4	=	1				
64	=	8	=	2	=	1		
128	=	16	=	8	=	4	=	1

Exercises: Change each unit of measurement into an equivalent measurement.

1. 3 gallons = _____ quarts

                = _____ pints

                = _____ cups

                = _____ ounces

2. 4 quarts = _____ pints

              = _____ cups

              = _____ ounces

3. 10 ounces = _____ cups and _____ ounces

4. 250 ounces = _____ cups and _____ ounces

5. 5 pints = _____ cups and _____ ounces

Dry Measures

Ounces		Pounds		Tons
16	=	1		
		2000	=	1

Exercise: Change each unit of measurement into the equivalent measurement.

6. 12,000 pounds = _____ tons

7. 7,500 pounds = _____ tons

8. 80 ounces = _____ pounds

9. 4.5 pounds = _____ ounces

10. Mary bought three pounds of turkey at the deli counter. How many ounces of turkey did she buy?

11. An apple orchard harvested 2.5 tons of apples last year. How many pounds of apples were harvested?

12. A cheesecake recipe called for two quarts of heavy cream and 2 cups of sour cream. How many pints of heavy cream and sour cream were needed to make this cake?

Customary Measurement *(cont.)*

Linear Measures

Inches		Feet		Yards
12	=	1		
36	=	3	=	1

To change a measurement of feet into a measurement of inches, multiply by 12.

> *Example:* How many inches are equal to 4 feet?
> 4 feet x 12 inches = 48 inches

Exercise: Change the following measurements into inches.

1. 7 feet = _____ inches

3. 9 feet = _____ inches

2. 12 feet = _____ inches

4. 24 feet = _____ inches

To change a measurement of inches into feet, divide by twelve.

> *Example:* How many feet are equal to 60 inches?
> $$\frac{60 \text{ inches}}{12 \text{ inches}} = 5 \text{ feet}$$

Exercise: Change the following measurements into feet.

5. 48 inches = _____ feet

7. 7,200 inches = _____ feet

6. 9,816 inches = _____ feet

8. 24 inches = _____ feet

To change a measurement of yards to feet, multiply by three.

> *Example:* How many feet are equal to 7 yards?
> 7 yards x 3 feet = 21 feet

Exercise: Change the yards to feet.

9. 15 yards = _____ feet

11. 6 yards = _____ feet

10. 3 yards = _____ feet

12. 9 yards = _____ feet

To change feet to yards, divide by three.

> *Example:* $\frac{66 \text{ feet}}{3 \text{ feet}} = 22 \text{ yards}$

Exercise: Change the feet to yards.

13. 366 feet = _____ yards

15. 915 feet = _____ yards

14. 27 feet = _____ yards

16. 1,536 feet = _____ yards

Customary Measurement *(cont.)*

Time

Seconds		Minutes		Hours
60	=	1		
3600	=	60	=	1

To find the total number of hours and minutes in an addition problem, you must regroup the sum of the problem. Your answer should contain 59 minutes or less.

Example:　　　2 hours 24 minutes
　　　　　　　+ 7 hours 45 minutes
　　　　　　　―――――――――――
　　　　　　　9 hours 69 minutes

69 minutes is more than 1 hour. It is equal to 1 hour 9 minutes.

9 hours + 1 hour + 9 minutes = 10 hours 9 minutes

Solve the following problems. Remember to regroup.

1.　　　9 hours 15 minutes
　　　+ 4 hours 50 minutes
　　　―――――――――――

2.　　　14 hours 25 minutes
　　　+ 12 hours 42 minutes
　　　―――――――――――

3.　　　6 hours 59 minutes
　　　+ 5 hours 3 minutes
　　　―――――――――――

4.　　　7 hours 37 minutes
　　　+ 6 hours 32 minutes
　　　―――――――――――

To find the difference, regroup before subtracting.

Example:　　　$\overset{4}{\cancel{5}}$ hours $\overset{74}{\cancel{14}}$ minutes
　　　　　　　– 3 hours 22 minutes
　　　　　　　―――――――――――
　　　　　　　1 hour 52 minutes

5 hours can be regrouped to 4 hours 60 minutes. When we add the existing 14 minutes to the 60, the problem can be solved.

Exercise: Regroup to find the difference.

5.　　　8 hours 12 minutes
　　　– 6 hours 8 minutes
　　　―――――――――――

6.　　　12 hours 34 minutes
　　　– 5 hours 57 minutes
　　　―――――――――――

7.　　　15 hours 11 minutes
　　　– 13 hours 45 minutes
　　　―――――――――――

8.　　　2 hours 29 minutes
　　　– 1 hour 30 minutes
　　　―――――――――――

Distance–Time–Rate

Most of *Tuck Everlasting* is set in the 1880s, a time when people usually depended on horses for transportation. The epilogue takes place in 1950, and although the Tucks continue to use their horse-drawn buggy, cars are predominant. Solve the following problems (round to the nearest hundredth). Then compare the speeds of both methods of transportation.

1. It was 20 miles from Treegap to the Tuck's house. The man in the yellow suit and the constable had a 3- or 4-hour ride ahead of them on horseback. Fill in the chart below to tell the speed of the horse for each time listed. (Remember that the rate is calculated by dividing the distance by the time.)

Distance	Time	Rate (m.p.h.)
20 mi.	3 hrs.	
20 mi.	3.25 hrs.	
20 mi.	3.50 hrs.	
20 mi.	3.75 hrs.	
20 mi.	4 hrs.	

2. Today we usually travel by car to go 20 miles. If you were moving at an average speed of 45 miles per hour, how long would it take you to get to the Tuck's house from Treegap?_____

   At 60 miles per hour? _____

3a. Using a map of North America, estimate the distance from your home to Washington, D.C. How long would it take you to get there by car going 50 m.p.h.? by horse going 5 m.p.h.?

   Distance to Washington, D.C. = _____

   Time by car = _____

   Time by horse = _____

3b. Using a map of North America, estimate the distance from your home to Disneyland, located in Anaheim, California. How long would it take you to get there by car going 50 m.p.h.? by horse going 5 m.p.h.?

   Distance to Disneyland = _____

   Time by car = _____

   Time by horse = _____

3c. Using a map of North America, estimate the distance from your home to Vancouver, Canada. How long would it take you to get there by car going 50 m.p.h.? by horse going 5 m.p.h.?

   Distance to Vancouver = _____

   Time by car = _____

   Time by horse = _____

Metric Measurement

Metric Measurement Tips:

- A *meter* (m) is about the length from your fingertips to the end of your opposite shoulder if your arms are extended outward from your shoulder.

- One *centimeter* (cm) is about the distance across the nail of your pinky.

- A *millimeter* (mm) is about the thickness of a dime.

- A *kilometer* (km) is the distance a person can walk in about 10–12 minutes.

Circle the best estimate.

1. length of a workbook	a. 35 m	b. 35 mm	c. 35 cm	d. 2 km
2. length of a bus	a. km	b. m	c. cm	d. ml
3. length of a new pencil	a. 20 kg	b. 20 mm	c. 20 cm	d. 20 m
4. distance on plane from NY to CA	a. km	b. kg	c. m	d. L
5. width of your hand	a. 12 cm	b. 1.2 cm	c. 120 m	d. 12 mm

Choose the most appropriate measurement: mm, cm, m, km

6. height of a tree _____

7. diameter of Mars _____

8. length of a turtle _____

9. width of a paper clip _____

10. diameter of a penny _____

11. height of a vase _____

12. perimeter of a room _____

13. Nile River _____

Match the best estimate for each picture below. Remember that the width of your pinky is 1 cm.

14. lips

15. fish

16. pencil

A. 4.5 cm

B. 40 mm

C. 7 cm

Measurement Practice

10 mm = 1 cm	1 cm = 10 mm
100 cm = 1 m	1 m = 100 cm
1000 mm = 1 m	1 m = 1000 mm
1000 m = 1 km	1 km = 1000 m
1 L = 1000 mL	1 kL = 1000 L
1 kg = 1000 g	1 g = 1000 mg

Complete the conversions.

1. 10 mm = _____ cm
2. 50 cm = _____ mm
3. 30 mm = _____ cm
4. 10 cm = _____ mm
5. 50 mm = _____ cm
6. 90 cm = _____ mm
7. 65 mm = _____ cm
8. 33 cm = _____ mm
9. 100 cm = _____ m
10. 1,000 m = _____ km
11. 600 cm = _____ m
12. 5,000 m = _____ km
13. 800 cm = _____ m
14. 7,000 m = _____ km
15. 753 cm = _____ m
16. 8,350 m = _____ km
17. 4 m = _____ cm
18. 3 km = _____ m
19. 7 m = _____ cm
20. 6 km = _____ m
21. 9 m = _____ cm
22. 10 km = _____ m
23. 6.8 m = _____ cm
24. 15.5 km = _____ m

Complete the equations.

25. 4 mL = _____ L
26. 7 mm = _____ m
27. 650 mm = _____ cm
28. 70 mm = _____ m
29. 650 mm = _____ m
30. 4 mL = _____ L
31. 650 cm = _____ m
32. 4 L = _____ mL
33. 4 g = _____ kg
34. 7.5 L = _____ mL
35. 4 kg = _____ g
36. 6,500 L = _____ kL
37. 225 g = _____ kg
38. 3.5 kL = _____ L
39. 225 kg = _____ g
40. 57 g = _____ kg

Problem Solving: Measurement and Decimals

1. A fisherman uses a fishing pole that is about 350 cm long. How many millimeters is the fishing pole? How many meters is this pole?

_____

2. Which race is longer: a 5 kilometer (km) walk, a 700 meter (m) walk, or a 6,500 meter (m) walk?

_____

3. The football was thrown 1,350 meters in the first half of the Super Bowl. At the end of the second half, the football had traveled a total of 2.875 kilometers in the air. During which half did the football travel farther?

_____

4. The mass of a golf ball is about 75 grams (g). What is the mass of 18 new golf balls? How many kilograms is this?

_____

5. Sean has a set of checkers whose total mass is 36 grams. There are 24 checkers in the set. What is the mass of each checker?

_____

6. A vase has a capacity of 240 mL. A 650 mL pitcher is used to fill it. How much water is left in the pitcher?

_____

7. Each science book is 2 centimeters thick. There are 30 books stacked on the shelf. How high is the stack in meters?

_____

8. Kristen poured 175 mL of milk into a 3 L pitcher. How much more milk must be added to fill the pitcher?

_____

9. Jan is 1,600 cm tall, Christina is 1,250 cm tall, and Cindy is 1,500 cm tall. What is the average height of the girls? What is the average height in meters?

_____

Geometric Terms

Match each definition in column A with the correct picture in column B.

Column A	**Column B**

_____ 1. A *point* is a particular location.

A.

_____ 2. A *line* contains a set of points. It has arrows on the ends to indicate that it extends outward in the same direction.

B.

_____ 3. A *line segment* is part of a line marked by points.

C.

_____ 4. A *ray* is part of a line with one end point.

D.

_____ 5. *Intersecting lines* cross each other. In doing so, the lines create *angles*.

E.

_____ 6. *Perpendicular lines* are lines that intersect, forming right angles.

F.

_____ 7. *Parallel lines* are lines that run in the same direction but never intersect.

G.

_____ 8. A *plane* is a flat figure that continues out in all directions.

H.

Angles

• *Angles* are formed when two or more rays intersect. The point of intersection is called the *vertex*.

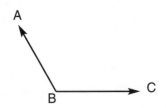

Ray BA intersects with ray BC at point B.
Point B is the vertex of angle ABC.

• Any angle that measures less than 90° is called an *acute angle*.

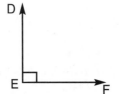

• A *right angle* measures 90°.
Angle DEF measures 90°.
Point E is the vertex.

• Any angle that measures less than 180° but measures more than 90° is an *obtuse angle*.

Using a protractor, measure the following angles and label them as *acute*, *right*, or *obtuse* angles.

1.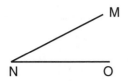

2.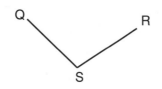

3.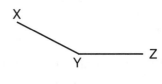

_____   _____   _____

Draw angles that measure the following degrees:

   4. 50°   5. 78°   6. 125°   7. 60°   8. 30°

Use the following diagram to answer these questions.

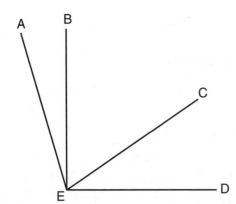

9. The right angle is _____ .

10. One acute angle is _____ .

11. A second acute angle is _____ .

12. A third acute angle is _____ .

13. The obtuse angle is _____ .

14. The vertex is _____ .

Triangles

- A *right triangle* has one angle that measures 90°.

- An *isosceles triangle* has two equal angles and two sides of equal length.

- An *equilateral triangle* has three equal angles and three sides of equal length.

- A *scalene triangle* has no equal angles and no sides of equal length.

- The sum of all three angles in any triangle is equal to 180°.

Directions: Label each triangle as *right, isosceles, equilateral,* or *scalene.*

1. _____

2. _____

3. 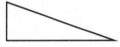 _____

4. 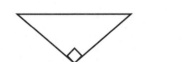 _____

5. a triangle with sides of 9 in., 9 in., 9 in.

6. a triangle with sides of 4 cm, 8 cm, 8 cm _____

7. a triangle with angles of 95°, 55°, 30° _____

8. a triangle with angles of 110°, 35°, 35° _____

Find the measurement of the third angle for each unfinished triangle below.

9. 110°, 60° _____   12. 90°, 43° _____

10. 45°, 58° _____   13. 45°, 66° _____

11. 75°, 35° _____   14. 120°, 30° _____

Perimeter

Perimeter is the distance around the outside edges of a figure. It can be found by adding the lengths of all the sides of a figure together.

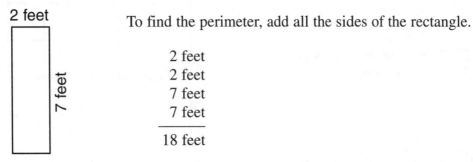

To find the perimeter, add all the sides of the rectangle.

$$
\begin{array}{r}
2 \text{ feet} \\
2 \text{ feet} \\
7 \text{ feet} \\
7 \text{ feet} \\
\hline
18 \text{ feet}
\end{array}
$$

Exercises: Find the perimeter of each of the following figures.

1.

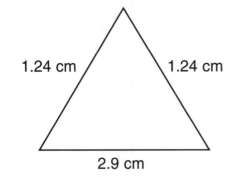

2.

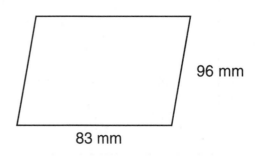

3.

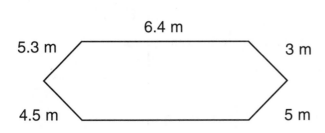

4.

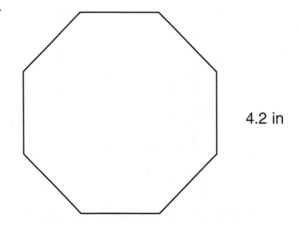

5. Jane skates around a rectangular ice rink three times each day. The length of the rink is 12.4 meters, and the width is 8.6 meters. What is the total distance she skates in a day?

6. Mr. Beecher purchased fencing to go around the outside edge of his property. How much fencing does he need to buy if the length of his yard is 30 feet and the width is 75 feet?

7. Mrs. Curtis needs to frame a picture that is 11 inches by 8 inches. How many inches of wood does she need?

Finding the Area of a Rectangle

The *area* of an object is the number of square units that fit inside the figure. For a rectangle, area is measured by multiplying the length by the width.

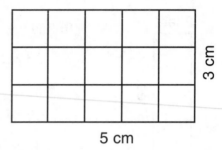

L x W = A
L = 3 cm, W = 5 cm
3 x 5 = 15 sq cm
A = 15 sq cm

3 cm

5 cm

Exercise: Find the area of the following figures:

1.

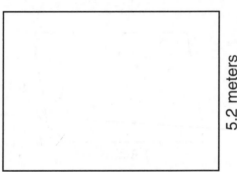

5.2 meters

7.3 meters

2.

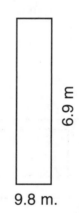

12 in.

2 in

3.

3.7 cm

4.

6.9 m

9.8 m.

5. a rectangle with a length of 9.2 meters and a width of 11 meters _____

6. a square with a length of 4 cm _____

7. a rectangle with a length of 1.3 cm and a width of 0.5 cm _____

8. a rectangle with a length of 2.4 cm and a width of 4.7 cm _____

9. a square with a length of 30 meters _____

10. a rectangle with a length of 8.1 inches and a width of 8 inches_____

Finding the Area of a Parallelogram

The area of a parallelogram can be found by multiplying the base by the height. This will tell how many square units are needed to fill the figure.

Area = base x height

A = b x h

height

base

Example: A parallelogram has a base of 15 centimeters and a height of 6 centimeters.
What is the area?
A = b x h
A = 15 x 6
A = 90 square centimeters

Directions: Find the area of the following parallelograms.

1.

4.6 in.

10 in.

_____

2.

7.2 ft.

5.8 ft.

_____

3.

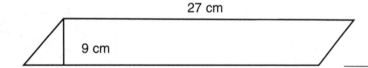

27 cm

9 cm

_____

4. Bill is building a greenhouse with four windows. Each window has a base of 4 feet and a height of 6 feet. What is the area of the piece of plastic that he will need to cover the four windows?

_____

5. Philip and Margie selected carpeting for their den. The length of the room is 8 feet 5 inches and the width is 9 feet. What is the area that will be covered by the rug?_____

6. Tim made a parallelogram with an area of 15 square centimeters. If the height was 3 cm, what was the base?

_____

Circles

Directions: Match the following definitions in column A with the correct pictures in column B.

| Column A | Column B |

Column A   **Column B**

1. The *center* of the circle is the *midpoint*. All lines drawn from the center to the outer edge are of equal distance.

_____ A.

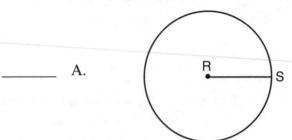

2. The *diameter* is a line segment that begins on one edge of the circle and passes through the center point, ending on the other edge of the circle.

_____ B.

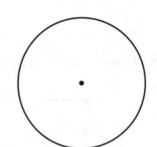

3. The *radius* is a line starting from the center point and ending on the outer edge. It is equal to one-half the diameter.

_____ C.

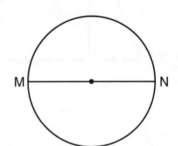

4. A *chord* is any line beginning at one edge of the circle and ending on the other edge. It need not pass through the center.

_____ D.

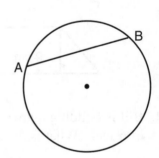

Directions: Identify each segment of the circle.

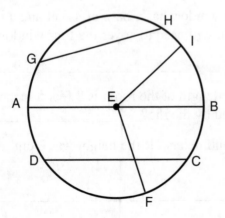

1. The diameter is _____ .

2. The center point is _____ .

3. Four radii are _____ .

4. Two chords are _____ .

Finding the Circumference of a Circle

The distance around the outer edge of a circle is the *circumference*. To find the circumference, you can use this formula:

$$C = \pi \text{ x diameter}$$

Pi (π) is equal to 3.14 or, if used as a fraction, $\dfrac{22}{7}$.

Example: Find the circumference of a circle with a diameter of 6 centimeters.
C = π x diameter
C = 3.14 x 6 cm
C = 18.84 centimeters

Exercise: Find the circumference of each circle.

1.

 8 mm diameter

2.

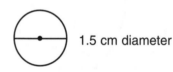 1.5 cm diameter

3.

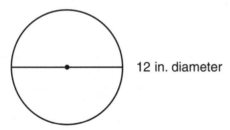 12 in. diameter

4.

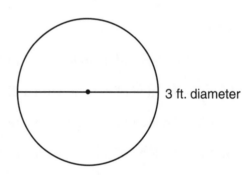 3 ft. diameter

If a circle has a radius given, then use the following formula:

$$C = 2 \pi \text{ x radius}$$

Example: 3 cm = radius
C = 2 π x radius
C = 2 π x 3
C = 2(3.14) x 3
C = 6.28 x 3
C = 18.84 cm

Exercises: Find the circumference of the following circles.

5. a circle with a radius of 2 mm_____

6. a circle with a radius of 10 in._____

7. a circle with a diameter of 26 centimeters _____

8. a circle with a radius of 13 mm_____

Finding the Area of a Circle

The *area of a circle* is the amount of space within that circle. Area is computed by squaring the length of the radius of a circle and multiplying that number by pi. Remember that the radius is equal to one half the length of the diameter.

The formula we use is this:

$$A = \pi r^2$$

Example: Find the area of a circle with a radius of 6 inches.

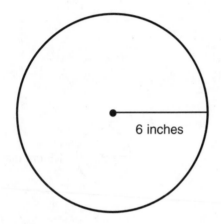

6 inches

$A = \pi r^2$
$A = 3.14 \times 6 \times 6$
$A = 113.04$ sq. in.

Exercises

1. Find the area of a circle with a radius of 8 centimeters._____

2. Find the area of a circle with a diameter of 8 inches._____

3. Find the area of a circle with a radius of 5 millimeters._____

4. Find the area of a circle with a radius of 4.2 centimeters. _____

5. Find the area of a circle with a diameter of 6 meters. _____

6. Find the area of a circle with a diameter of 10.4 feet. _____

7. Tom bought a plate with a diameter of 18 inches. What is the area of the entire plate?

8. Phyllis dug a circle in her garden. A smaller circle with a diameter of 5 feet had a tree planted in the center. The larger circle that went around the circle with the tree had a diameter of 22 feet. Phyllis wanted to plant flowers between the outer edge of the small circle and large circle. What is the difference in the area between the two circles?

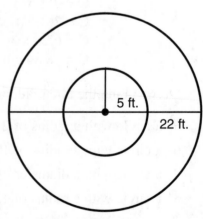

5 ft.

22 ft.

Volume of a Rectangular Prism

The amount of space that an object occupies is its *volume*. To find the volume of a rectangular prism, you can use this formula:

Volume = length x width x height

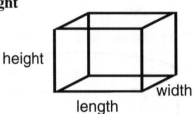

height

width

length

Example: Find the volume of the rectangular prism.

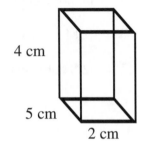

4 cm

5 cm

2 cm

V = L x W x H
V = 5 x 2 x 4
V = 40 cm³

A *cube* is a special rectangle. Since all its sides are equal in length, we can use this formula:

V = S³

3 cm

V = S³
S = Side
S = 3 cm
V = 3 x 3 x 3
V = 9 cm³

Exercises

What is the volume of each object?

1.

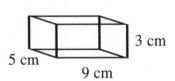

3 cm

5 cm

9 cm

2.

4 cm

3.

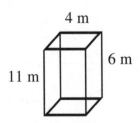

4 m

6 m

11 m

4. What is the volume of a box with a length of 1.7 in, a width of 2.3 in, and a height of 6.2 in.?

Volume of a Cylinder

Many objects are *cylinders*, such as cans, jars, and hat boxes. The volume of a cylinder can be found by multiplying the area of the base of the cylinder by the height. The base of the cylinder is a circle, so we can use the formula for the area of a circle, $\pi \times r^2$. Volume is expressed in *cubic units*.

π is equal to 3.14.

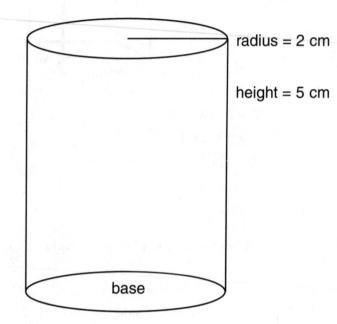

radius = 2 cm

height = 5 cm

base

V = area of base x height

$V = (3.14 \times 2^2) \times 5$

V = 62.8 cubic centimeters

Exercises: Find the volume of the cylinders with the following measurements.

1. R = 7 cm, h = 10 cm _____

2. R = 3 cm, h = 8 cm _____

3. R = 5 in., h = 9 in. _____

4. R = 2 m, h = 4 m _____

5. R = 12 cm, h = 2 cm _____

6. R = 8 cm, h = 4 cm _____

7. R = 11 cm, h = 11 cm _____

Symmetry

If a figure can be cut or folded in half so that each half exactly matches the other half, the two figures are called *figures of symmetry*. The line that divides each figure exactly in half is called the *line of symmetry*. Some figures may have more than one line of symmetry.

Examples:

Draw the lines of symmetry for each figure.

1.
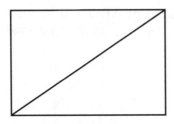

2.
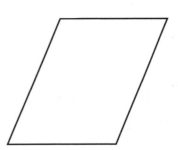

3.
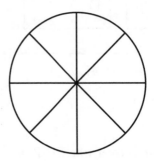

4.
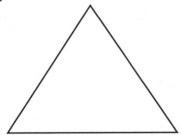

5.
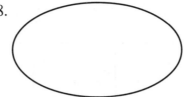

6.

7.

8.
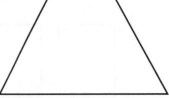

9.

Reflections, Translations, and Rotations

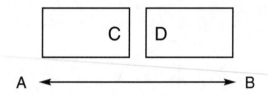

You can slide a figure along a straight line. If figure C slides along line AB, it will fit on figure D. This is called *translation*.

If you flip figure S over line EF, it will fit over figure T. This is called *reflection*.

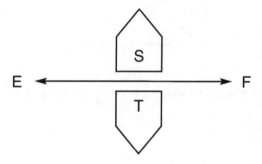

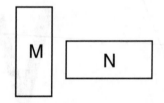

If figure M is turned, we say it is *rotated*.

Label each figure as a *reflection*, *translation*, or *rotation*.

1.

2.

3.

4.

5.

6.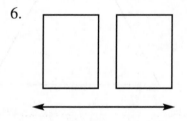

7.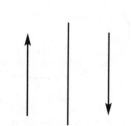

8.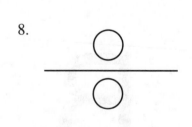

Similar and Congruent Figures

Two figures which have the same shape but are not the same size are called *similar* figures.

Example:

Two figures that have the same shape and the same size are *congruent* figures.

Example: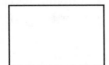

Exercises: Label each set of figures as *congruent* or *similar*.

1.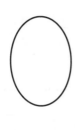

2.

3.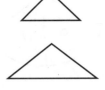

Pick the figure that is congruent to the first one shown.

4.

figure A	figure B	figure C	figure D

5.

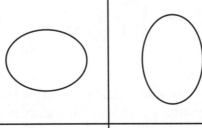

Probability

What is the probability of landing on the number 9 after the wheel stops spinning?

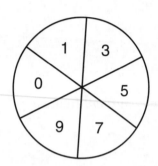

There is only one 9 on the wheel.

There are six spaces on which a spinner can stop.

The probability of the spinner landing on the number 9 is one chance out of six, or $P = \dfrac{1}{6}$ or 1 out of 6.

Directions: Find the probability for each question.

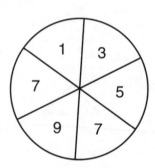

1. What is the probability of spinning a 7?

    A.   There is/are _____ number 7.

    B. $P = \dfrac{\square}{\square}$ or _____ out of _____ .

2. What is the probability of landing on the number 3?

    A.   There is/are _____ number 3.

    B.   There are _____ numbers on the spinner.

    C. $P = \dfrac{\square}{\square}$ or _____ out of _____ .

3. What is the probability of *not* landing on 5?

    A.   There are _____ numbers that are not 5.

    B.   There are _____ numbers on the spinner.

    C. $P = \dfrac{\square}{\square}$ or _____ out of _____ chances.

Ben puts 2 black (B) marbles, 7 red (R) marbles, and 1 clear (C) marble in a bag. He then shakes the bag to mix all the marbles together. The marbles are the same size, weight, and texture.

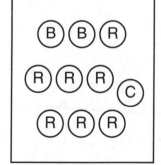

4. What is the probability of choosing a clear marble?_____

5. What is the probability of choosing a red marble? _____

6. What is the probability of choosing a black marble? _____

7. What is the probability of choosing a clear or black marble?_____

8. What is the probability of choosing a yellow marble? _____

Combinations

Melinda has two blouses and four skirts. How many different outfits can she make by combining her blouses and skirts in different ways?

Blouses	Skirts	Combinations
pink	white	pink and white
pink	yellow	pink and yellow
pink	black	pink and black
pink	brown	pink and brown
blue	white	blue and white
blue	yellow	blue and yellow
blue	black	blue and black
blue	brown	blue and brown

Melinda had two blouses and four skirts that she was able to combine in eight different ways. If we multiply the number of blouses by the number of skirts, we have the number of combinations.

2 blouses x 4 skirts = 8 combinations

Combinations *(cont.)*

Directions: Find the number of combinations.

1. A restaurant offers an omelet for breakfast. It can be made by using eggs with a choice of ham or bacon or cheese as a filling. How many different omelet choices are on the menu?

   Egg   Filling   Combination

   eggs

   _____ egg x _____ fillings = _____ combinations or choices.

2. Mark has a pair of boots and a pair of sneakers. He has one pair of white socks, one pair of black socks, and one pair of brown socks. How many combinations can Mark form?

   _____ shoes x _____ pairs of socks = _____ combinations.

3. Karen wants to buy an ice-cream sundae with vanilla ice cream. She has a choice of strawberry, hot fudge, or caramel sauce. Her sundae can be topped with chocolate sprinkles or nuts. How many combinations are there from which to choose?

   vanilla ice cream x _____ sauces x _____ toppings = _____ choices

4. Ben had five television sets in his home. Each set can be tuned to seven channels. How many combinations can Ben tape at one time?

   _____ televisions x _____ channels = _____ combinations

5. The school cafeteria offers three sandwiches, four vegetables, and five juice drinks daily. How many combinations are available to the students each day?

   _____ sandwiches x _____ vegetables x _____ drinks = _____ choices.

Check Test

1. Which represents the ratio 12 to 45?

    A. $\dfrac{45}{12}$ B. $2\dfrac{1}{3}$ C. $\dfrac{12}{45}$ D. not here

2. $\dfrac{3}{9} = \dfrac{n}{63}$

    A. 32   B. 24   C. 18   D. 7   E. 21

3. What is the fraction for 60%?

    A. $\dfrac{3}{4}$ B. $\dfrac{3}{5}$ C. $\dfrac{2}{3}$ D. $\dfrac{8}{16}$

4. What is the percent for $\dfrac{19}{25}$?

    A. 95%   B. 82%   C. 14%   D. 75%   E. 76%

5. What is the exponent form for 10 x 10 x 10?

    A. 10   B. 10^3 C. 10^2 D. 2^{10} E. 3^{10}

6. $2 = \dfrac{24}{\square}$

    A. 12   B. 8   C. 4   D. 16

7. What sign is missing? $\dfrac{1}{2} \bigcirc \dfrac{4}{5}$

    A. <   B. =   C. ≠   D. >

8. $5 = \dfrac{\square}{5}$

    A. 11   B. 25   C. 14   D. not here

9. $\begin{array}{r} 5{,}637 \\ \times \quad 835 \\ \hline \end{array}$

    A. 4,706,895   B. 5,544,813   C. 4,745,712   D. 4,124

10. $\begin{array}{r} 31{,}657 \\ \times \quad 307 \\ \hline \end{array}$

    A. 10,031,125   B. 9,718,699   C. 9,707,699   D. 8,012

Check Test (cont.)

11. $18\overline{)136}$

    A. 7 r55   B. 6 r16   C. 6 r8   D. not here

12. $307\overline{)50,985}$

    A. 210 r14   B. 201 r4   C. 1377 r9   D. not here

13. 34.1 + 16.959 = _____

    A. 578.3   B. 487.5   C. 51.059   D. 62.059

14.   0.066
    − 0.009

    A. 0.057   B. 0.055   C. 0.042   D. 0.054

15. $\dfrac{7}{16} + \dfrac{1}{4} =$

    A. $\dfrac{2}{12}$ B. $2\dfrac{1}{2}$ C. $1\dfrac{3}{4}$ D. $1\dfrac{1}{8}$ E. $\dfrac{11}{16}$

16. $\dfrac{5}{9} - \dfrac{3}{9} =$

    A. $\dfrac{8}{9}$ B. $\dfrac{1}{9}$ C. $\dfrac{3}{9}$ D. $\dfrac{7}{9}$ E. $\dfrac{2}{9}$

17. $8\dfrac{7}{12} + 4\dfrac{6}{12} =$

    A. $3\dfrac{1}{12}$ B. $13\dfrac{1}{12}$ C. $3\dfrac{1}{3}$ D. not here

18. What is the greatest common factor of 72 and 30?

    A. 15   B. 6   C. 8   D. 4

Check Test (cont.)

19. What is the least common multiple of 5 and 20?

    A. 10   B. 20   C. 5   D. not here

20. $4 - 1\frac{3}{4} =$ _____

    A. $2\frac{1}{8}$ B. $2\frac{4}{8}$ C. $2\frac{1}{4}$ D. $2\frac{3}{5}$

21. What is the name of this figure?

    A. right angle   B. obtuse angle
    C. acute angle   D. not here

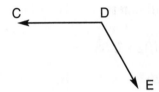

22. What is the name of this figure?

    A. rectangle   B. triangle
    C. rhombus   D. parallelogram

23. What type of lines are these?

    A. rectangular   B. parallel
    C. crossing   D. intersecting

Use the figure to answer the questions 24 through 27.

24. Which is a radius?

    A. AD   B. AB   C. EF

25. Which is a diameter?

    A. EF   B. CD   C. AB

26. Which is a chord?

    A. AB   B. CD   C. EF

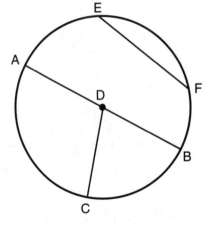

Check Test *(cont.)*

27. Complete: 3 hours 30 minutes = _____ minutes.

    A. 150 minutes   B. 90 minutes   C. 210 minutes

28. Complete: 4 quarts = _____ cups

    A. 16 cups   B. 18 cups   C. 12 cups

29. What is the circumference of a circle with a diameter of 30 centimeters? (pi = 3.14)

    A. 80 centimeters   B. 85 centimeters   C. 94.2 centimeters

30. Multiply: 0.102 x 0.081 =

    A. 0.008262   B. 0.000826   C. 0.082810

31. What is the probability of landing on a circle?

    A. 1 in 6
    B. 2 in 6
    C. 3 in 6
    D. 4 in 6
    E. 0 in 6

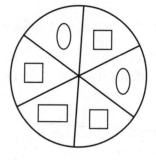

32. What is the volume of this figure?

    A. 130 cubic inches
    B. 140 cubic inches
    C. 150 cubic inches

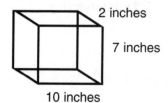

2 inches

7 inches

10 inches

33. Multiply: $1\frac{3}{5} \times \frac{1}{8} =$

    A. $\frac{1}{5}$ B. $\frac{1}{6}$ C. $\frac{1}{3}$

34. Are these polygons congruent?

    A. Yes   B. No

35. Is this figure symmetrical?

    A. Yes   B. No

36. 24 millimeters = _____ centimeters

    A. 2.5 centimeters   B. 2.4 centimeters
    C. 24 centimeters   D. 1.4 centimeters

Check Test *(cont.)*

37. A cruise ship sails with a total of 225 passengers. There are 75 passengers on each of the first two decks. How many passengers are on the third deck?

    A. 65   B. 73   C. 75   D. 84

38. Mrs. Bittle can type two letters in 20 minutes. At that rate, how long will it take her to type 10 letters?

    A. 1 hour 40 minutes   B. 1 hour 35 minutes
    C. 1 hour 37 minutes   D. 1 hour 30 minutes

39. Each baseball team has 9 players. If 81 players joined the league, how many teams would they need to form?

    A. 72   B. 81   C. 65   D. 88   E. 9

40. A farmer harvested 64 bushels of peaches. He kept 25% of them. How many did he sell?

    A. 16 bushels   B. 48 bushels   C. 24 bushels

41. What is the area of a triangle with a base of 12 centimeters and a height of 7.2 centimeters?

    A. 18.7 square centimeters   B. 19 square centimeters
    C. 14.6 square centimeters   D. 14.4 square centimeters
    E. 43.2 square centimeters

42. Four of sixteen children came to school wearing sneakers. What percent didn't wear sneakers?

    A. 25%   B. 75%   C. 50%   D. 12%

43. A runner can run 2.5 miles per hour. How many miles will he run in one week if he runs for two hours each day of the week?

    A. 33 miles   B. 35 miles   C. 31 miles

Check Test *(cont.)*

44. A group of 244 people are going on a bus tour. Each bus holds thirty people. How many buses will they need for the tour?

    A. 7 buses   B. 8 buses   C. 9 buses

45. The soccer team charged $8.75 per dinner. If 163 were attending, what would be the total amount collected?

    A. $1,426.23   B. $1,476.23   C. $1,423.21   D. $1,426.25

46. How much fencing would be needed to fence the outer edge of a property measuring 60 feet by 120 feet?

    A. 400 feet   B. 350 feet   C. 360 feet

47. Lines that never cross each other are called _____ .

    A. parallel lines   B. intersecting lines   C. lines of longitude   D. lines of force

48. There were 22 red flowers in Mary's garden and 15 yellow flowers. What is the ratio of red to yellow flowers?

    A. 22:37   B. 22:15   C. 15:22

49. A class of 22 students took a spelling test using white lined paper. How many pages would be used if there were 35 units of spelling tested during the year?

    A. 750 papers   B. 770 papers   C. 819 papers

50. The vibrations from an earthquake took 2 hours 20 minutes to reach city A. If the earthquake started at 1:45 P.M., what time were the vibrations felt in city A?

    A. 4:07 P.M.   B. 4:03 P.M.   C. 4:05 P.M.

Scientific Method Review

Complete the paragraphs about the scientific method of conducting an experiment with the following science words.

• laboratory	• control	• experiment
• conclusion	• data	• observations
• procedure	• graph	• manipulated variable
• hypothesis	• chart	• scientific method
• problem	• theory	• materials

To conduct an (1) _____ , a scientist follows a specific set of standard guidelines. The

scientist works in his or her (2) _____ , obeying safety rules. Once the scientist identifies

the (3) _____ , he/she tries to determine the outcome by proposing an answer or

(4) _____ . If the scientist is conducting a controlled study, care must be taken so that there

is only one (5) _____ _____ at a time. Otherwise, the scientist might

not be able to determine the cause of the outcome.

The scientist is ready to start. Having gathered all the necessary (6) _____ , the scientist is

able to begin the (7) _____ . The scientist must determine which directions must be

followed and record the steps in order to interpret his/her results. While conducting the experiment, the

scientist must make careful (8) _____ of what he or she sees, hears, smells, tastes, feels, etc.

The scientist collects and records the (9) _____ on a prepared (10) _____ .

After the experiment is over, the scientist will convert his or her information into a

(11) _____ . A pie, bar, or line type is easily read and helps to interpret the data at a glance.

The scientist analyzes the results of the experiment in order to draw a (12) _____ .

He or she compares this to the original hypothesis.

A scientist generally conducts an experiment many times before converting the conclusion into a

(13) _____ . By comparing the manipulated variable to a (14) _____ , the

scientist is better able to decide why something occurred. This precise, orderly system of conducting

an experiment is the (15) _____ _____ . It is used to answer questions of a

scientific, social, or psychological nature.

Scientific Instruments

Scientists use a variety of instruments to conduct experiments. Match the instrument listed in the word bank to its definition.

Word Bank

- Petri dish
- cover slip
- slide
- thermometer
- beaker
- microscope
- Bunsen burner
- telescope
- double-pan balance scale
- triple-beam balance scale
- graduated cylinder
- magnifying lens

_____ 1. used to examine objects too small to be seen with the unaided eye

_____ 2. lens that causes objects to look larger than reality

_____ 3. used to measure mass or weight by balancing standard weights against the object being weighed

_____ 4. used to observe objects in the distant sky by making them appear closer or larger

_____ 5. small, shallow, circular glass or plastic dish with a loose cover used in the preparation of specimens

_____ 6. rectangular piece of glass or plastic on which is placed a specimen to be viewed under a microscope

_____ 7. instrument with a hot, blue flame, generally used in laboratories

_____ 8. type of scale with one pan

_____ 9. instrument used to measure air temperature

_____ 10. small, square piece of plastic used to keep a specimen in place on a slide

_____ 11. glass or metal cup with a flat bottom, no handle, and a small lip for pouring

_____ 12. used to measure liquid volume or capacity

Science in Real Life

Read the selection about an experiment conducted in a sixth-grade classroom. Then answer the questions about the experiment, using your knowledge of the scientific method of inquiry.

> The students in Ms. Foster's science class wanted to see if different types of music would have any effects on the growth of plants. They played jazz, opera, classical, rock, and country music for five (5) ivy plants for 30 minutes each day. They watered the ivy plants the same amount and kept them in sunlight for the same amount of time. They played the music for the plants in different rooms, so the plants were exposed to only the one specific type of music. A sixth ivy was exposed to no music at all.
>
> The students measured the plants at the beginning of the experiment and then weekly for four weeks. After the fourth week, the students compared and analyzed the results.

1. What is the problem in this experiment? _____

_____

2. What is your hypothesis? _____

_____

_____

3. What materials would you need to conduct this experiment? _____

_____

_____

4. What is the manipulated variable in this experiment? _____

_____

_____

5. What are the controls in this experiment? _____

_____

_____

Science in Real Life (cont.)

Data and Conclusions

The students recorded the following data:

Height of Ivy Plants

	Start	Week 1	Week 2	Week 3	Week 4	Total Growth
Jazz	6"	6.2"	6.7"	7.0"	7.0"	_____
Opera	6"	6.5"	7.1"	7.8"	8.5"	_____
Rock	6"	6.0"	6.2"	6.3"	6.5"	_____
Country	6"	6.5"	6.9"	8.0"	8.5"	_____
Classical	6"	6.9"	7.5"	8.5"	9.0"	_____
No Music	6"	6.5"	7.0"	7.3"	7.5"	_____

6. Calculate the total growth of each plant exposed to the different types of music.

   Jazz _____ , Opera _____ , Rock _____ ,

   Country _____ , Classical _____ , No Music _____

   Which plant grew the least? _____ the most? _____

7. Make a bar graph to show your results.

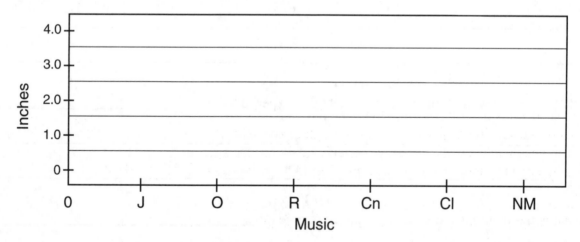

8. What conclusions can you draw from this experiment?_____

   _____

9. What could you do to make sure your conclusions are valid? _____

   _____

10. What type of follow-up experiment could you conduct to try this experiment in a different way?

   _____

Reviewing the Microscope

The microscope is a scientific instrument with one (1) lens or a combination of lenses for making small things look larger. Objects not visible to the unaided eye, like blood, bacteria, or plant cells, are clearly visible through a microscope.

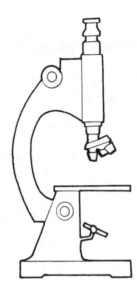

A *simple microscope* has only one (1) lens. A *compound microscope* has two (2) or more lenses which increase the magnifying ability of the instrument. An *electron microscope,* which has much greater power than an ordinary microscope, uses beams of electrons instead of beams of light to focus on the specimen being observed.

A microscope must be handled very carefully. It is carried close to the body with one hand on the arm, while the other hand is under the base. It is then placed gently on a flat table or working surface. The lenses should be cleaned with lens paper before examining any specimen.

In order to observe a specimen under the microscope, always turn the coarse adjustment knob (the higher one) toward the viewer. It raises the body tube so that a prepared slide can be placed on the stage. Be sure to click the low power objective lens into place first. (A specimen should be viewed through the low powered objective lens first.) Once the stage clips are in place, holding the slide so it does not move, the viewer can turn the coarse adjustment knob back, lowering the body tube. Carefully continue this procedure until the specimen appears in view through the eyepiece. Continue looking through the eyepiece while slowly lowering the body tube until the specimen is clear. Any more adjustments should be made with the fine adjustment knob for a distance image.

Other more powerful lenses may be clicked into place for closer or clearer observations. In addition, the diaphragm could be adjusted to allow more or less light to shine on the specimen, as needed. Care must be taken to raise the body tube before changing objective lenses, since they vary in size and could crack the slide.

When the observer is finished using the microscope, the slide should be removed, cleaned, and stored. The microscope should then be stored with the lowest powered objective lens in place.

Reviewing the Microscope *(cont.)*

Answer the questions about the care and handling of a microscope.

1. Why do scientists use a microscope? _____

_____

2. What is the difference between a simple and a compound microscope? _____

3. What is used in an electron microscope to focus on the specimen that differs from a simple or compound microscope?_____

4. How does a person carry a microscope?_____

5. Why must you be careful handling a microscope?_____

6. What is used to clean the lens of a microscope? _____

7. Which knob is turned first when adjusting a microscope?_____

8. What does the coarse adjustment knob do? _____

9. Where is the slide placed?_____

10. What holds a slide so it does not move?_____

11. Through what do you look to see the specimen? _____

12. Which knob is used to get a more distinct image?_____

13. Which part of the microscope allows light to enter? _____

14. How should the microscope be stored?_____

15. What should be done to the slide after viewing the specimen? _____

_____

Match the part of the microscope in the word bank to its corresponding number on the diagram.

Word Bank
_____ arm
_____ base
_____ stage
_____ stage clips
_____ diaphragm
_____ mirror/light
_____ eyepiece
_____ body tube/barrel
_____ revolving nosepiece
_____ low power objective lens
_____ high power objective lens
_____ coarse adjustment knob
_____ fine adjustment knob

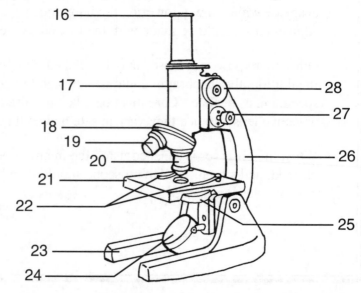

Measuring Temperature

Temperature is the degree of heat or cold. It is measured with a thermometer, an instrument which usually contains mercury or alcohol in a narrow tube. The liquid goes up by expanding when the heat rises, and the liquid drops by contracting when the temperature outside the tube goes down.

A thermometer is like a ruler, a scale for measuring the temperature in degrees. In the metric system, the *Celsius scale* is generally used. *Centigrade* is another term for Celsius. The zero degree (0°) marks the freezing point of water, and 100 degrees (100°) marks the boiling point of water. The Celsius scale is named for the Swedish astronomer *Anders Celsius* (1701–1744), who invented it in 1742.

Another thermometer, named for *Gabriel Fahrenheit* (1686–1736), the German physicist who introduced it, is marked off according to a scale for measuring temperature in which 32 degrees (32°) marks the freezing point of water. The boiling point of water is marked at 212 degrees (212°).

A third type of thermometer, the *Kelvin thermometer,* is based on a scaled for measuring temperature on which 273 degrees (273°) marks the freezing point of water, 373 degrees (373°) marks the boiling point, and 0 degrees (0°) marks absolute zero. It is named for *Lord Kelvin* (1824–1907), a British physicist.

Answer the following questions about thermometers.

1. Name the three different types of thermometers.

   _____ _____ _____

2. Thermometers are like _____ .

3. The unit of measurement on a thermometer is a _____ .

4. Thermometers measure the degree of _____ or _____ .

5. What is inside the glass tube of a thermometer? _____

6. What is the basic principle upon which thermometers are based?_____

   _____

7. Which thermometer was invented first? _____ second?_____

8. All three thermometers are based upon the freezing and boiling point of _____ .

9. 0° C = _____ ° F = _____ on the Kelvin scale.

10. 100° C = _____ ° F = _____ on the Kelvin scale.

Reading a Celsius/Fahrenheit Thermometer

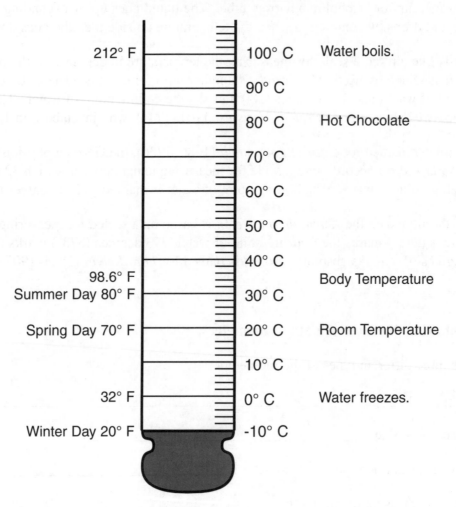

Answer the following questions using the thermometer above.

1. At which temperatures would water be ready to make spaghetti? _____

2. At which temperatures could ice cubes start to form? _____

3. Which temperatures are good for building snowmen? _____

4. At which temperatures would you set your thermostat at home so you would be comfortable in the winter? _____

5. What is the temperature of hot chocolate when it is served? _____

6. At which temperature would you most likely be wearing a jacket while riding your bike? _____

7. At which temperatures would you most likely be going to the neighborhood pool or beach? _____

8. What is your temperature when you are healthy? _____

Reading a Thermometer

The markings on a thermometer indicate *degrees*. All markings above zero are *positive*. All markings below zero are *negative* and are read as below zero. A minus sign is placed to the left of the number read when it is below zero. No sign is placed to the left of the degree indicated when it is above zero.

Always count down if the portion of the thermometer being observed is below zero. Some thermometers are scaled by twos, while others are marked by ones. Therefore, when reading the thermometer, first determine how it is scaled. Then determine if the mercury or alcohol has leveled off at a point above or below zero.

Record the temperatures shown.

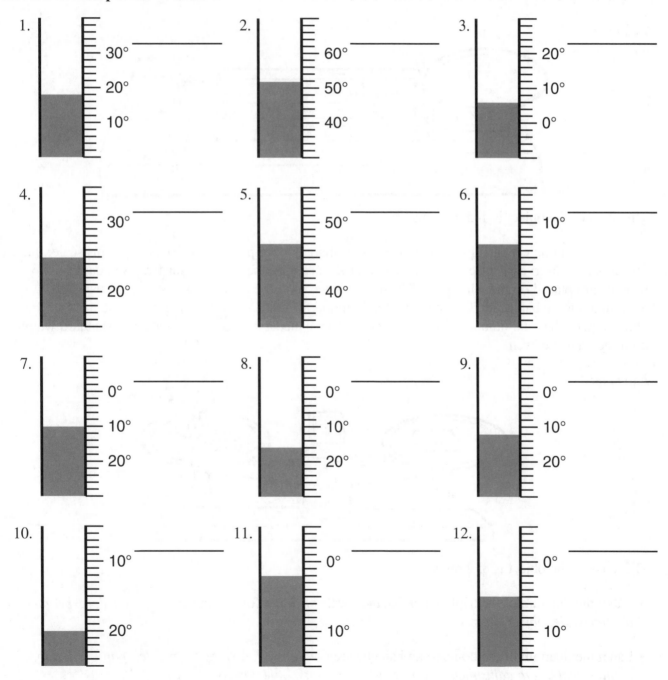

Measuring Mass

The *mass of* an object is the amount of matter a body contains, giving it the ability to stay still or continue to move. The mass of an object is always the same. Its weight, however, varies depending upon the force of gravity.

The mass of an object can be measured by finding its weight on a triple-beam balance scale. This scale uses three beams to register weight in grams or kilograms. The riders are moved on each beam to the appropriate notch—e.g., 100, 20, 30, 5.6, 3, etc. When the pointer is in the center of the scale, the mass of the object on the pan can be determined.

Calculate the total weight or mass by adding the number of grams indicated by the riders.

Example:

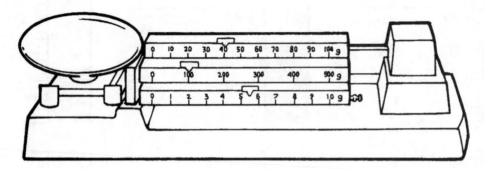

The mass of the object is 145.5 grams.

The mass of an object can also be measured by using a double-pan balance scale. On this scale, the object being observed is placed on one pan after the scale has been zero-adjusted. Standard gram weights are placed on the other pan. When the pointer is in the center of the scale, the pans are determined to be balanced. Compute the total number of gram weights in the pan. The mass of the object equals the total number of gram weights. To balance the scale, add or subtract standard weights until the pans are even.

Example:

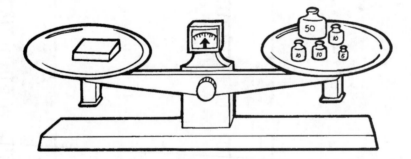

The mass of the object is 85 grams.

• Label the diagram of the triple-beam balance scale with the following terms: *pan, riders, beams, pointer scale, object mass.*

• Label the diagram of the double-pan balance scale with the following terms: *left pan, right pan, pointer, scale, zero adjustment knob, standard weights, object mass.*

Practice Measuring Mass

Find the gram weights indicated on the triple-beam balance scale.

1. g

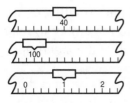

2. g

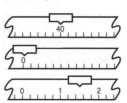

3. g

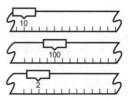

4. g

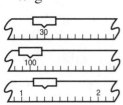

5. g

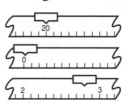

6. g

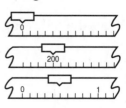

Calculate the mass of the objects on the double-pan balance scale.

7. g

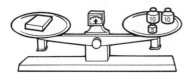

8. g

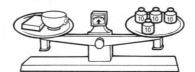

9. g

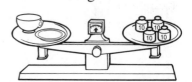

10. g

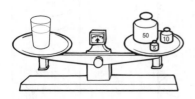

11. g

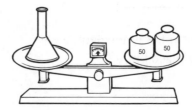

12. g

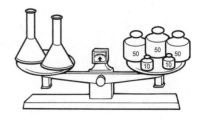

Reading a Graduated Cylinder

A *graduated cylinder* is an instrument used to measure small amounts of a liquid. The scientist uses this cylinder to measure liquid volume. There are many sizes of graduated cylinders. Some measure 1,000 milliliters (mL) or 1 liter (L). Some measure 500 milliliters (mL). Some measure only 10 milliliters (mL). The lines on the graduated cylinder are called *graduations*. The liquid usually curves up the side of a graduated cylinder. To achieve an accurate reading, it is important to remember to read the measurement at the lowest point or the bottom of the curve. This low point is called the *meniscus*.

Sometimes scientists need to find the volume of small, irregularly-shaped solid objects. They use the graduated cylinder and the *water displacement method* to calculate the volume. The graduated cylinder is filled to a specific height and recorded. The object is then placed inside the graduated cylinder. The water will rise above the object. Then a second reading of the cylinder is recorded. The first reading is subtracted from the second or higher reading. The difference is the volume of the solid object in milliliters or cubic centimeters.

Read the following volumes in the graduated cylinders.

1. mL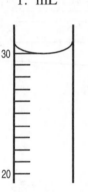

2. mL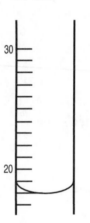

3. mL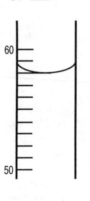

4. mL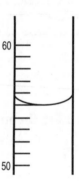

Calculate the volume of the marbles, using the water displacement method.

5. What is the volume of the water in the graduated cylinder?

   _____

6. What is the volume of the water in the graduated cylinder after five marbles were placed in it?

   _____

7. What is the volume of the five marbles?

   _____

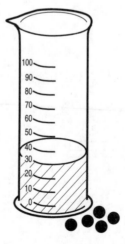
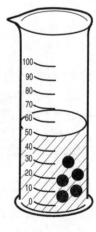

Metric Math

Metric measures that will help you:

- 10 millimeters = 1 centimeter
  (about the width of a dime)

- 100 centimeters = 1 meter
  (about the height of a desk)

- 1,000 meters = 1 kilometer
  (about the distance you can walk in 10 to 12 minutes)

Abbreviations that will help you:

mm = millimeters   cm = centimeters   m = meters   km = kilometers

Practice

1. 20 mm = _____ cm

2. 4 cm = _____ mm

3. 200 cm = _____ m

4. 8 m = _____ cm

5. 5,000 meters = _____ km

6. 7 km = _____ meters

How would you measure the following?

7. the length of a pen   (a) cm   (b) meters   (c) km

8. the width of a paper clip   (a) mm   (b) cm   (c) km

9. the height of an adult   (a) cm   (b) m   (c) mm

10. the length of a river   (a) mm   (b) cm   (c) km

Measure each line segment to the nearest millimeter.

11. _____

12. _____

13. _____

14. _____

Measure each object to the nearest centimeter.

15.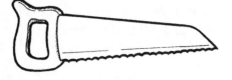

16.

17.

18.

Reviewing Interdependence of Life

Green plants are called *producers* in the chain of life. They use carbon dioxide, water, minerals, and sunlight to produce their own food. The food that they produce is a simple form of sugar which gives them energy to grow. During this process, called *photosynthesis,* the plant releases oxygen and water through its leaves. Producers are important because they not only produce food for themselves but for others as well.

Consumers are the living organisms that get energy from eating others. Animals may eat plants or other animals to obtain energy to maintain life. Decomposers are organisms that help break down dead organisms or their parts. *Decomposers* break down leaves, wood, and animals and help the cycle of life continue.

In a community, organisms live together and pass energy on to each other. This is called the *food chain.* For example, a plant would be eaten by an insect which would be eaten by a bird. The bird would be eaten by a snake which would then be eaten by a hawk.

Food chains form *food webs.* A plant or animal in a food chain might also be linked to another part of the food web. For example, the insect might also be a part of a food chain for a frog and a snake. There are many links that make up a food web in a community.

Energy for life is available to organisms at each level of the feeding order. The producers, or green plants, have the most energy. They use some of the energy for themselves. They need the energy to grow and perform photosynthesis. Some of the energy is passed along to others when plants are eaten. The animal that eats the plant gets energy from this food. The energy can be used to help that animal stay alive and function. The energy that is contained in the animal is passed on to other animals when the animal is eaten. This chain of life would take on the form of a pyramid with the most energy available at the bottom and the least amount of energy at the top of the pyramid.

People have an effect on food chains and food webs. When a forest is cleared, both producers and consumers are affected. The wood comes from a tree, which is a producer. Within that forest are other consumers and producers that may be linked to that tree for their needs. Clearing land to build new cities or highways can be destructive to the community of life that once lived there.

Reviewing Interdependence of Life *(cont.)*

Chemicals present another danger to certain environments and communities. The Environmental Protection Agency is a federal government agency that works to ensure that pollution and chemicals are not harming communities. They do studies on pollution and enforce environmental laws.

Directions: Use the information on page 254 to complete the outline.

I. Producers and Consumers

   A. _____ are producers.

      1. They need _____ , _____ , _____ , _____ .

      2. _____ is the process of producing their own food.

      3. They give off _____ and _____ when they produce their own food.

   B. Consumers

      1. They get energy from _____ .

      2. They include _____ —organisms that break down wastes and dead organisms.

II. Food Chains

   A. They start with _____ .

   B. Energy is passed on from one organism to the next when _____ .

III. Food Webs

   A. Food webs are made of many food _____ .

   B. Many animals can be links in the same _____ .

IV. The Energy Pyramid

   A. _____ are the bottom of the energy pyramid.

   B. Energy is passed from the bottom of the pyramid to the _____ .

   C. The most energy is available at the _____ of the pyramid to the _____ of the pyramid.

V. People Affect the Environment

   A. Clearing

   B. Clearing

   C. Using

VI. The Environmental Protection Agency

   A. Conducts

   B. Enforces

The Water Cycle

Directions: Use the word bank to complete the paragraphs correctly.

Word Bank				
• waste	• clouds	• rain	• soil	• precipitation
• snow	• sleet	• die	• hail	• evaporates
		• condensation		

Water in the water cycle goes in a series of steps that lead back to the same point. Water that falls from clouds is called   1   which can take the form of   2,   3,   4,   or   5.   Water that reaches the earth might be absorbed into the ground or fall into bodies of water such as rivers, streams, and oceans.

Plants use their root systems to take water in from the   6.   Some water is released by the plant through the leaves. This water   7   and is returned as water vapor in the air. Animals drink water and return that water to the ecosystem through their   8   products. When plants and animals   9, they decompose, and the water in their body becomes part of the ecosystem once again.

When water evaporates from the land and from bodies of water, it circulates in the air as water vapor. As the water vapor rises higher in the air, it cools, and tiny droplets of water form. This is called   10. The droplets form   11 , which release the water when the droplets become too heavy.

Answers

1. _____

2. _____

3. _____

4. _____

5. _____

6. _____

7. _____

8. _____

9. _____

10. _____

11. _____

The Water Cycle *(cont.)*

Directions: Label the parts of the water cycle.

| A—evaporation | B—precipitation | C—condensation |

The Carbon Dioxide-Oxygen Cycle

Directions: Use the words in the word bank to complete the paragraph correctly.

Word Bank

- glucose
- photosynthesis
- oxygen
- carbon dioxide
- exhale

Plants are called producers because they not only make food that other animals need to live but they can also make their own food. Plants produce their own food in a process called _1._ The plants use a gas called _2,_ which they obtain from the air, and combine it with sunlight, minerals from the soil, and water to create their food, a form of sugar. This simple sugar is called _3._ During this chemical reaction, certain products are given off by the plants. Once such substance is a gas called _4,_ which is very important to people, animals, and other organisms. During a process called respiration, animals use this gas, along with other materials, to produce the energy they need to live. When animals _5,_ they release a by-product too. This by-product is a gas called _6,_ which can be used by plants. This cycle repeats over and over again in the environment.

Answers

1. _____   4. _____

2. _____   5. _____

3. _____   6. _____

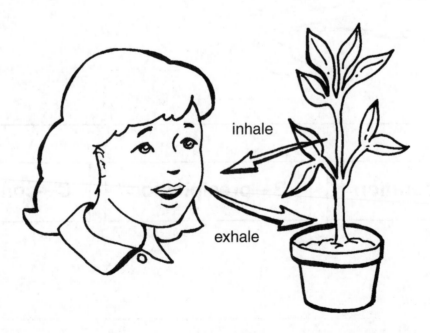

inhale

exhale

The Nitrogen Cycle

Word Bank

- nitrogen compounds
- nitrogen
- bacteria
- die
- roots
- oxygen
- waste

Nearly eighty percent of air is made up of nitrogen gas. When lightning passes through the air, nitrogen in the air combines with __1__ to form __2__ in the soil. Plants can use this by taking it in through their __3__ which are spread out in the soil. Nitrogen gas in the ground is acted on by __4__ to form compounds. Animals __5__ and decompose. Their return to the soil also contributes to the nitrogen cycle. Dead leaves and other __6__ products decompose and form __7__ compounds. This too is returned to the soil. Nitrogen can be changed back into a gas which can be released into the air. This happens after __8__ in the soil changes it back into a gas.

Answers

Directions: Label the diagram, using the word bank below.

1. _____
2. _____
3. _____
4. _____
5. _____
6. _____
7. _____
8. _____

9. _____

10. _____

11. _____

12. _____

13. _____

Word Bank

A—lightning

D—bacteria

B—roots

E—nitrogen gas

C—nitrogen compounds

Weather

Directions: On the lines below, write the word that matches the definition. Use the word bank to help.

Word Bank

- thermometer
- anemometer
- high
- psychrometer
- satellites
- cirrus clouds
- relative humidity
- tornado warning
- hurricane
- National Weather Service
- Doppler radar
- meteorologist
- barometer
- precipitation
- cumulus clouds
- front
- forecast
- air mass
- clear
- tornado

---

1. An instrument that measures air pressure _____

2. An instrument that measures air temperature _____

3. An instrument that measures wind speed _____

4. Instruments that detect the direction in which a storm is moving _____

5. A scientist who studies the weather _____

6. Instruments that have been used since 1960 to send information to earth about atmospheric conditions_____

7. A large body of air that has similar properties or weather conditions _____

8. An instrument used to measure relative humidity_____

9. The boundary between two air masses _____

10. A prediction of weather conditions_____

11. Rain, sleet, snow, hail _____

12. A ratio that compares the amount of water vapor present in the air to the total amount of water vapor that can be held in the air at a particular temperature_____

13. Fair weather usually accompanies this area of greater _____ air pressure surrounded by an area of lower air pressure.

14. A violent funnel-shaped cloud with extremely strong winds _____

15. A tropical storm that forms over warm oceans and contains an eye and sometimes moves onto land. _____

16. This is issued once a tornado has been seen. _____

17. Puffy clouds_____

18. Feathery clouds _____

19. A term used to describe the appearance of the sky on a given day _____

20. A network of weather stations around the United States _____

Weather Word Search

E	N	I	W	R	D	D	E	F	T	S	R	A	R	R
E	R	O	W	E	O	N	H	O	C	U	E	E	E	E
M	N	U	N	P	P	I	R	R	I	L	H	A	T	I
S	S	A	S	O	P	W	E	E	R	U	T	N	E	P
V	V	S	C	S	L	T	T	C	R	M	A	E	M	S
E	A	L	A	I	E	A	A	A	U	U	E	M	O	A
S	W	P	A	M	R	R	W	S	S	C	W	O	M	T
I	H	H	O	E	R	R	P	T	C	S	O	M	R	E
R	O	R	P	R	A	I	U	S	L	E	C	E	E	L
A	A	M	H	I	D	T	A	H	O	I	E	T	H	L
B	E	I	N	R	A	E	L	C	U	T	A	E	T	I
T	G	N	I	N	R	A	W	O	D	A	N	R	O	T
H	T	C	U	M	U	L	O	U	S	E	Z	O	O	E
N	O	I	T	A	T	I	P	I	C	E	R	P	R	S
R	E	T	E	M	O	R	H	C	Y	S	P	O	S	F

Weather Words

1. air mass
2. anemometer
3. barometer
4. cirrus clouds
5. clear
6. cumulus
7. doppler radar
8. forecast
9. front

10. hail
11. high
12. hurricane
13. ocean
14. precipitation
15. pressure
16. psychrometer
17. rain
18. satellite

19. snow
20. thermometer
21. tornado warning
22. vane
23. vapor
24. water
25. weather
26. wind

Weather Instruments

Directions: Choose the correct name for each weather instrument and then label each picture correctly.

Word Bank		
• thermometer	• wind vane	• barometer
• weather map	• anemometer	• rain gauge

used to determine wind speed

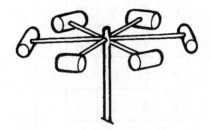

1. _____

used to determine the amount of precipitation

2. _____

used to determine wind direction

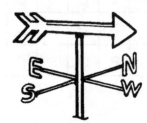

3. _____

used to determine temperature

4. _____

used to track weather patterns

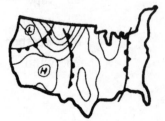

5. _____

used to determine air pressure

6. _____

Geography Terminology–Part I

Match the land term to its corresponding definition.

_____ 1. valley

_____ 2. plain

_____ 3. mountain

_____ 4. cape

_____ 5. plateau

_____ 6. archipelago

_____ 7. coast

_____ 8. isthmus

_____ 9. peninsula

_____ 10. mountain range

_____ 11. island

_____ 12. delta

_____ 13. hill

_____ 14. basin

_____ 15. canyon

A. a group of islands

B. narrow strip of land that connects two larger land areas

C. raised area lower than a mountain with a rounded top and sloping sides

D. soil that collects at the mouth of a river, usually three-sided

E. body of land smaller than a continent, surrounded by water

F. very high hill

G. large, high plain

H. land drained by a river, land surrounded by higher land

I. flat stretch of land, prairie

J. land nearly surrounded by water

K. low land area between hills or mountains

L. row of connected mountains

M. land along the ocean, seashore

N. narrow valley with high, steep sides, usually with a stream at the base

O. point of land extending into a sea, ocean, or lake

Label the land forms below using the terms from above.

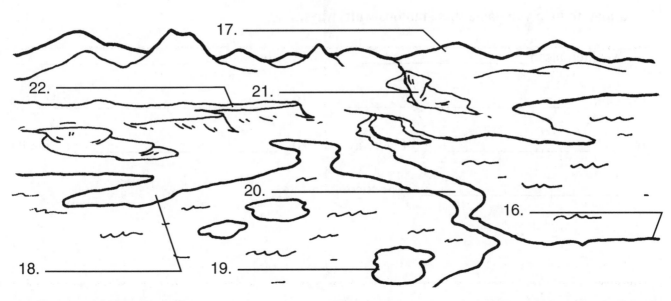

Geography Terminology–Part II

Match the water words with the corresponding definitions.

_____ 1. bay   A. place at which a river's waters empty into a large body of water

_____ 2. tributary   B. large body of water, usually fresh, surrounded by land

_____ 3. cove   C. part of an ocean or sea extending into land, a large bay

_____ 4. strait   D. area of deep water forming a shelter where ships can anchor safely

_____ 5. gulf   E. large body of saltwater smaller than an ocean, enclosed by land

_____ 6. sound   F. narrow strip of water running from a larger body of water into
                           land or between islands

_____ 7. harbor   G. large, natural stream of water that flows through the land into a
                           lake, ocean, etc., containing freshwater

                        H. stream or small river that flows into a larger river or body of water

_____ 8. sea   I. narrow channel connecting two larger bodies of water

_____ 9. inlet   J. long, narrow body of water connecting two larger bodies of water
                           or separating an island from the mainland; larger than a strait
_____ 10. fjord

                        K. long, narrow bay bordered by steep cliffs

_____ 11. river   L. small, sheltered bay

_____ 12. mouth   M. part of the sea or lake extending into the land; usually smaller than
                           a gulf and larger than a cove
_____ 13. lake

Use a map to help you name these famous waterways.

14. Mediterranean _____   18. Long Island _____

15. Ohio _____   19. _____ Erie

16. _____ of Norway   20. _____ of Gibraltar

17. _____ of Mexico

Ancient Greece

Directions: Find the correct match. On the line provided, write the letter from Column 2 that matches the number in Column 1.

Column 1

_____ 1. Homer

_____ 2. Olympic Games

_____ 3. Aristotle

_____ 4. city-state

_____ 5. democracy

_____ 6. Pericles

_____ 7. Socrates

_____ 8. Hippocrates

_____ 9. Parthenon

_____ 10. Herodotus

_____ 11. Plato

_____ 12. Phidias

Column 2

A. a type of government run by the people

B. the leader during the Golden Age

C. the temple honoring Athena

D. the author of *The Iliad* and *The Odyssey*

E. the "Father of History"

F. Alexander the Great's teacher

G. the author of *The Republic*

H. a competition to honor Zeus

I. a famous Greek sculptor

J. studied the human body; referred to as the "Father of Medicine"

K. a teacher who taught by using a series of questions

L. an independently ruled city

Directions: Sparta and Athens were two cities that held different beliefs and followed different ways of life. On the line provided, write the name of the city that the sentence is about.

_____ 1. Boys were educated in literature, writing, and philosophy.

_____ 2. Boys started military training at seven years of age.

_____ 3. Male citizens voted in the assembly.

_____ 4. Trials were judged by a jury.

_____ 5. Women owned and operated their own businesses.

_____ 6. Males and females were citizens.

Map of Ancient Rome

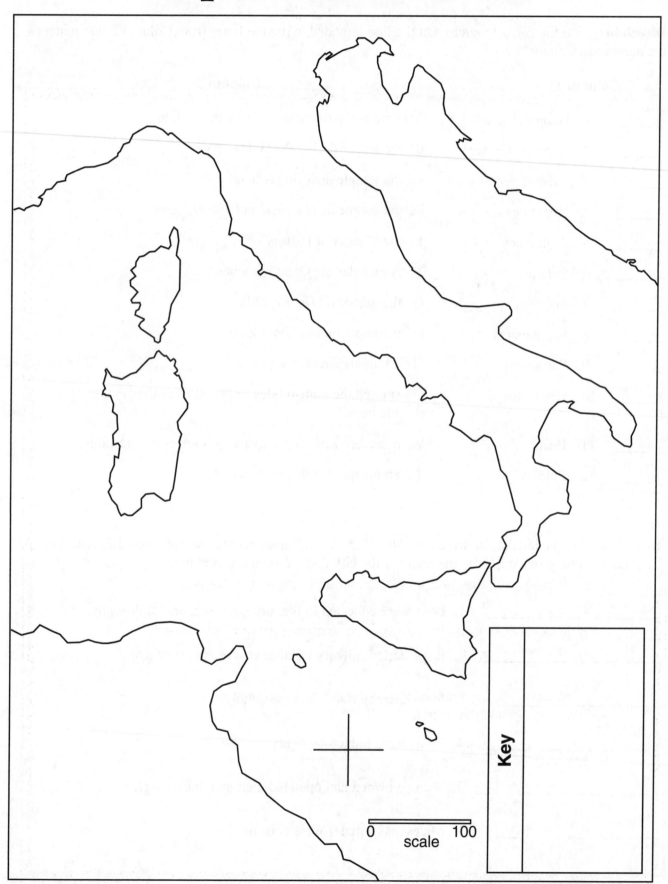

Key

0   100
scale

Map of Ancient Rome *(cont.)*

Use the map on page 266 and the directions below to make a map showing the physical features of Ancient Rome.

1. Locate, draw, and label the Apennine Mountains and the Alps. Color these two mountain ranges brown.

2. Label the Mediterranean Sea, the Adriatic Sea, and the Ionian Sea. Color the seas blue.

3. Locate, draw, and label the Tiber River and the Po River. Color the rivers blue.

4. Locate and label the islands of Corsica, Sardinia, and Sicily. Color the islands yellow.

5. Locate, draw, and label the Tuscan Plain, the Latium Plain, and Campanian Plain. Color the plains green.

6. Color the rest of the Italian coastline yellow.

7. Locate and label Northern Africa.

8. Locate, indicate, and label the cities of Rome and Naples.

9. Make a compass rose on your map showing north, south, east, and west.

10. Make a map key showing what each symbol and color represents on your map.

11. Make a scale showing that 1 inch equals 100 miles.

12. At the top clearly write The Geography of Ancient Rome.

Ancient Rome

Directions: Choose the answer that best completes each sentence.

1. _____ was a legendary twin brother who founded Rome.

   A. Mars   B. Romulus   C. Zeus

2. The form of government used in Rome was that of a _____ .

   A. republic   B. democracy   C. dictatorship

3. Two elected officials, called _____ , were the commanders of the government.

   A. plebeians   B. tribunes   C. consuls

4. The noble families of Rome were called _____ .

   A. patricians   B. plebeians   C. republicans

5. The common people of Rome were called _____ .

   A. patricians   B. plebeians   C. republicans

6. All citizens had to serve in the army and pay taxes, but only _____ could then become consuls or senators.

   A. patricians   B. plebeians   C. republicans

7. Ten _____ were elected yearly to stop the passage of laws that were unfair to the plebeians.

   A. soldiers   B. senators   C. tribunes

8. _____ means "I forbid" in Latin and was used to stop the passage of unfair laws.

   A. Veto   B. Verdad   C. Verify

9. The first written code of Roman law was called the _____ .

   A. Laws of Hammurabi   B. Twelve Tables   C. The Republic

10. The Roman calendar was based on _____ calendar and Latin.

    A. Julius Caesar's   B. Constantine's   C. Hannibal's

Ancient Rome (cont.)

11. The Romans built 50,000 miles of roadway. The _____ , built in 312 B.C., is still used today by tourists and residents.

    A. Parthenon   B. Acropolis   C. Appian Way

12. The Romans were excellent plumbers. They designed and built a water supply system that used channels called _____ to bring fresh water into their cities.

    A. pipe lines   B. aqueducts   C. tunnels

13. A speech given by _____ at the Forum in Rome (as immortalized by William Shakespeare) began with the words, "Friends, Romans, countrymen, lend me your ears."

    A. Horatio   B. Julius Caesar   C. Mark Anthony

14. _____ was a powerful leader who was voted dictator by the Senate and was later assassinated on the Senate steps.

    A. Brutus   B. Cassius   C. Julius Caesar

15. _____ became the first Emperor of the Roman Empire.

    A. Julius Caesar   B. Mark Anthony   C. Octavian/Augustus Caesar

16. _____ consorted with Julius Caesar and Mark Anthony while ruling Rome from Egypt.

    A. Cleopatra   B. Constantine   C. Nero

17. All but one of the following statements is true about Hannibal. Place an X next to the false piece of information.

    _____ A. He traveled by land and not by sea.
    _____ B. He was a general sent from Rome.
    _____ C. He crossed the Alps using elephants.
    _____ D. He was a general from Carthage.
    _____ E. He fought in the second Punic War.

18. All but one of the following statements is true about the geography and location of Italy. Place an X next to the false piece of information.

    _____ A. The rivers were not a good means of transportation.

    _____ B. It is located in the middle of the Mediterranean region.

    _____ C. United Rome allowed for easy travel throughout Italy.

Roman Times

Directions: Use the words in the word bank to complete the sentence correctly.

Word Bank		
• Byzantine Empire	• aqueducts	• Constantine
• Pax Romana	• Byzantium	• Constantinople

1. The "Peace of Rome" that lasted for 200 years started under the rule of Augustus was called the
   _____ .

2. _____ were channels that were designed by engineers and used to bring water into cities from far away places.

3. A Roman Emperor who became a Christian was _____ .

4. The city of _____ in Asia Minor was made the new capital of the Roman Empire and named _____ .

5. Greece, the Balkans, and Asia Minor were part of the _____ created by Constantine.

Directions: Match the answers in Column 2 with the correct word in Column 1.

Column 1	Column 2
1. forum	A. an indoor yard with trees
2. atrium	B. an author who wrote about life in the Roman Republic
3. Cicero	C. the main square; all roads began here; location for all temples, shops, and government buildings
4. gladiators	D. performers who battled with other people or animals for the amusement of others

Directions: Place each statement number under the proper heading below to show the role of each member in a Roman household unit.

Father	Mother	Girls
_____	_____	_____

Boys	Slaves
_____	_____
	_____

1. the head of the family
2. did the housework
3. were schooled at home

4. were sometimes teachers
5. between the ages of twelve to eighteen attended school
6. entertained guests at home and assisted in businesses

Greek and Roman Gods and Goddesses

Directions: Circle the name of a Greek god or goddess that completes the sentence correctly.

1. The king of the gods, (Zeus, Hades), lived on Mount Olympus and ruled over the weather and the skies.

2. (Ares, Neptune) was the god of war and violence. A red planet was named for his Roman counterpart.

3. The queen of the gods and goddesses, (Demeter, Hera) is the protector of marriage.

4. Zeus and Hera had twins, (Artemis, Dionysus), the goddess of the moon, and (Hermes, Apollo), the god of the sun.

5. The goddess of love and beauty was (Aphrodite, Athena). Her son Eros, called Cupid by the Romans, caused people to fall in love.

6. (Athena, Hera), the goddess of wisdom and protector of Athens, sprang fully grown from the head of Zeus.

7. (Poseidon, Apollo), ruler of the seas, and (Hermes, Hades), ruler of the underworld, were Zeus's brothers.

8. (Hestia, Demeter) was goddess of springtime and the harvest. Her daughter (Persephone, Hera) lived in Hades during the winter and returned to her mother during the spring and summer when all new things began to bloom and grow.

9. The goddess of the hearth and protector of home and family was (Aphrodite, Hestia).

10. All the gods and goddess lived on (Mount Olympus, Mount Sinai).

Greek and Roman Gods and Goddesses *(cont.)*

Directions: The chart gives the Roman name of a god or goddess and his or her importance. Place the matching Greek name for the god or goddess in the correct space on the chart.

Roman Name	Job	Greek Name
Jupiter	king of all the gods and goddesses	_____
Juno	wife and sister of Jupiter	_____
Pluto	god of the underworld	_____
Venus	goddess of love and beauty	_____
Diana	goddess of the moon	_____
Mars	god of war and violence	_____
Neptune	god of the sea	_____

Ancient Egypt

Directions: Use the words in the word bank to complete each sentence correctly.

+--+
| **Word Bank** |
| |
| • delta   • pharaoh   • Menes |
| • Memphis   • Mediterranean   • Africa |
+--+

1. Egypt is located on the continent of _____ .

2. The Nile River flows from the mountains and empties into the _____ Sea.

3. The _____ of the Nile River contains rich soil left behind after the annual flooding of the river.

4. _____ was the king of Egypt who united the northern part of Egypt with his southern kingdom.

5. The capital of the united kingdom of Egypt was _____ .

6. The ruler of Egypt was the _____ .

Directions: Match the gods listed in Column 1 with their responsibilities listed in Column 2.

Column 1		Column 2
_____ 1. Re		A. the god of science and wisdom
_____ 2. Thoth		B. the sun god
_____ 3. Anubis		C. judge of the dead in the underworld
_____ 4. Osiris		D. the god of embalming
_____ 5. Horus		E. leads the dead to the underworld to be judged

Directions: Match the names of the gods and goddesses with their symbol.

+---+
| **Egyptian Gods and Goddesses** |
| • Re   • Thoth   • Anubis   • Isis   • Osiris   • Horus |
+---+

_____ 1. the god with a large crown and the sun

_____ 2. the god with the head of a jackal

_____ 3. the god with the head of an ibis

_____ 4. a god with the head of a falcon or a falcon wearing a crown

_____ 5. a god represented by a mummy

_____ 6. A goddess with a headdress shaped like a seat

Ancient Egypt *(cont.)*

Directions: Read the clue that is given and then complete the puzzle by inserting the missing letters in the spaces provided.

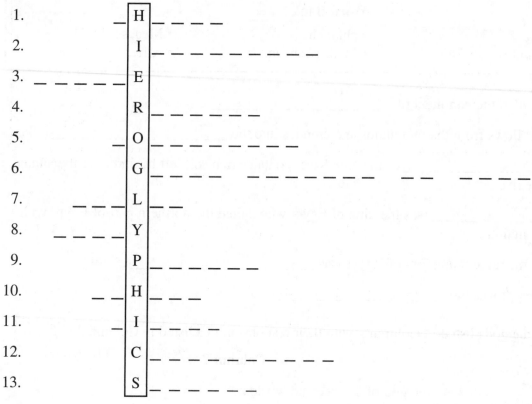

1. _ H _ _ _ _
2. I _ _ _ _ _ _ _
3. _ _ _ _ _ E
4. R _ _ _ _ _
5. _ O _ _ _ _ _
6. G _ _ _ _ _ _ _ _ _ _ _ _ _ _ _
7. _ _ _ L _ _
8. _ _ _ _ Y
9. P _ _ _ _
10. _ _ H _ _
11. _ I _ _ _ _
12. C _ _ _ _ _ _ _ _
13. S _ _ _ _ _ _

Clues

1. a statue with the body of a lion and the head of King Khafre, built to guard the dead in the pyramid at Giza

2. a piece of stone containing three languages; translated in 1822

3. a preserved body wrapped in linen

4. a mummy-like statue buried with the dead to work as servants in the fields during the afterlife

5. a famous scholar who decoded the Rosetta Stone which led to the understanding of Egyptian writing

6. the flooding season of the Nile River

7. jewelry that was sometimes shaped as a scarab beetle and worn to bring good luck

8. an important crop that grew in the Nile River and could be made into paper

9. the person whom the pharaoh relied upon to oversee his kingdom

10. the largest pyramid ever built; constructed under the rule of King Khufu

11. a person who could read and write

12. the practice of worshipping many gods

13. rolled pieces of paper that were used for writing

Early Middle Ages

Complete the following text on the Early Middle Ages with words from the word bank.

Word Bank

- east
- sick/poor
- Latin
- Franks
- Vikings
- empire
- feudalism
- convents
- Gregory I
- A.D. 800
- Magyarz
- Holy Roman Empire
- missionaries
- monastery
- Charlemagne
- education
- Louis the Pious
- Muslims
- nuns
- monks
- trade
- 1066
- pope
- north

After the fall of the Roman Empire, battling Germanic armies brought much destruction to Europe. Despite all the confusion, leaders in the Catholic Church in Rome still wanted a united Europe. In 590, (1) _____ became pope, or the leader of the Roman Catholic Church. His dream was for a united Christian kingdom that would stretch (2) _____ from Italy to England and (3) _____ from Spain to Germany. He tried to carry on the Roman traditions like prayer in (4) _____ . He organized armies to defend Rome and attempted to spread Christianity throughout Europe.

Special teachers, or (5) _____ , were sent to foreign countries to spread religion and have people convert or adopt that religion. Some of these people were monks and nuns. (6) _____ were men who lived in a (7) _____ and devoted themselves to prayer and the Church. They performed many tasks, including hand-copying religious writings.

(8) _____ , women who also devoted themselves to the Church, lived in (9) _____ . Monasteries and convents became home to many people who were (10) _____ or _____ .

Gregory I's dream of a united kingdom with a (11) _____ , the most prominent religious Roman Catholic leader, at its head became an important part of life in the Middle Ages.

Early Middle Ages *(cont.)*

In 768, (12) _____ , "Charles the Great" in French, became king of the

(13) _____ , a Germanic people in western Europe. He, like the popes, dreamed

of a united Christian kingdom, or (14) _____ . For 32 years he increased his

powerful empire by conquering many European nations, including Rome. On December 25 in

(15) _____ , Charlemagne and a Roman Catholic pope joined together to create

an empire known as the (16) _____ . This empire lasted for 46 years. During

his rule, Charlemagne's major contributions included spreading (17) _____ and

reviving learning. He also did much to restore (18) _____ between Asia and

Europe.

Charlemagne's Empire →

Charlemagne's kingdom passed to his son (19) _____ and then to his grandsons.

Conflict continued among differing nations to conquer or reconquer land. Warriors attacked from the

south. They were (20) _____ , followers of Islam.

(21) _____ from the plains of central Asia invaded Germany, France, and Italy

from the east. Warriors from the north, (22) _____ or Norsemen, presented the

greatest threat because their ships could sail in shallow water, so they eventually conquered Ireland,

Russia, England, and northern France. They had come from present-day Norway, Sweden, and

Denmark.

By (23) _____ , William, the Duke of Normandy, conquered England and

declared himself king. A new way of life was to emerge to help the people of Europe to govern

themselves, a system of government based on agreements. This system is known as

(24) _____ .

Middle Ages I

Circle the term that is described in the definition.

1. System of government based on agreements between rulers and local warriors.

    (a) democracy
    (c) communism
    (b) feudalism
    (d) aristocracy

2. A warrior who swore an oath of allegiance to a lord in return for land.

    (a) serf
    (c) vassal
    (b) missionary
    (d) viceroy

3. A ruler to whom a vassal would swear loyalty.

    (a) king
    (c) prince
    (b) servant
    (d) lord

4. Vassals who were given special training as soldiers.

    (a) squires
    (c) monks
    (b) knights
    (d) pages

5. The age at which a page became a squire.

    (a) 6
    (c) 14
    (b) 21
    (d) 30

6. Which of the following was not a nobleman or noblewoman during the Middle Ages?

    (a) Roland of France
    (c) Eleanor of Aquitaine
    (b) Sir Lancelot of England
    (d) King Henry VIII

7. This small community included acres of farmland, a huge house for the lord and his family, huts for workers, a flour mill, a church, and an oven.

    (a) cathedral
    (c) manor
    (b) castle
    (d) village

8. People who worked on a manor.

    (a) serfs/peasants
    (c) slaves
    (b) knights
    (d) vassals

9. Massive stone churches, usually filled with stained glass windows.

    (a) mosques
    (c) cathedrals
    (b) synagogues
    (d) temples

Middle Ages II

Use the terms in the word bank to complete sentences 1–21.

Word Bank

- plague
- crusade
- knight
- lute
- justice
- portcullis
- charters
- squire
- apprentice
- armor
- nationalism
- Joan of Arc
- jury
- moat
- page
- guilds
- quintain
- accolade
- Magna Carta
- drawbridge
- duel
- coat of arms
- donjon
- castles

---

1. A war fought for religious reasons is a _____ .

2. _____ were organizations of people who worked at the same type of occupation like weavers, goldsmiths, or tailors.

3. An _____ is a young person who lived in a master's home for 3–12 years, without pay, learning a craft.

4. At the end of the Middle Ages, _____ , or written agreements giving townspeople the right to self-government, were bought by citizens of towns from nobles who needed money.

5. _____ , fairness under the law, was upheld when kings sent judges to towns and cities to help determine the facts in criminal cases.

6. A _____ was a group of 12 good men who were chosen to hear the facts in criminal cases and eventually decide if the accused were guilty or not.

7. The _____ _____ was a charter that said even kings could not do certain things. It guaranteed trial by jury and no raise in taxes without the approval of the Great Council of Nobles.

8. A sense of loyalty to one's country or king or queen is known as _____ .

Middle Ages II (cont.)

9. _____ of the Middle Ages were places to live and places of defense.

10. A _____ learned to hunt with hawks and falcons, ride and use guns, and respect superiors.

11. A _____ participated in _____ , a sport in which he jousted with a dummy. He was always at the side of his lord in battle.

12. To become a _____ , a person must learn the codes of chivalry.

13. A knight receives an _____ , a touch on the shoulder with a sword, as he is knighted.

14. During the Middle Ages, a _____ was fought to settle simple disputes.

15. Important musical instruments during the Middle Ages were the _____ and harp.

16. A castle of the Middle Ages was surrounded by a _____ and had a _____ which could be raised and lowered.

17. An armored gate called a _____ protected a medieval castle at the main entrance.

18. The _____ , or keep, was a tower-like structure which had thick walls and was the strongest part of the castle.

19. A knight wears a metal suit of _____ into battle and has a special _____ on his shield.

20. _____ was an important heroine who led the French armies against the English, but was burned to death after being condemned as a witch. She was made a saint in 1920.

21. The disease that killed 25 million Europeans during the 1340s was called the _____ , or Black Death.

The Renaissance and Beyond

The period in Europe that began around the mid-1300s when there was a renewed interest in Greek, Roman, and Islamic ideas is known as the *Renaissance*. It means "rebirth." Many of the people who lived during that time had a profound impact upon the course of history and continue to influence the world during the twentieth century.

Match the names below to the accomplishments.

- King Henry VIII
- Martin Luther
- Miguel de Cervantes
- Michelangelo
- William and Mary
- Estates General
- Oliver Cromwell

- Ignatius Loyola
- Geoffrey Chaucer
- Johannes Gutenberg
- Dante
- Marie Antoinette
- guillotine
- Whigs

- John Calvin
- William Shakespeare
- Leonardo da Vinci
- Thomas More
- Napoleon Bonaparte
- Parliament
- Tories

1. He was an inventor, scientist, and artist who painted the Mona Lisa. He is

   _____ .

2. He is famous for painting scenes from the Bible, especially the ceiling of the Sistine Chapel of the Vatican in Rome. He is _____ .

3. He is famous for writing *The Divine Comedy,* a poem mixing religious ideas from the Middle Ages with political ideas from Italy. It was written in Italian, not Latin. He is

   _____ .

4. He is a famous English writer. He wrote *The Canterbury Tales,* which is a set of stories about a group of travelers on their way to a religious shrine. He is _____ .

5. He is a famous Spanish writer. He wrote *Don Quixote,* a story about a hero who thinks he is a brave knight in shining armor trying to defend honor and fight evil in the world. He is

   _____ .

6. He is a famous English author. He wrote many plays about ancient Romans and English Kings. Some of his plays are *Julius Caesar* and *King Richard III.* He is _____ .

7. He is a famous German printer who used movable type to print the Bible in 1456. He is

   _____ .

8. He is a famous English writer. He wrote *Utopia*, a story about an ideal society where everyone lived in peace and happiness. He is _____ .

9. He is a famous German Protestant leader who translated the Bible into German. He is

   _____ .

The Renaissance and Beyond *(cont.)*

10. He is a famous French Protestant religious leader. His followers in France were called Huguenots. In England they were called Puritans. He is _____ .

11. He is a famous Spanish knight who tried to strengthen the Catholic Church by helping people better understand its teachings. He founded the Jesuits. He is _____ .

12. He is an English king who broke away from the Catholic Church and started the Church of England. He is _____ .

13. This English organization is made up of the House of Lords and the House of Commons. This is called _____ .

14. This famous English leader worked with Parliament on a plan for a government, or a constitution. He is _____ .

15. Political parties are groups of people who share similar ideas about government. The first political parties were English. They were called the _____ and the _____ .

16. This famous French queen was married to King Louis XVI. They lived a very luxurious lifestyle while the people in France were poor and starving. She is _____ .

17. In 1789 King Louis XVI called a meeting of the three estates or groups to approve new taxes. The First Estate was composed of officials from the Roman Catholic Church. The Second Estate was made up of nobles. The Third Estate was made up of peasants, bankers, merchants, lawyers, and doctors. This meeting was called _____ .

18. This French general was elected consul, or ruler, for life. He then made himself emperor and tried to build an empire. He was defeated at the Battle of Waterloo in Belgium. He is _____ .

19. In 1688 these two leaders accepted Parliament's invitation to rule England. They took an oath to obey the laws passed by Parliament. When they came to power without any warfare, it was known as the Glorious Revolution. They are _____ .

20. This instrument was used to behead people during the French Revolution. It is a _____ .

The Industrial Revolution

The time period from about 1750–1900 is known as the Industrial Revolution because of all the technological changes that took place. It was an age of change that turned society from an agrarian or agricultural economy into a manufacturing economy.

Match the inventor to the invention.

_____	1. James Hargreaves	A. elevator
_____	2. John Deere	B. steel
_____	3. James Watt	C. telephone
_____	4. Samuel F. B. Morse	D. modern automobile
_____	5. Alexander Graham Bell	E. spinning wheel
_____	6. Richard Trevithick	F. steam engine
_____	7. Henry Bessemer	G. light bulb, electricity through wires, phonograph
_____	8. G. Daimler and K. Benz	H. vulcanized rubber
_____	9. Thomas Edison	I. telegraph
_____	10. Otis	J. locomotive
_____	11. Charles Goodyear	K. sewing machine
_____	12. Elias Howe	L. steel plow

Choose the correct answer. (*cholera, strike, union, factories, assembly line*)

13. Large buildings set up with machines that can manufacture or produce goods are called _____ .

14. People who work together form a _____ to advance the interests and working conditions of its members.

15. Many times workers will go on _____ , or refuse to work, until their demands for better conditions are met.

16. In a factory, an _____ , of rows of workers and machines pass along a product until it is completed.

17. _____ , a disease caused by contaminated drinking water, resulted from unhealthy conditions in manufacturing cities.

Answer Key

Page 6

Vocabulary
1. confident
2. glider
3. aerodynamic
4. exceeded

Comprehension
1. Most people believed that flight was not possible because the machines used to fly were heavier than air.
2. Three achievements Orville Wright made prior to 1886 were
   a. he built a printing press
   b. he started a printing business
   c. he developed a weekly newspaper edited by Wilbur
3. Both brothers were involved in
   a. a weekly newspaper
   b. renting and selling bicycles
   c. manufacturing bicycles
4. When Otto Lilienthal, a pioneer glider died, the brothers, upon reading about his work, became interested in aerodynamics.
5. 1900, Kill Devil Hill near Kittyhawk, North Carolina.
6. They felt that the data that they had on air pressure and curved surfaces was inaccurate, so they built a wind tunnel to make their own pressure tables.

Page 7

| 1900 | D | 1901 | B | 1902 | F |
| 1903 | E | 1905 | C | 1908 | A |

Page 9

Vocabulary
1. C   2. E   3. B
4. F   5. A   6. D

Page 9

Comprehension
1. April 1912; The vessel was luxurious, having the best of everything. It was believed to be unsinkable.
2. The hull had sixteen watertight compartments and even if two compartments flooded, the ship would still float.
3. Mr. and Mrs. John Jacob Astor and Isidor and Ida Strauss
4. It departed from Southampton, England, and was to arrive in New York City.
5. They only had room for 1,200 people, fewer than the persons on board.

Page 10

Cause and Effect
2. Effect—The steel became brittle from the cold, causing cracks to appear instantly in the hull of the ship and the seams to unrivet. Water poured inside, further weakening the hull.
3. Cause—The radio operator on the California was not on duty.
4. Effect—Accept all reasonable answers. Many passengers died and the *Titanic* went down. Help was too far away.
5. Effect—Water flooded through the hull to the ship's bow.
6. Effect—The passengers were encouraged.
7. Effect—Accept all reasonable answers such as:
   a. The ship's captain goes down with his ship.
   b. Many people died.
8. Cause—Accept all reasonable answers such as:
   a. The steel composition of the hull was faulty.
   b. The boat was traveling too fast.
Summary—Accept all reasonable answers.

Page 12

Vocabulary
1. gentleman's agreement   2. ban
3. immigrants   4. quota
5. excluded   6. restriction

Comprehension
1. The Chinese Exclusion Act was passed because people in the United States feared that Chinese laborers would work for less money.
2. American laborers were afraid they would lose their jobs to immigrants willing to work for lower pay. Others believed the newcomers were inferior to the people already living in the United States.
3. Prior to the 1880s—countries in Northern and Western Europe.
4. It sought to establish severe quotas for immigrants from southern and eastern European countries.

Page 13

5. Italy   5,082 people per year
   Russia 2,784 people per year
   Greece 307 people per year

Prefixes
(Sentences will vary.)
1. ex
2. in
3. pre
4. re
5. im
6. in

Page 15

Vocabulary
1. agriculture
2. resent
3. conserve
4. prosper

Cause and Effect
1. C
2. A
3. D
4. B
5. E

Comprehension
1. A. They moved on to new land after depleting fertile soil.
   B. They plowed up natural grasses to plant wheat.
2. Californians called the people who migrated from the Great Plains region to California, "Okies," (derived from Oklahoma). It was used by some to mean dumb and lazy.
3. Some farmers, not wanting to share their surplus food with the Okies, destroyed it.
4. Labor camps in the San Juaquin Valley were created giving relief and education to the migrants.
5. A. Steinbeck wrote the novel, *The Grapes of Wrath*
   B. Lange photographed and documented the misery of the migrants.
   C. Guthrie sang songs about the lives and the problems of migrants.

Page 17

I. Pat Nixon
   A. renovated the White House
   B. made the White House into a Museum of American Heritage
   C. supported volunteerism in the community
   D. acted as the goodwill ambassador to Europe
II. Betty Ford
   A. public awareness of breast cancer
   B. supporter of Equal Rights Amendment
   C. made the public aware of alcohol and pain medication addiction

Answer Key (cont.)

D. founder of the Betty Ford Clinic for Substance Abuse
III. Rosalyn Carter
  A. presidential advisor
  B. official presidential representative to Central and South American countries
  C. took notes at cabinet meetings
  D. supported mental health reform, Society Security reform legislation, and the approval of the Equal Rights Amendment

Comprehension
  1. Pat Nixon
  2. Rosalyn Carter
  3. A. Pat Nixon—community volunteerism
     B. Betty Ford—breast cancer/addiction
     C. Rosalyn Carter—mental health reform, Social Security reform, Equal Rights Amendment

Page 19
VCR video cassette recorder—taped programs when people were not at home
CD compact disc—enhanced sound for listeners of recorded music
PC personal computer—entertainment and productivity
Comprehension
  1. A. Buy or rent video tapes of movies and watch whenever they chose.
     B. Record a movie or show from television to watch at their leisure.
     C. Watch a show on one channel while taping a show on another channel.
     D. A new line of stores that sold and rented videos was the fastest growing 1980s industry.
  2. Television studios recorded programs for viewing in different time zones or for repeat usage
  3. A. Sony introduced the Betamax in 1975
     B. Matsushita released a VHS, video home system
  4. Microchip technology, modems, and user friendly software

Page 20
VCRs
  #7—It helped form a new line of business.
  #8—It was the fastest growing industry in the 1980s.
  #9—It was used in the entertainment industry.
  #10—It is used for home entertainment.
Alike
  #1—It is more affordable.
  #3—Prices became lower.
  #10—It is used for home entertainment.
Computers
  #2—It is expensive.
  #4—It advanced because of microchip technology.
  #5—It was used by schools.
  #6—It used a modem and software.
  #10—It is used for home entertainment.

Page 22
Sequences
  A. 9   F. 6
  B. 3   G. 2
  C. 1   H. 7
  D. 4   I. 5
  E. 10   J. 8
Sequence of Creating a Painting
  A. He sketched a picture.
  B. He made individual drawings of each element in each scene.
  C. He made full-size charcoal drawings.
  D. He made color sketches.
  E. He painted the picture.
Paragraph (Accept all reasonable efforts.)

Vocabulary
  1. C
  2. B
  3. A
  4. B
  5. C
  6. A
Complete the sentence
  1. mother of the civil rights movement
  2. Tuskegee, Alabama
  3. NAACP (National Association for the Advancement of Colored People); Voters' League
  4. seamstress
  5. vacate her seat on the bus for a white man
  6. Edgar Daniel Nixon; Dr. Martin Luther King
  7. A. Blacks were harassed, black leaders were arrested; many people lost their jobs.
     B. The United States Supreme Court ruled the Alabama bus segregation laws unconstitutional.
     C. The bus company lost $75,000 in revenues.

Page 25
  8. A. walking
     B. carpooling
     C. riding bicycles
     D. riding mules
  9. 381
  10. Unconstitutional
Paragraph (Accept all reasonable answers.)

Page 27
True or False
  1. True
  2. False; Sweden
  3. False; Brazilian and Swedish
  4. False; Brazilian
  5. True
  6. True
  7. False; junior league
  8. False; knee

Fact or Opinion
  2. Fact
  3. Opinion
  4. Fact
  5. Opinion
  6. Fact

Page 29
I. Early Life
  A. August 9, 1808
  B. Salem, Massachusetts
II. Education
  A. private school
  B. Public Latin School
  C. Harvard College
  D. Harvard Medical School
III. Places of Study
  A. Massachusetts
  B. France
  C. England
IV. Employment
  A. Pre-Civil War
     1. Boston Medical practice
     2. Worked for the abolitionists to help slaves escape to the North
  B. Civil War
     1. Doctor for the Union soldiers fighting in Virginia
     2. Campaigned for and succeeded in having the Senate begin an army ambulance corps

Answer Key (cont.)

V. Accomplishments
   A. improved public health by making people aware of how TB was spread.
   B. helped create health boards to monitor public health
   C. served on health boards
   D. in 1879 became the president of the American Medical Association
   E. spokesman for public health issues
   F. encouraged women to enter careers in medicine
Evaluation (Accept all reasonable answers)

Page 31
   1. flour
   2. five
Rhyming Patterns
Stanza 2
Line 1: fair, 3, wear, 4, there
Line 2: claim, 5, same
Stanza 3
Line 1: lay, 3, day, way
Line 2: black, 5, back
Stanza 4
Line 1: sigh 3, I, 4, by
Line 2: hence, 5, difference

Page 32
Line 3, Line 4
Line 5
Comprehension
   1. nine
   2. in a wooded area with two roads that diverged in different directions
   3. the author, Robert Frost
   4. Which road shall he take?
   5. He took the road that was grassy and less traveled.
   6. It has made all the difference in his life.

Page 33
   1. It indicates that he is not afraid to explore a less familiar area
   2. curiosity
      individuality
      confidence
      sense of adventure
   3. It is easier, more accepted, and chosen by the majority.
   4. a. Doing what is conventional does not always lead to the best outcome.
      b. You must make decisions for yourself and have the courage to carry them out.

Page 35
Vocabulary
   1. A
   2. E
   3. D
   4. B
   5. C
Comprehension
   1. A. metaphor—*like* or *as* is not used
      B. Accept all reasonable answers, such as *a rock is strong and holds up well over time.*
   2. simile—uses the word *like*, in *like a rock*
   3. the poet, Edna St. Vincent Millay

Page 36
   4. a brooch
   5. It is not something she really needs, but she treasures it more than anything else she owns.
   6. Accept all reasonable answers such as, it is not a necessary item in her life.

   7. She wishes she had inherited her mother's courage.
   8. Accept all reasonable answers.

Page 43
Section I
   1. melancholy
   2. ceased
   3. oppressive, staggering
   4. galls
   5. exasperated
   6. accessible
   7. ambled
   8. reluctantly
   9. brooch
   10. isolation
   11. intrusions
   12. meager
   13. stationary
   14. dimensions, gallows
   15. veered

Page 44
   1. troupe
   2. elated
   3. reservoirs
   4. assaults
   5. helter-skelter
   6. revolutionary
   7. populated
   8. revived
   9. receded
   10. enveloped
   11. parson
   12. comprehend
   13. bridle
   14. camphor
   15. vigorous
   16. penetrate

Page 45
Section III
   1. roust
   2. constable
   3. cahoots
   4. disarray
   5. accommodations
   6. threadbare
   7. fragrant
   8. wheezed
   9. flapjacks
   10. illiterates
   11. ordeal
   12. lingered
   13. rigid
   14. anguish
   15. peril

Page 46
Sections IV and V
   1. swivel
   2. verandah
   3. flailing
   4. prostrate
   5. revulsion
   6. accomplice
   7. custody
   8. mantel
   9. furrowed
   10. ignorant
   11. staunchly
   12. wistful
   13. hearth
   14. tarnation
   15. remorseless

Page 47
   1. Natalie Babbitt was born on July 28, 1932, in Dayton, Ohio.
   2. Natalie Babbitt graduated from Smith College in Massachusetts in 1954.
   3. She married Samuel F. Babbitt who was the vice president of Brown University.
   4. Natalie Babbitt began her career as the illustrator of her husband's books.
   5. Natalie began writing herself because her husband became too busy to continue writing, so she decided to write and illustrate her own books.
   6. Natalie Babbitt has written six books.
   7. Natalie Babbitt has written the following books:
      Search for Delicacies
      Kneeknock Rise
      Goody Hall
      The Devil's Storybook
      The Eyes of the Amaryllis
      Tuck Everlasting
   8. *Kneeknock Rise* and *The Devil's Storybook* both were awarded the ALA Notable Book Award and were placed on the *Horn Book* Honors List.
   9. Natalie Babbitt has received six awards for *Tuck Everlasting.*
   10. Accept all reasonable responses.

Page 48
   1. Accept appropriate descriptions.

Answer Key (cont.)

2. Cottage was not inviting, visitors not welcome.
3. Woods appeared peaceful, as if they should be disturbed.
4. They have looked the same for 87 years.
5. Little music box painted with roses and lilies of the valley
6. Angry about always being told what and what not to do
7. She had heard it many years before, and it was the music of elves.
8. Accept any appropriate answer.
9. Met Jesse Tuck.
10. Accept any appropriate answer.

Page 49
1. Kidnappers seemed friendly and had no intention of hurting her. Said they would return her home the next day.
2. Accept any appropriate answer.
3. It had come from Mae's music box.
4. They have not changed in 87 years because they drank from a spring in the wood by Treegap.
5. See pages 38 and 39, Chapter 7.
6. They wanted her to understand the consequences.
7. Accept any appropriate response.
8. Jesse thinks of it as fun and good times. Miles, more seriously, is wary of consequences.
9. Tucks were messy, cluttered, dusty. Fosters were clean, neat, orderly.
10. They are afraid people will notice they never changed.

Page 50
1. She was no longer afraid; she loved the Tucks.
2. Gentle, kind insightful, caring.
3. Life is everchanging.
4. The Tucks do not grow and change; they are not really living.
5. Everyone would come running for some spring water and everyone would stay the same forever. Life would go on without them.
6. They haven't had a chance to interact with other people in 20 years.
7. Drink from the spring when she turns 17 so they could go off together forever.
8. He didn't realize what had happened to him until it was too late.
9. Accept reasonable responses.
10. He would tell them where Winnie was in exchange for the ownership of the wood.

Page 51
1. Accept appropriate summaries.
2. His grandmother knew Miles' wife.
3. He recognized the tune of the music box.
4. Accept reasonable responses.
5. She felt she had to save the secret of the spring.
6. He longed to have a normal life span.
7. She would not be able to die, and their secret would be revealed.
8. She did what she had to do because she loved the Tucks and felt it was right.
9. She was happy with herself, and other children respected her.
10. Accept reasonable and complete responses.

Page 52
1. Helped Mae escape in order to keep their secret.
2. Accept appropriate responses.
3. Both made decisions about who should have everlasting life. Winnie gave her gift because she cared; the man only wanted to have financial gain.
4. Accept reasonable responses.
5. He was glad she chose to live a natural life and remain part of the "wheel."

6. Accept reasonable responses

Page 53
Answers will vary. Accept any reasonable response and supporting details.

Page 55
1. A stranger dressed in a yellow suit arrives in Treegap.
2. Mysterious activity takes place in the Foster woods.
3. Winnie Foster disappears.
4. A horse is stolen outside of Treegap.
5. The Fosters sell their wood.
6. Winnie Foster is found unharmed.
7. Mae Tuck is put in jail for murder.
8. An unusual summer storm hits Treegap.
9. Mae Tuck escapes.
10. Winnie Foster, age 78, dies.

Page 56
Intention: Winnie wants to make a difference in the world.
Initial Barrier: Winnie is stuck at home, not able to do what she wants.
Barrier Reversal: Learns about Tuck and the spring.
High Point: Loves the Tucks.
Rug Pulling: Man with yellow suit wants the spring.
Catastrophe: Mae kills the man.
Resolution: Winnie helps Mae escape.

Page 57
1. metaphor
2. simile
3. simile
4. personification
5. simile
6. personification
7. simile
8. metaphor
9. personification
10. metaphor
11. metaphor
12. simile

Page 58
1. Answers will vary, but could include a son, younger brother or cousin, or any young person admiring a role model.
2. The "little chap" trails after the narrator, copies all actions and words, believes everything the narrator says, and admires the narrator.
3. The "little chap" loves and adores the narrator. He seems to worship him. He thinks the narrator is a good person.
4. The poet must be careful since the "little person" is modeling himself after the speaker. He must set a good example for the youngster to follow.
5. The poet is making a difference in the world because he is teaching a younger person how to think and act appropriately.
6. Answers will vary, but could include that Winnie made a difference by helping her friends. She also prevented the world from discovering the Tucks' secret, which they believed would destroy mankind.
7. Answers will vary.
8. There are four stanzas in the poem.
9. The rhyming pattern is AABB.
10. This poem is told in the first person because of the references to "I."

Page 65
Matching
1. Mae
2. Tuck
3. Jesse
4. man in the yellow suit
5. Winnie
True or False
6. True
7. True

Answer Key (cont.)

8. False—Although that is a matter of opinion, they knew the importance of keeping the spring a secret.
9. False—The stranger did not have a good idea because his idea would have caused irreparable damage to the world.
10. True
11. The music box helped to calm down Winnie.
12. Their cat did not drink the water and had a normal life.
13. The man in the yellow suit found Winnie by following the Tucks.
14. The constable knew that Mae should be arrested because he saw her hit the stranger.
15. The thunder during the summer storm helped the escape plan to work.

Page 66

Contrasts (Accept all reasonable and appropriate responses.)

21. Winnie said this because she wanted to be able to help others. She wanted to be responsible and show that she, all by herself, could do something that was important.
22. Angus said this. It meant that being part of the cycle of life is better than living a life in isolation. Every part of life should be experienced, including death at its appropriate time.
23. The Man in the Yellow Suit said this to the Fosters. He knew where Winnie was located, and he would exchange it for the wood that they owned.
24. Winnie knew that Mae must not go to the gallows because she would not die if hanged, and then the secret would be revealed.
25. This question refers to Winnie. Would she drink the water when she was 17 so she could meet Jesse again to marry?

Essay

Accept fully supported appropriate responses.

Page 67

1. C	2. D	3. B
4. A	5. B	6. C
7. A	8. B	9. D
10. C	11. E	12. C
13. A	14. B	15. D

16. Answers will vary.

Page 73

Section I

1. submarine	2. torpedo
3. schooner	4. channel
5. calypso	6. parched
7. hurricane	8. flimsy
9. pontoon bridge	10. destroyer
11. Nazi	12. oil refinery
13. stubborn	14. mutiny
15. tanker	16. hinged
17. ballast	18. stern

Section II

19. langosta

Page 74

20. biscuits	21. anxiously
22. plunged	23. haze
24. drone	25. ignore
26. doused	27. gasping
28. spicy	29. tensely
30. cay	31. Panama
32. Denmark	33. harass
34. dishearten	

Section III

35. reef	36. bamboo
37. support	38. mussels
39. scorpion	40. driftwood
41. smoldering	

Page 75

42. palm fronds	43. vines
44. catchment	45. funnel
46. patient	47. squall
48. satisfaction	49. carnival
50. miserable	

Section IV

51. stranded	52. faint
53. abrupt	54. treacherous
55. melons	56. slope
57. tethered	58. keg
59. voodoo	60. convinced

Page 76

61. dependent
62. foundations
63. diameter
64. damp
65. skate
66. echo

Section V

67. fury, debris	68. locate, rattle
69. receded, inspect	70. groped
71. scallops	72. moray eel
73. tatters	74. burrow
75. limp	76. screech
77. swirl	78. gusted
79. described	80. slithering

Page 77

I. Early Life
  A. June 23, 1921, Statesville, North Carolina
  B. Edward and Elmora Taylor
II. Education
  A. Craddock Elementary School
  B. Craddock High School
    1. a. A
      b. A
      c. poor
    2. graduated a year late
  C. High school activities
    1. 1934-39: cub reporter, *Evening Star*
    2. 1939-42: sports editor, *Evening Star*
  D. College
    1. Merchant Marine Academy
    2. Columbia University
III. First Career
  A. Joined the merchant marines
  B. 1. Seaman
    2. Third Mate
  C. U.S. Navy Cargo Officer
IV. Second Career
  A. Produced films
  B. Writer
    1. *McCall's*
    2. *Redbook*
    3. *Saturday Evening Post*
V. Accomplishments
  A. 1. Commonwealth Club of America Silver Medal
    2. Best Book Award
  B. *Battle in the Arctic Seas*
  C. *Walking Up a Rainbow*
  D. 1. *Maldonado Miracle*
    2. *The Trouble with Tuck*
    3. *Tuck Triumphant*
    4. *The Teetoncey Trilogy*
    5. *Timothy of the Cay*

Page 78

  1. Accept appropriate responses.

Answer Key (cont.)

2. They are at war with the Germans.
3. The refinery is sending oil to England for the war. The Germans want the oil.
4. Phillip's father is an expert at fuel production.
5. She is worried about her family, and she does not like the oil smell.
6. They are taking a boat to Florida and a train to Virginia. Mrs. Enright's family is in Virginia.
7. Their ship is torpedoed.
8. Timothy is on the raft. He is a very old Negro, ugly, with a flat nose and broad face. He has wiry gray hair and a scar on his face. He is very big.
9. She might not approve since she has a fear of blacks. She always warns Phillip that they are "different."
10. Phillip is afraid of Timothy. He is also angry at him for not giving him enough water and food. He also feels superior to Timothy because Timothy is black.

Page 79
1. Accept appropriate responses.
2. Timothy is an orphan from St. Thomas, Virgin Islands. Phillip thinks he is from Africa because he looks like men he has seen in jungle pictures.
3. The problem is that now Phillip is blind.
4. He blames them for his situation.
5. Phillip could be characterized as self-centered.
6. Timothy is afraid Phillip will fall into the shark-infested waters.
7. He attempts to generate a smoke flare from a piece of burning cloth on a stick.
8. Phillip falls into the shark-infested waters.
9. Timothy decides to abandon the raft so he can signal for help. He also thinks it will be safer away from the sharks.
10. Timothy is afraid to kill the cat because he is superstitious and thinks it would cause bad luck.

Page 80
1. Accept appropriate responses.
2. He fails to take into consideration that the war is more important, and everyone is busy.
3. He makes a hut.
4. He is worried about scorpions and snakes.
5. He is angry about being left alone.
6. Timothy is telling Phillip that they better work together and be friends since there is no one else to help them.
7. Timothy prepares an ongoing rescue fire and spells out the word "Help" with rocks and sticks in the sand.
8. Phillip can spell, and Timothy cannot.
9. He strikes Phillip because Phillip refuses to even try to help make sleeping mats. Phillip makes fun of Timothy because he cannot spell.
10. Phillip discovers that Timothy has been making a rope for his safety. Phillip realizes that all along Timothy has been trying to help him.

Page 81
1. Accept appropriate responses.
2. Phillip is able to walk around the island by keeping his feet in the damp sand near the water's edge.
3. He realizes that Timothy worries that he might die, and Phillip will be left defenseless.
4. Timothy says Stew Cat is the cause of their troubles.
5. Timothy solves the problem by putting Stew Cat on the raft. Then he makes a carving of the cat and kills the jumbi by nailing the carving on the roof. The nails drive out the jumbi.
6. The fever drives Timothy into the water. He needs to clear the burning fever from his head.
7. After the fever, Timothy helps Phillip by making extra fishing poles and fish hooks. He takes Phillip to a safe

fishing hole where Phillip is able to fish for himself. He teaches Phillip how to use mussels for bait.
8. Phillip climbs the palm tree to get the coconuts.
9. Timothy hears the waves crack like rifle shots on the reefs.
10. He lashes the water keg high on the palm tree. He ties extra rope onto the tree for hand and arm holds. He dismantles the raft and saves the parts. He prepares a huge meal in case they cannot eat for days. He gives Phillip cups of coconut milk for nourishment. He lashes his knife to a tree for recovery later.

Page 82
1. Accept appropriate responses.
2. The storm that hit the island began slowly with dark clouds and a hot wind. Soon the wind was howling, and the rain was pelting down.
3. Timothy put his body between the storm and Phillip to take the brunt of the storm.
4. The storm stops because they are in the eye of the hurricane.
5. Timothy's body is lashed and torn by the storm winds and sand. The result is that he dies.
6. Phillip finds that Timothy has lashed at least 12 poles and many hooks and sinkers to the palm tree for him.
7. The birds attack Phillip because he is in the their nesting ground.
8. Phillip is attacked by a moray eel.
9. Phillips gets the smoke to blacken by using the oily sea grapes in the fire.
10. Phillip seems to change by becoming more mature. He becomes self-reliant and stops being prejudiced. He learns to trust someone.

Page 83
1. A fisherman follows the fish. Certainly the fish are here.
2. Long ago, I, Timothy, could have climbed this very palm tree by myself.
3. This is a western storm, I would guess. They are outrageously strong when they arrive.
4. This island is about one mile long and a half a mile wide, shaped like a watermelon.
5. Phillip, did you every think that I might be sick again some morning?
6. Don't worry, Young Boss. Someone will find us. Many schooners pass here, and this is the ship track to Jamaica and beyond.
7. We have good luck, Young Boss. The water keg didn't break when the raft was launched, and we have a few biscuits, some chocolate, and dry matches in the tin. So, we have rare good luck.

Page 84
1. before the storm	2. Henrik
3. Chinese sailors	4. S. S. *Hato* explodes
5. the palm tree	6. the cay
7. Phillip's mother	8. the sea before the storm
9. malaria fever	10. the rain
11. Stew Cat	12. the hut
13. Phillip's father	14. Timothy
15. Phillip	16. Virginia

Page 85
1. Phillip and Henrik go to Punda to watch the war preparations.
2. The S.S. *Hato*, with Phillip and his mother on board, is torpedoed.
3. Timothy pulls Phillip onto a raft.
4. Phillip loses his eyesight.
5. Timothy makes a vine rope to guide Phillip to the beach.
6. Timothy teaches Phillip how to weave mats.

7. A hurricane blows over the island.
8. Timothy dies.
9. Phillip is bitten by a moray eel.
10. Phillip is reunited with his parents.

Page 86
Answers will vary. Accept all appropriate answers.

Page 87
1. Aruba
2. Caribbean Sea
3. Venezuela
4. Caracas
5. Colombia
6. Netherlands
7. Northeast
8. Willemstad

Page 88
1. sea urchins
2. mussels
3. sea grape leaves
4. moray eel
5. flying fish
6. sharks
7. pompano
8. seaweed
9. organpipe coral
10. langosta

1. flying fish
2. langosta
3. moray eel
4. mussels
5. organpipe coral
6. pompano
7. sea grape leaves
8. sea urchins
9. seaweed
10. sharks

Page 89
Matching
1. Mr. Enright
2. Mrs. Enright
3. Timothy
4. Phillip
5. sailor

True or False
1. False—Phillip's mother was prejudiced.
2. False—Mrs. Enright and Phillip boarded the ship.
3. True
4. False—Timothy died because of the hurricane.
5. False—Phillip was rescued.

Short Answer
1. The S.S. *Hato* was bound for Panama and then to Miami, Florida.
2. Mr. Enright felt the oil production was necessary to win the war.
3. They were making sure none of the oil or fuel resources reached their enemies.
4. He placed Stew Cat on the raft out at sea.
5. Phillip's mother returned to be with her husband at Willemstad.
6. Answers will vary.
7. Phillip is rescued and reunited with his parents. He has several operations to restore his eyesight.
8. Answers will vary.
9. Answers will vary.
10. Accept all reasonable responses.

Page 90
1. D
2. C
3. B
4. E
5. A
6. B
7. E
8. D
9. C
10. A
11. C
12. A
13. E
14. B
15. D
16. D
17. F
18. I
19. G
20. A

Page 91
1. pitcher
2. league
3. outfield
4. shortstop
5. catcher
6. baseman
7. stadium
8. home run
9. triple
10. double
11. cleats
12. mitt

13. glove
14. summer
15. dugout
16. steal

Page 92
Alphabetical Order
1. baseman
2. catcher
3. cleats
4. double
5. dugout
6. glove
7. home run
8. league
9. mitt
10. outfield
11. pitcher
12. shortstop
13. stadium
14. steal
15. summer
16. triple

Dictionary Usage
1. 2
2. 1
3. noun
4. 1
5. pit

Page 93
1. N
2. O
3. A
4. B
5. C
6. D
7. E
8. F
9. G
10. H
11. I
12. J
13. P
14. K
15. L
16. M

Page 94
1. pitcher
2. league
3. outfield
4. shortstop
5. catcher
6. baseman
7. stadium
8. triple
9. home run
10. double
11. cleats
12. mitt
13. glove
14. summer
15. dugout
16. steal

Completion
1. pitcher
2. steal
3. dugout
4. shortstop
5. baseman, double
6. cleats
7. mitt
8. triple

Page 96
1. ac com´ mo da´ tions
2. ac com´ plice
3. cus´ to dy
4. flail´ ing
5. fra´ grant
6. ghast´ ly
7. ig´ nor ant
8. il lit´ er ate
9. ling´ ered
10. or deal´
11. re morse´
12. re vul´ sion
13. rig´ id
14. staunch
15. ver an´ dah

Syllables
1. staunch
2. flailing fragrant ghastly lingered ordeal remorse rigid
3. accomplice custody ignorant revulsion verandah
4. illiterate
5. accommodations

Page 97
Across
3. ordeal
6. staunch
9. accomplice
12. illiterate
14. verandah
15. rigid

Down
1. custody
2. ignorant
4. remorse
5. ghastly

Answer Key (cont.)

7. accommodations
8. flailing
10. fragrant
11. revulsion
13. lingered

Page 98
1. C	2. A	3. C
4. D	5. B	6. A
7. D	8. B	9. C
10. A	11. B	12. D
13. B	14. A	15. D

Sentences
16.–20. Answers will vary.

Page 100
Alphabetical Order/Accent Marks
1. am´ bled	2. ceased
3. dis´ ar ray	4. e lat´ ed
5. en vel´ oped	6. gal´ lows
7. in´ fin ite	8. in tru´ sion
9. i´ so la´ tion	10. mel´ an chol´ y
11. re ced´ ed	12. re luc´ tant ly
13. tan´ gent	14. tran´ quil
15. van´ i ty	

Syllables
one: ceased
two: tangent ambled tranquil gallows
three: infinite intrusion elated disarray vanity enveloped receded
four: melancholy reluctantly isolation

Page 101
1. reluctantly	2. melancholy
3. tranquil	4. ambled
5. infinite	6. ceased
7. gallows	8. tangent
9. recede	10. enveloped
11. disarray	12. vanity
13. isolation	14. elated
15. intrusion	

Page 102
1. C	2. D
3. B	4. D
5. A	6. B
7. C	8. A
9. B	10. D
11. C	12. A
13. B	14. C
15. D	16. infinite, interest
17. envelope	18. recede
19. elate	20. amble

When a word ends with a silent *e* and it is preceded by a consonant, drop the *e* and add *ed*.
Unit IV

Page 104
1. anx´ ious
2. bal´ last
3. chan´ nel
4. con´ scious
5. de bris´
6. de scribe´
7. drone
8. hur´ ri cane
9. mu´ tin y
10. sat´ is fac´ tion
11. smol´ der
12. stub´ born
13. sub´ mar ine
14. tor pe´ do
15. treach´ er ous

Syllables
one: drone
two: debris describe conscious smolder anxious channel ballast stubborn
three: treacherous torpedo submarine mutiny hurricane
four: satisfaction, 2, third

Page 105
1. drone	2. described
3. debris	4. mutiny
5. hurricane	6. smolder
7. anxious	8. treacherous
9. conscious	10. channel
11. ballast	12. submarines
13. torpedoes	14. stubborn
15. satisfaction	

Page 106
1. C	2. A	3. D
4. A	5. C	6. D
7. A	8. B	9. B
10. C	11. D	12. A
13. D	14. D	15. B
16. describe	17. channel	18. hurricane
19. anxious	20. debris	

Unit V

Page 108
1. Atlantic Ocean	2. Pacific Ocean
3. North America	4. South America
5. Africa	6. Europe
7. Arctic Ocean	8. Asia
9. Indian Ocean	10. Australia
11. Antarctica	12. equator

Page 109
1. Asia	2. America
3. Europe	4. latitude
5. Africa	6. Pacific
7. longitude	8. Arctic
9. oceans	10. meridian
11. Atlantic	12. equator
13. Indian	14. Antarctica
15. continents	16. hemisphere

See our planet Earth.
Alphabetical Order: Continents
Africa
Antarctica
Asia
Australia
Europe
North America
South America
Alphabetical Order: Oceans
Arctic
Atlantic
Indian
Pacific

Page 110
1. A	2. C	3. D
4. A	5. B	6. A
7. D	8. C	9. D
10. C	11. A	12. D
13. C	14. B	15. B
16. C	17. longitude	18. oceans
19. continents	20. latitude	

Answer Key (cont.)

Page 112
1. ad´ dends or ad dends´
2. ad di´ tion
3. de nom´ i na´ tor
4. dif´ fer ence
5. div´ i dend
6. di vi´ sion
7. di vi´ sor
8. fac´ tors
9. frac´ tions
10. math´ e mat´ ics
11. mul´ ti pli ca´ tion
12. nu´ mer a tor
13. pro´ duct
14. quo´ tient
15. sub trac´ tion
16. sum

Syllables
one: sum
two: quotient fractions product factor addends
three: subtraction division divisor dividend difference addition
four: numerator mathematics
five: multiplication denominator
accent marks: 2

Page 113
1. D   2. E   3. F
4. C   5. A   6. B
7. H   8. G   9. J
10. I

Page 114
1. C   2. C   3. D
4. B   5. D   6. B
7. C   8. C   9. B
10. D   11. C   12. D
13. B   14. A   15. mathematics
16. difference   17. quotient   18. numerator
19. addition   20. division

Page 116
1. verb   2. conjunction
3. imperative   4. noun
5. interrogative   6. adjective
7. pronoun   8. declarative
9. sentence   10. adverb
11. exclamatory   12. preposition
13. fragmen   14. subject
15. capital   16. predicate
17. fragment   18. fragment
19. sentence   20. sentence

Page 117
1. verb
2. noun
3. adjective
4. conjunction
5. adverb
6. preposition
7. pronoun(s)
8. E (W !)
9. Int. (D ?)
10. Imp. (P .)
11. D (T .)
12. The fluffy white cat | slept all afternoon on the soft couch.
13. The little red wagon | is filled with apples from the orchard.

Page 118
1. B   2. C   3. A
4. D   5. C   6. A

7. B   8. C   9. D
10. A   11. B   12. D
13. C   14. D   15. A
16. C   17. noun   18. verb
19. adverb   20. preposition

Page 120

1. conclusion   2. observation   3. experiment
4. graph   5. theory   6. laboratory
7. hypothesis   8. scientific   9. materials
10. procedure

Page 121
1. O   2. G   3. F
4. C   5. N   6. B
7. M   8. K   9. J
10. I   11. L   12. A
13. H   14. D   15. E
16. C   17. D   18. E
19. B   20. A

Page 122
1. B   2. D
3. C   4. B
5. A   6. C
7. B   8. C
9. A   10. B
11. C   12. B
13. D   14. A
15. C   16. materials
17. problem   18. hypothesis
19. observation   20. manipulated variable

Page 124
1. B   2. I   3. E
4. H   5. F   6. D
7. J   8. A   9. C
10. G   11. C   12. E
13. B   14. A   15. J
16. D   17. H   18. I
19. G   20. F   21. B
22. C   23. A   24. E
25. D

Page 125
1. Where   2. There eight
3. toe   4. grown
5. would   6. which roll
7. hair tail   8. know sew
9. air   10. road steel
11. Too sea   12. fair pair

Answer Key (cont.)

13. hear planes   14. Four boars
15. They're seen   16. role witch

Grammar

Page 126

1. The snow | was falling heavily during the night, depositing one foot on the ground.
2. The streets and highways | were closed for many hours.
3. All the schools in the area | had delayed opening for two hours.
4. Most of the elementary school students | did not attend school at all.
5. Many high school students | were stranded on an overturned bus.
6. A helicopter and an ambulance | transported the injured students to the hospital.
7. Another major storm | pounded the area, dumping another four feet of snow.
8. The board of education | decided to close the schools for two weeks.
9. At first the children | enjoyed ice skating, building snowmen, and sledding.
10. The regular school year | was extended for two weeks into the month of July.
11. The Little League baseball game schedule | was revised and altered.
12. The local pools and beaches | changed their lifeguard schedules.
13. Many vacation plans | needed to be adjusted or cancelled.
14. The highlight of the summer, the county fair, | continued as planned.

Page 127

1. is the strongest muscle in the body— is
2. is enclosed in the skull— is enclosed
3. attaches the eye to the brain— attaches
4. broke his femur during the baseball game— broke
5. could distinguish color at an early age— could distinguish

Simple Subject	Simple Predicate
1. puzzles—	help develop
2. clues—	are
3. students—	check
4. Maryanne—	keeps
5. cryptogram—	is
6. puzzle—	has
7. puzzle—	includes
8. puzzle solver—	hunts
9. children—	like
10. Summertime—	is
11. Michael/Joe—	join
12. Joan—	read
13. Heather—	was
14. lifeguards—	awarded
15. librarian—	distributed

Page 128

1. equipment is—inverted
2. whales are—inverted
3. Susan greeted—natural
4. tiger climbed—inverted

Page 129

1. (you)   2. we   3. you
4. animals   5. (you)   6. (you)
7. relatives   8. priests   9. Jessica
10. Sam   11. mural   12. pyramids

Page 130

1. summer time year
2. weather children swimming
3. schools people time vacations
4. days hours sunlight
5. pool beach lake
6. teacher Mr. Dawson Metropolitan Museum of Art New York City July
7. care concern visitors
8. friends Tim Carol Statue of Liberty Ellis Island
9. scent flowers Central Park lunch
10. hamburgers grill backyard

Person	Place	Thing	Idea
Ms. Lizt	France	clouds	happiness
Dr. Forest	city	shoelaces	science
	building	bicycles	loyalty
	Texas	sounds	fairness
		glasses	love
		table	pain

Page 131

1. President of the United States—proper
   George Washington—proper
2. Eiffel Tower—proper
   attraction—common
   Paris—proper
3. John Glenn—proper
   astronaut—common
4. bridges—-common
   Golden Gate Bridge—proper
   California—proper
   George Washington Bridge—proper
   New York—proper
5. Space Needle—proper
   attraction—common
   Seattle, Washington—proper

1. D   2. F   3. H   4. J   5. G
6. A   7. C   8. I   9. E   10. B
1. P   2. C   3. C   4. P   5. P
6. P   7. P   8. C   9. C   10. P

Page 132

1. foxes
2. knives
3. apples
4. stereos
5. ladies
6. families
7. monkeys
8. giraffes
1. singular, plural
2. plural, plural, plural, singular
3. singular, singular, singular
4. plural, plural
5. plural, plural, plural, plural, singular
6. plural, plural
7. singular, plural
8. plural, singular, singular, plural
9. plural, plural, plural
10. singular, singular

Page 133

1. Mr. Briggs' or Briggs's
2. men's
3. birds' or bird's
4. sister's
5. puppies'
6. mouse's
7. libraries'
8. women's

9. Fred's
10. guitar's
1. girls'
2. teacher's
3. babies' or baby's
4. players'
5. deer's
1. cat's, cats'
2. mouse's, mice's
3. runner's, runners'

Page 134

Days of the Week
Sun.
Mon.
Tues.
Wed.
Thur.
Fri.
Sat.

Months
Jan.
Feb.
Mar.
Apr.
May
Je
Jul
Aug.
Sept.
Oct.
Nov.
Dec.

Titles
Mr.
Dr.
Rev.
Pres.
Sen.
Gov.
Capt.
Gen.
Prof.
Jr.
Sr.

Streets
Dr.
Ave.
Rd.
Blvd.
Pkwy.
Hwy.
St.
Pl.
Ln.

Places
Ft.
Mt.
Riv.
Nat'l Pk.

States
NY
NJ
CA
TX
WN
IL
KY

General

° C
° F
U.S.N.
D.A.

Page 135
1. I
2. We
3. he
4. They
5. she
6. She, I
7. he
8. They
1. she
2. he
3. It
4. he
5. They
Carl and he like to water-ski in the summer.
He and I like to water-ski in the summer.

Page 136
1. My
2. mine, yours
3. Your, mine
4. her
5. My, our
6. his
7. Their
8. their
1. themselves
2. ourselves
3. herself
4. himself
5. yourselves
6. herself
7. yourself
8. ourselves

Page 137
1. it
2. her
3. him
4. them
5. us
6. her, him
7. me
8. us
1–6. Answers will vary.

Page 138
1. she, Wanda
2. it, Biking
3. they, Craig and Bill
4. she, Carla
5. her, Louise
6. their, Bob and Jim
1. their
2. it
3. He
4. her
5. their
6. she
7. their
8. He

Page 139
1. Everybody
2. Neither
3. anyone
4. Each
5. Somebody
1. no one, his
2. one, she
3. each, his
4. either, his

Page 140
1. flashed—PA
2. raced—PA
3. is—linking
4. looked-linking
5. smelled—linking
6. captured—PA
7. are—linking
8. covered—PA
9. skidded—PA
10. formed—PA
11. pulled—PA
12. appears—linking
13. seems—linking
14. became—linking

Page 141
1. has sketched
2. have visited
3. is elected
4. can serve
5. will be needed
6. has planted
7. were dressed
8. has been closed
9. will reopen
10. are circling

Answer Key (cont.)

11. could control 12. have collected
13. will be going 14. have won

Page 142
1. will take off—future 2. left—past
3. landed—past 4. was—past
5. steers—present 6. waits—present
7. meets—present 8. beats—present
9. will shine—future 10. played—past
11. rises 12. protected
13. launched 14. will circle
15. roamed

Page 143
1. drove, us
2. brought, it
3. read, newspaper
4. picked, apples
5. collected, papers
6. found, us
1. A. bought
   B. CD
   C. Us
2. A. send
   B. letter
   C. Him

Page 144
Subject	Predicate	Predicate Adjective
1. soup	was	hot, delicious
2. room	was	dark, cool
3. Statue of Liberty	is	famous
4. wind	was	fierce, cold
5. We	felt	happy
6. Jodi	felt	relaxed
7. lights	are	colorful
8. game	was	unbelievable
9. whistle	sounds	low
10. rain	was	cool, chilling

1–5. Answers will vary.

Page 145
1. rush(es) rushed rushed
2. ruin(s) ruined ruined
3. pass(es) passed passed
4. try(tries) tried tried
5. grade(s) graded graded
6. provide(s) provided provided
7. slip(s) slipped slipped
8. roam—present
9. climbed—past participle
10. live—present
11. killed—past participle
12. studied—past

Page 147
1. said 2. ran 3. chosen
4. stolen 5. grow 6. written
7. took 8. fallen 9. flew
10. froze 11. saw 12. ridden
13. broken 14. froze 15. eaten
16. gave 17. grew 18. caught

Page 148
1. given
2. known
3. spoken
4. torn
5. ran/runs

6. written
7. gone
1. go(es) went gone
2. come(s) came come
3. throw(s) threw thrown
4. eat(s) ate eaten
5. fly(ies) flew flown
6. forget(s) forgot forgotten
7. begin(s) began begun
8. buy(s) bought bought
9. hear(s) heard heard
Correct Principal Parts: 2, 6, 9, 10, 13, 14, 16, 19

Page 149
1. May 2. can 3. laid
4. lie 5. left 6. Let
7. Leave 8. set 9. sat
10. raised 11. rises 12. raised
13. risen 14. learn 15. taught
16. teach 17. learned 18. taught
19. Let 20. Can

Page 150
1. holds 1. is
2. protect 2. are
3. places 3. have
4. cross 4. Were
5. gives 5. have

Page 151
Subject	Verb
1. one	hurts
2. neither chicken nor fish	tasted
3. Jim and Steve	play
4. dog	seems
5. people	are
6. You	are
7. you	have heard
8. Everyone	loves
9. James and Carla	have
10. All	were
11. Someone	took
12. English and science	are
13. No one	knows
14. Either Lisa or I	will call
15. Aunt Maggie and Uncle Fred	ran

Page 152
1. favorite—which kind
2. front—which kind
3. Eight—how many
4. cloudy, rainy—which kind
5. chocolate—which kind
6. well-baked cheese-covered—which kind
7. Nine—how many
8. cute little Dalmation—which kind
9. The—which one
10. flashing, two—which kind, how many
11. tourist—which kind
12. long, winding—which kind
13. many large, small—how many, which kind
14. Five hot, tired, happy—how many—which kind (3)
15. Several—how many
1. The big hairy
2. six
3. wet
4. this

Answer Key (cont.)

Page 153
1. these
2. Those
3. This
4. this
5. this
6. These
7. those
8. those
9. The
10. the
11. These
12. them
13. those
14. Those

Page 154
1. small
2. funnier
3. bigger
4. tallest
5. more thrilling
6. most difficult
7. better
8. fewest

1. better
2. happy
3. biggest
4. lonelier
5. more enjoyable
6. most
7. nice

Page 155
1. accidentally—was discovered
2. usually—is prescribed
3. badly—were treated
4. very—famous
5. really—slender
6. best—grow
7. greatest—English
8. swiftly—rode
9. always—delivered
10. financially—were ruined
11. elaborately—how
12. usually—when
13. thickly—how
14. Often—when
15. here—where

Page 156
1. firmer—C
2. fastest—S
3. usually—P
4. less—C
5. most often—S
6. steadily
7. farther
8. higher
9. hardest
10. most skillfully

Page 157
1. adjective—teacher
2. adverb—waited
3. adverb—ended
4. adjective—desserts
5. adverb—paints
6. slowly—steadily
7. smoothly—quickly
8. terribly—fierce
9. suddenly—ferociously
10. famous—amazing
11. beautifully—beautiful
12. sure—surely
13. attentive—attentively
14. real—really

Page 158
1. good
2. well
3. badly
4. good
5. well
6. good
7. any
8. ever
9. anything
10. anywhere
11. any
12. any

Page 159
1. I enjoy going to the theater and ice skating.
2. I eat lunch with Mary and Brian in the school cafeteria.
3. Debra can swim faster than Henry, but Henry won the race.
4. I don't like to go mountain climbing, and I don't like building things.
1. "Oh!" said Sylvia . . . forward.
2. Ouch! The hammer hit my finger.
3. Hey, wait for me.
4. Oh no! What did I do with my homework?
5. Well, that might just work.
6. Ah, I see what you mean.
7. Ssh, be quiet so he doesn't hear you.
8. Ugh! What an ugly shirt!
9. Wow! I've never seen a bug like that before.

Page 160
1. alongside
2. into
3. around
4. over
5. in front of
6. among
7. against
8. beneath
9. through
10. across

1. C
2. I
3. H
4. D
5. E
6. B
7. G
8. J
9. A
10. F

Page 161
1. around the playground
2. one the next block
3. except the broccoli
4. out of the front door
5. over the foul line
6. like me
7. since breakfast
8. with a shout of hello
9. from Aunt Rose
10. Into the mailbox
11. near the road
12. Alongside the stable

Page 162
1. C
2. D
3. B
4. A
5. J
6. G
7. H
8. I
9. F
10. E

uncooperative	illogical	irregular
disapprove	incorrect	misunderstand
improper	nonsense	unbalance

power ful	farm er	count less
soft ness	Swed ish	produc tion
respons ible	fool ish	appli cant
govern ment	art ist	tight en
danger ous	accept ance	
humid ity	gent ly	

auto | matic	multi | media	kilo | watt
micro | surgery	thermo | meter	tele | vision
geo | logy	peri | scope	photo | graph
geo | graphy	photo | genic	auto | graph
tele | phone	tele | scope	tri | pod

thermo	auto	multi
meter	photo	ology
geo	tele	micro
scope	phone	kilo

Page 163
1. Two—to
2. rode—road
3. knights—nights
4. know
5. wear—new
6. won—role
7. sun—pier
8. steak
9. steel
10. pair
11. clothes
12. plane
13. birth
14. toes
15. guests

Page 164
1. P—13
2. F—6
3. A—1
4. B—2
5. T—16
6. A—1
7. P—13
8. M—11
9. Z—20
10. L—10
11. S—15
12. P—13

Answer Key (cont.)

Page 165
1. atlas/almanac
2. almanac
3. atlas/almanac
4. almanac
5. almanac
6. atlas/almanac
7. atlas
8. almanac
9. almanac/atlas
10. almanac
11. atlas
12. almanac/atlas
13. atlas/almanac
14. almanac/atlas
15. almanac

Page 166
1. Bert
2. 475 Homedale Avenue, Lakewood, New York
3. Bert invited Pete to come spend a weekend.
4. Bert told Pete to write back telling him if he can come and how his team is doing.

Page 168
1. *Heading* Use your own address/date
2. *Inside Address* All About Toy Company
   2471 Game Lane
   Happyville, New York 17555
3. *Greeting* Gentlemen: Dear Sir: Dear Madam
4. *Body*
   I have always enjoyed the toys that your company produces and sells. Recently I purchased the Whammer Radio Car and remote control. It is not working properly. The toy moves in reverse when it should go forward. The buttons on the remote sometimes stick. I am shipping this toy back to you, so that you can either fix it or replace it with a working model. Thank you for your help.
5. *Closing* Sincerely,
6. *Signature* Robert Singleton

Page 169
Susan Hanker
42 Lightning Street
Bayview, New Hampshire 18923
The Fun to Read Book Company
89 Tulip Blvd.
Evans, Maine 90906

Page 171
1. The Eiffel Tower is located in Paris, France.
2. Rhode Island, Delaware, Connecticut, Hawaii, and New Jersey are the five smallest states by area in the U.S.
3. *The Nutcracker*, a famous ballet, is performed during the Christmas season.
4. Edgar Allan Poe wrote the thrilling short story "The Fall of the House of Usher."
5. The flight is scheduled to depart from La Guardia Airport at 10:30 A.M. and arrive in San Francisco at 5:30 P.M.
6. I am going to receive the magazine *Car and Driver* on the first Tuesday of March.
7. The novel The *Castle in the Attic* is an adventure story based on the Middle Ages.
8. The Statue of Liberty, a gift to the United States from France, is visible from New York City.
9. Did you see the Thanksgiving Day Parade as it proceeded down Fifth Avenue?
10. The Taj Mahal, an Indian tomb, is an example of the blending of Hindu and Muslim architecture.
11. Dr. Erica Weiss
12. *Sports Illustrated*
13. Mr. James Frank
14. Dallas, Texas
15. Park Place
16. George Washington Bridge
17. 5:40 A.M.
18. *The Island of the Blue Dolphins*

Page 172 (continued)
19. Pres. Ronald Reagan
20. The Civil War

Page 172
1. How do male humpbacks communicate to the female humpback whales?
2. What an incredible landing the pilot made!
3. Great! Your performance on the test was nearly perfect!
4. The New York Knicks played the Chicago Bulls in Madison Square Garden.
5. The Super Bowl was broadcast at 6:00 P.M. on Jan. 31, 1999.
6. Which president was elected first, Franklin D. Roosevelt or Rutherford B. Hayes?
7. Mrs. B. B. Johnson, Jr. was chosen to lead the parade.
8. Watch out! A deer is crossing the highway.
9. Oh, no! The elephants are stampeding the audience!
10. Wow! My bedroom will be 20 ft. long and 15 ft. wide.
11. Mr. James Mulligan
12. Mt. Rushmore
13. the year 456 B.C.
14. P.O. Box 345
15. Rev. Jesse Jackson
16. J. H. Thompson and Co.
17. I. Museums of New York
    A. Guggenheim
    B. Metropolitan Museum of Art
    C. Museum of Natural History

Page 173
1. "Please give our guest a warm welcome," said the host of the talk show.
2. "Governor, how will the new tax increase affect the local schools?" asked the reporter.
3. "Be careful driving to work," warned the meteorologist. "Freezing temperatures have caused black ice to form on the roads."
4. Mars, Jupiter, Venus, and Saturn are planets in our solar system.
5. The baby's tears wouldn't stop for hours.
6. The *Titanic* sank in the Atlantic Ocean on April 15, 1912.

Page 174
1. B	2. C	3. A
4. C	5. D	6. B
7. C	8. C	9. C
10. B	11. B	

Page 175
12. C	13. C	14. A
15. B	16. D	17. A
18. C	19. D	20. C
21. B	22. D	23. C

Page 176
24. B	25. C	26. A
27. C	28. D	29. C
30. C	31. B	32. B

Page 177
33. C	34. A	35. B
36. C	37. A	38. A
39. B	40. D	41. D
42. B		

Page 178
43. D	44. C	45. B
46. B	47. B	48. C
49. D	50. B	

Answer Key (cont.)

Page 181
1. edge
2. divisor
3. quotient
4. product
5. sum
6. difference
7. dividend
8. addends
9. even
10. odd
11. fraction
12. numerator; denominator
13. estimate

Page 182
14. factors
15. mixed
16. prime
17. positive; negative
18. mean or average
19. median
20. range
21. capacity
22. mass
23. discount
24. mode
25. volume
26. variable
27. congruent
28. exponent
29. integers
30. multiple

Page 185
1. E
2. C
3. D
4. B
5. A
6. I
7. H
8. G
9. J
10. K
11. F
12. 7
13. 3
14. 6
15. Answers will vary.
16. 8
17. $0 + 6 = 6; 6 - 6 = 0$
18. 4
19. 3
20. 7
21. $8 \times (4 + 6)$
22. $(5 + 9)$
23. $n = 8$
24. $n = 8$
25. $n = 64$

Page 186
1. 60
2. 3,700
3. 458,000
4. $3.00
5. $17.80
6. $351.70
7. 36,200
8. 460,000
9. $58.00
10. 74,500
11. 19,500
12. 52,500,000
13. 850,000
14. 36,499
15. 84,999
16. 37,499,999
17. 649,999
18. $73,900,000

Page 187
1. 389 $389 + 359 = 748$
2. 1,245 $1,245 - 789 = 456$
3. 12,164 $12,164 - 3,489 = 8,657$
4. 1,999 $1,999 + 6,975 = 8,974$
5. 1,919 $1,919 + 13,989 = 15,908$
6. 19,806 $19,806 + 16,565 = 36,371$
7. $40,000 + 90,000 = 130,000$
8. $80,000 - 20,000 = 60,000$
9. $40,000 + 40,000 = 80,000$
10. $70,000 - 30,000 = 40,000$
11. $90,000 + 30,000 = 120,000$
12. $3,000 + 6,000 = 9,000$
13. $6,000 - 2,000 = 4,000$
14. $5,000 + 3,000 = 8,000$
15. $6,000 - 4,000 = 2,000$

Page 188
1. Est. Ans.—700 coins, Act. Ans.—621 coins
2. Est. Dif.—$6,000, Act. Ans.—$5,423
3. Est. Attend.—500 people, Act. Attend—431 people
4. Est. Mileage—1,200 mi., Act. Mileage—1,228 mi.
5. App. Profit—$50,000, Act. Profit—$49,499

Page 189
1. $3 + 7 = 10$ 9.63
2. $5 - 2 = 3$ 2.99
3. $10.00 + 0.00 = 10$ 10.01
4. $0.6 - 0.4 = 0.2$ 0.045
5. $7 + 3 = 10$ 9.57
6. $15 - 8 = 7$ 7.8
7. $19 + 40 = 59$ 55.7
8. $4 - 1 = 3$ 3.477
9. $27 - 23 = 4$ 4.4
10. $>$
11. $<$
12. overestimate
13. overestimate
14. No. Cindy will not have enough ribbon to wrap the gifts. She needs 6.65 meters, and she only has 5 meters.

Page 190
1. 20.484
2. 20.924
3. 10.3
4. 38.85
5. $73.14
6. 12.496
7. 24.824
8. 41.266
9. 57.7037
10. 60.755
11. $93.36
12. 5,488.31
13. 3.5
14. 35.655
15. 6.25
16. 162.61
17. 71.082
18. 4.325
19. 57.68
20. 4.71
21. 72.146
22. 67.0242
23. 29.36
24. 362.13

Page 191
1. 22.2 inches
2. 25 yards
3. 4.50 miles per hour
4. $30.20
5. $202.14
6. $1254.46
7. 11.97
8. $2.80
9. $41.49

Page 192
1. 1 and 6; 2 and 3; composite
2. 1 and 8; 2 and 4; composite
3. 1 and 7; prime
4. 1 and 18; 2 and 9; 3 and 6; composite

Page 193
1. $3 \times 2 \times 3 = 2 \times 3^2$
2. $2 \times 2 \times 2 \times 2 = 2^4$
3. $2 \times 2 \times 5 = 2^2 \times 5$
4. $2 \times 2 \times 2 \times 3 = 2^3 \times 3$
5. $3 \times 3 = 3^2$
6. $2 \times 2 \times 2 \times 2 \times 2 = 2^5$
7. $5 \times 5 \times 3 = 5^2 \times 3$
8. $2 \times 2 \times 3 = 2^2 \times 3$
9. $2 \times 2 \times 3 \times 3 = 2^2 \times 3^2$
10. $(4 = 2 \times 2)$; $(12 = 2 \times 2 \times 3)$ GCF = 2
11. $(10 = 2 \times 5)$; $(30 = 2 \times 3 \times 5)$ GCF = 5
12. $(20 = 2 \times 2 \times 5)$; $(30 = 2 \times 3 \times 5)$ GCF = 5
13. $12 = 2 \times 2 \times 3)$; $(18 = 2 \times 3 \times 3)$ GCF = 3
14. $(12 = 3 \times 5)$; $(50 = 2 \times 5 \times 5)$ GCF = 5
15. $(18 = 2 \times 3 \times 3)$; $(20 = 2 \times 2 \times 5)$ GCF = 2

Page 194
Multiples of 4 (4, 8, 12, 16, 20, 24, 28, 32, 36, 40)
Multiples of 2 (2, 4, 6, 8, 10, 12, 14, 16, 18, 20)
Multiples of 3 (3, 6, 9, 12, 15, 18, 21)
Multiples of 5 (5, 10, 15, 20, 25, 30 35)
Least common multiple of 3 and 5 is 15
A. 6 and 12
B. 18 and 36
C. 40 and 80
D. 20 and 40
E. 24 and 48
F. 28 and 56
G. 4 yellow, 5 blue

Answer Key (cont.)

Page 195
Estimations will vary. Accept reasonable responses.

1. <	2. <
3. <	4. B
5. B	6. A
7. 640	8. 25,000
9. 1,700	10. 2,500
11. 2,698	12. 4,984
13. 36,624	14. 634,150
15. 350,980	16. 2,226,566
17. 20,369,349	18. 24,180,052
19. 22,217,203	20. 23,908,653

Page 196
Estimations will vary. Accept reasonable responses.

1. 63.08	2. 31.62
3. 4.452	4. 0.4185
5. 181.764	6. 226.2
7. 4.3715	8. 22,174.6
9. 50.0208	10. $10.76
11. $184.48	12. $21.89
13. 0.28	14. 789.645
15. 4.4346	16. 129.708
17. $1,0222.76	18. 43,413.311
19. 153,000	20. 53,600
21. 2.5	22. 88.4
23. 9,287.5	24. 8,600

Page 197
1. $24.97
2. 12 cm
3. 392 miles
4. 1,275 miles
5. 6,548 miles
6. $258.38
7. $28.89
8. 504 pictures $141.12

Page 198

1. C	2. D
3. C	4. C
5. 9 or 10	6. 60
7. 800	8. 79
9. 431	10. 729
11. 8,162 r5	12. 5,758 r1
13. 4684 r1	14. 4,021
15. 5342 r4	16. 5,201 r4

Page 199

1. 2	2. 0.8
3. 4	4. 2
5. 3	6. 4
7. 784	8. 25.36
9. 46.2	10. 3.5
11. 72.14	12. 23.6
13. 45.7	14. 0.57
15. 0.03584	16. 0.752 = $0.75
17. 229.714 = 229.71	18. 7.461 = 7.5

Page 200

1. 6	2. 5	3. 200
4. 500	5. 60 .	6. 700
7. 885 r14	8. 2052 r40	9. 7 r1
10. 1200	11. 173 r18	12. 86 r22
13. 3.6	14. 4.27	15. 5.896
16. 0.218	17. 0.606	18. 0.465

Page 201
1. 20 miles per minute
2. 29 trays

3. 40 class sets, 8 classes
4. 134 rooms
5. 42 rolls
6. $8.50/hour
7. 2,190 miles
8. $2.55

Page 202
1. A. 12, 25, 25, 35, 73
   B. 73 − 12 = 61
   C. (12 + 25 + 25 +35 + 73) ÷ 5 = 34
   D. 25
   E. 25
2. A. 23, 23, 30, 49, 51, 88, 100
   B. 100 − 23 = 77
   C. 52
   D. 49
   E. 23

Page 203
3. A. 18, 18, 24, 36
   B. 36 − 18 = 18
   C. 24
   D. 21
   E. 18
4. A. 22, 22, 36, 42, 70, 84
   B. 84 − 22 = 62
   C. 46
   D. 39
   E. 22
5. A. 170, 200, 305
   B. 135
   C. 225
   D. 200
   E. none
6. A. 22, 45, 66, 66, 69, 77, 89
   B. 67
   C. 62
   D. 66
   E. 66

Page 204
1. 120
2. 264
3. 1737.6
4. 66.24
5. 9
6. 37
7. 776.5
8. 15.5
9. 182
10. 31
11. 444
12. 13.78
13. 7.8
14. 3.5
15. a = 3: divide by 45
16. t = 30: divide by 35
17. m = 1600: multiply by 16
18. s = 215: multiply by 215
19. f = 9: divide by 81
20. p = 24: divide by 15

Page 205

1. 3/7	2. 6/8	3. 3/4
4. 7/10	5. 8/12	6. 52/100
7. 4/8	8. 3/9	9. 18/30
10. 10	11. 35	12. 21
13. 6	14. 24	15. 2/3
16. 40/100	17. 25	18. 1/3

Answer Key (cont.)

19. 2/5   20. 1/3   21. 2/3
22. 2/7   23. 1/4   24. 9/10
25. 87/500

Page 206
1. 4 1/6   2. 3 1/4   3. 8
4. 5 3/7   5. 3   6. 23/7
7. 28/5   8. 65/9   9. 35/8
10. 29/10   11. 2 1/5   12. 4 3/4
13. 9 3/5   14. 9 1/4   15. 0.25
16. 0.75   17. 6.20   18. 0.5
19. 0.25   20. 0.6   21. 3.6

Page 207
1. >
2. >
3. <
4. <
5. 2/8, 5/12, 3/6
6. 3/15, 2/3, 7/10
7. 2/9, 7/18, 4/6
8. 16/50, 10/25, 3/5
9. 5/16, 2/4, 5/8

Page 208
1. 1/3   2. 6/7   3. 1/4
4. 1/2   5. 17/20   6. 1 11/35
7. 5/18   8. 1/20   9. 1/5
10. 19/24   11. 11/20   12. 11/16
13. 10 7/12   14. 3 3/8   15. 3 2/9

Page 210
1. 3 3/4   2. 13 3/5
3. 4/9   4. 20/77
5. 45/48   6. 25 3/5
7. 3   8. 27 1/5
9. 12   10. 13/180
11. 14 6/7   12. 11 29/36
13. 5 5/7   14. 42 2/3
15. 1/15   16. 2/81
17. 25/24=1 1/24   18. 3/8
19. 4 11/48   20. 16/25
21. 37/116   22. 1/44
23. 29/32   24. 56
25. 72 cupcakes   26. 8 fireflies left for himself

Page 211
1. 12 quarts; 24 pints; 48 cups; 384 ounces
2. 8 pints; 16 cups; 128 ounces
3. 1 cup, 2 ounces
4. 31 cups, 2 ounces
5. 10 cups
6. 6 tons
7. 3.75 tons
8. 5 pounds
9. 72 ounces
10. 48 ounces
11. 5000 pounds
12. 4.5 pints

Page 212
1. 84   2. 144   3. 108
4. 288   5. 4   6. 818
7. 600   8. 2   9. 45
10. 9   11. 18   12. 27
13. 122   14. 9   15. 305
16. 512

Page 213
1. 14 hours, 5 minutes
2. 27 hours, 7 minutes
3. 12 hours, 2 minutes
4. 14 hours, 9 minutes
5. 2 hours, 4 minutes
6. 6 hours, 37 minutes
7. 1 hour, 26 minutes
8. 0 hours, 59 minutes

Page 214
1. 6.67, 6.15, 5.71, 5.33, 5.00
2. .44 hours
   .33 hours
3. a, b, c (answers will vary)

Page 215
1. C   2. B   3. C
4. A   5. A   6. m
7. km   8. cm   9. cm or mm
10. mm   11. cm   12. m
13. km   14. B   15. A
16. C

Page 216
1. 1   2. 500   3. 3   4. 100
5. 5   6. 900   7. 6.5   8. 330
9. 1   10. 1   11. 6   12. 5
13. 8   14. 7   15. 7.53   16. 8.35
17. 400   18. 3,000   19. 700   20. 6,000
21. 900   22. 10,000   23. 680   24. 15,500
25. 0.004   26. 0.007   27. 65   28. 0.07
29. 0.65   30. 0.004   31. 6.5   32. 4,000
33. 0.004   34. 7,500   35. 4,000   36. 6.5
37. 0.225   38. 3,500   39. 225,00   40. 0.057

Page 217
1. 3, 500 mm, 3.5 m
2. 6,500 m
3. 1,525 m (second half)
4. 1.35 kg
5. 1.5 g
6. 410 mL
7. 0.6 m
8. 2,825 mL
9. 1,450 cm = 1.45 m

Page 218
1. H
2. A
3. F
4. G
5. E
6. C
7. B
8. D

Page 219
1. acute; 35°
2. obtuse; 100°
3. obtuse; 140°
Questions 4 through 8: accept all reasonable measurements.
9. angle BED
10. angle CED
11. angle BEC
12. angle AEB
13. angle AED
14. E

Answer Key (cont.)

Page 220
1. right
2. scalene
3. equilateral
4. isosceles
5. equilateral
6. isosceles
7. scalene
8. isosceles
9. 10 degrees
10. 77 degrees
11. 70 degrees
12. 47 degrees
13. 69 degrees
14. 30 degrees

Page 221
2. 5.38 centimeters
2. 358 millimeters
3. 24.2 meters
4. 33.6 inches
5. 126 meters
6. 210 feet
7. 38 inches

Page 222
1. 37.96 m²
2. 24 in²
3. 13.69 cm²
4. 67.62 m²
5. 101.2 m²
6. 16 cm²
7. 0.65 cm²
8. 11.28 cm²
9. 900 m²
10. 64.8 in²

Page 223
1. 46 in²
2. 41.76 ft²
3. 2,430 cm²
4. 96 ft²
5. 10,908 in² or 75.75 ft²
6. 5 centimeters

Page 224
A. 3
B. 1
C. 2
D. 4
1. Line AB
2. E
3. EA; EI; EB; EF
4. DC; GH

Page 225
1. 25.12 millimeters
2. 4.71 centimeters
3. 37.68 inches
4. 9.42 feet
5. 12.56 millimeters
6. 62.8 inches
7. 81.64 centimeters
8. 81.64 centimeters

Page 226
1. 200.96 cm²
2. 50.24 in²
3. 78.5 mm²
4. 55.39 cm²
5. 28.26 m²
6. 84.91 ft²
7. 254.34 in²
8. 360.32 ft²

Page 227
1. 135 cm³
2. 64 cm³
3. 264 m³
4. 24.24 in³

Page 228
1. 1538.6 cm³
2. 226.08 cm³
3. 706.5 in³
4. 50.24 m³
5. 904.32 cm³
6. 803.84 cm³
7. 4,179.34 ft³

Page 229
Draw the lines of symmetry for each figure.

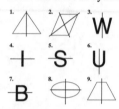

Page 230
1. translation
5. rotation
2. reflection
6. translation
3. reflection
7. rotation
4. rotation
8. reflection

Page 231
1. similar
2. congruent
3. similar
4. figure B
5. figure A

Page 232
1. A. 2 number sevens
   B. 2/6 or 2 out of 6
2. A. 1 number three
   B. 6
   C. 1/6 or 1 out of 6
3. A. 5
   B. 6
   C. 5/6 or 5 out of 6
4. 1 out of 10
5. 7 out of 10
6. 2 out of 10
7. 3 out of 10
8. 0

Page 233
1. *Fillings*   *Combinations*
   Eggs   Ham
   Eggs   Bacon
   Eggs   Cheese

   3 Eggs x 3 fillings = 9 combinations
2. 2 shoes x 3 socks = 6 combinations
3. 1 x 3 x 2 = 6 choices
4. 5 x 7 = 35 combinations
5. 3 x 4 x 5 = 60 choices

Page 235
1. C
2. E
3. B
4. E
5. B
6. A
7. A
8. B
9. A
10. B

Page 236
11. D
12. D
13. C
14. A
15. E
16. E
17. B
18. B

Answer Key (cont.)

Page 237

19. C	20. C	21. B
22. D	23. D	24. A
25. C	26. C	

Page 238

27. C	28. A	29. C
30. A	31. E	32. B
33. A	34. B	35. A
36. B		

Page 239

37. C	38. A	39. E
40. B	41. E	42. B
43. B		

Page 240

44. C	45. D	46. C
47. A	48. B	49. B
50. C		

Page 241

1. experiment
2. laboratory
3. problem
4. hypothesis
5. manipulated variable
6. materials
7. procedure
8. observations
9. data
10. chart
11. graph
12. conclusion
13. theory
14. control
15. scientific method

Page 242

1. microscope
2. magnifying lens
3. double-pan balance
4. telescope
5. Petri dish
6. slide
7. Bunsen burner
8. triple-beam balance
9. thermometer
10. cover slip
11. beaker
12. graduated cylinder

Page 243

1. Will different types of music affect the growth of ivy plants?
2. Accept all reasonable answers such as, *I think if I play jazz, opera, classical, rock, country music, and no music for five ivy plants for 30 minutes each day, then the ivy plant will grow best, next best, third best, fourth best, and fifth best.*
3. Accept all reasonable answers such as: *five types of music, a CD player, ivy plants, water and sunlight.*
4. different types of music
5. The same type of plant, the same size plant, the same amount of water and sunlight

Page 244

6. Type of Music	Growth
Jazz	1.0"
Rock	0.5"
Opera	2.5"
Country	2.5"
Classical	3.0"
No Music	1.5"

The least growth was by the plant exposed to rock music, and the greatest growth was the plant exposed to classical music.

7. Growth of Ivy Plants Exposed to Different Types of Music

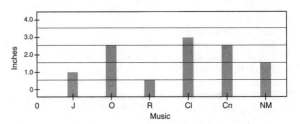

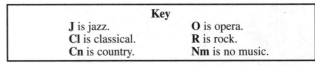

Key	
J is jazz.	**O** is opera.
Cl is classical.	**R** is rock.
Cn is country.	**Nm** is no music.

8. Conclusion—The plant exposed to classical music grew the best, followed by the plants exposed to country and opera which reached the same height. The plant exposed to no music grew fourth tallest, followed by the jazz plant and the least growth was by the plant exposed to rock music.
9. Repeat the same experiment many times.
10. Accept all reasonable answers, such as using different plants.

Page 246

1. to be able to view objects too small for the unaided eye
2. The simple microscope has one lens and the compound microscope has two lenses.
3. The electron microscope uses beams of electrons rather than beams of light to focus on the observed specimen.
4. Hold it close to the body with one hand on the arm and the other hand under the base.
5. The microscope is a delicate, precisely aligned instrument that can break or lose its alignment if not handled carefully.
6. Lens paper should be used.
7. coarse adjustment knob
8. It raises the body tube so the slide can be inserted.
9. on the stage
10. stage clips
11. eyepiece
12. fine adjustment knob
13. diaphragm
14. with the lowest power objective in place
15. The slide should be removed, cleaned, and stored.

Word Bank

26 arm
23 base
21 stage
22 stage clips
25 diaphragm
24 mirror/light
16 eyepiece
17 body tube/barrel
18 revolving nosepiece
20 low power objective lens
19 high power objective lens
28 coarse adjustment knob
27 Fine adjustment knob

Answer Key (cont.)

Page 247
1. Celsius, Fahrenheit, Kelvin
2. a ruler or scale
3. degree
4. heat or cold
5. mercury or alcohol
6. Heat causes the molecules in the liquid to expand, and cold causes the molecules in the liquid to contract.
7. Fahrenheit, Celsius
8. water
9. 32 degrees Fahrenheit or 273 degrees Kelvin
10. 212 degrees Fahrenheit or 373 degrees Kelvin

Page 248
1. 212 degrees Fahrenheit and 100 degrees Celsius
2. 32 degrees Fahrenheit and 0 degrees Celsius
3. 20 degrees Fahrenheit; -10 degrees Celsius
4. 70 degrees Fahrenheit and 20 degrees Celsius
5. 80 degrees Celsius
6. Between 10 degrees and 15 degrees Celsius.
7. 80 degrees Fahrenheit; 30 degrees Celsius.
8. 98.6 degrees Fahrenheit or 37 degrees Celsius.

Page 249
1. 18 degrees
2. 52 degrees
3. 6 degrees
4. 25 degrees
5. 47 degrees
6. 7 degrees
7. -10 degrees
8. -16 degrees
9. -12 degrees
10. -20 degrees
11. -2 degrees
12. -5 degrees

Page 250
1. riders
2. pointer scale
3. beam
4. pan
5. object mass
6. Triple Beam Balance
7. pointer
8. left pan
9. standard weights
10. zero adjustment knob
11. right pan
12. object mass
13. scale
14. Double-Pan Balance

Page 251
1. 141 grams
2. 41.5 grams
3. 112 grams
4. 131.3 grams
5. 22.8 grams
6. 200.5 grams
7. 25 grams
8. 40 grams
9. 40 grams
10. 65 grams
11. 100 grams
12. 170 grams

Page 252
1. 30 ml
2. 18 ml
3. 55 ml
4. 50 ml
5. 30 ml
6. 50 ml
7. 20 ml

Page 253
1. 2 cm
2. 40 mm
3. 2 m
4. 800 cm
5. 5 km
6. 7000 m
7. A
8. A
9. B
10. C
Accept all reasonable answers
11. 42 mm
12. 75 mm
13. 27 mm
14. 58 mm
15. 6 cm
16. 5 cm
17. 6 cm
18. 7 cm

Page 255
I.
  A. Green plants
     1. carbon dioxide, minerals, water, sunlight
     2. Photosynthesis
     3. oxygen and water
  B. Consumers
     1. eating others
     2. decomposers
II.
  A. plants
  B. they are eaten
III.
  A. chains
  B. food web
IV.
  A. producers/green plants
  B. top
  C. bottom/least at the top
V.
  A. forests affect producers and consumers
  B. land to build cities or highways
  C. chemicals endanger communities
VI.
  A. studies on pollution
  B. environmental laws

Page 256
Accept any order for questions numbered 2 through 5.
1. precipitation   2. rain
3. snow   4. sleet
5. hail   6. soil
7. evaporates   8. waste
9. die   10. condensation
11. clouds

Page 257
Evaporation
Condensation
Precipitation

Answer Key (cont.)

Page 258
1. photosynthesis
2. carbon dioxide
3. glucose
4. oxygen
5. exhale
6. carbon dioxide

Page 259
1. oxygen
2. nitrogen compounds
3. roots
4. bacteria
5. die
6. waste
7. nitrogen
8. bacteria

Left picture
A. lightning
B. nitrogen compounds

Middle picture
C. roots

Right picture
D. bacteria
E. nitrogen gas

Page 260
1. barometer
2. thermometer
3. anemometer
4. Doppler radar
5. meteorologist
6. satellites
7. air mass
8. psychrometer
9. front
10. forecast
11. precipitation
12. relative humidity
13. high
14. tornado
15. hurricane
16. tornado warning
17. cumulus clouds
18. cirrus clouds
19. clear
20. National Weather Service

Page 261
Weather

Page 262
1. Anemometer
2. Rain Gauge
3. Wind Vane
4. Thermometer
5. Weather Map
6. Barometer

Page 263
1. K
2. I
3. F
4. O
5. G
6. A
7. M
8. B
9. J
10. L
11. E
12. D
13. C
14. H
15. N
16. coast
17. mountain range
18. peninsula
19. island
20. isthmus
21. canyon
22. plateau

Page 264
1. M
2. H
3. L
4. I
5. C
6. J
7. D
8. E
9. F
10. K
11. G
12. A
13. B
14. Sea
15. River
16. Fjord
17. Gulf
18. Sound
19. Lake
20. Strait

Page 265
1. D
2. H
3. F
4. L
5. A
6. B
7. K
8. J
9. C
10. E
11. G
12. I

Sparta and Athens
1. Athens
2. Sparta
3. Athens
4. Athens
5. Sparta
6. Sparta

Page 268
1. B
2. A
3. C
4. A
5. B
6. A
7. C
8. A
9. B
10. A

Page 269
11. C
12. B
13. C
14. C
15. C
16. A
17. B
18. A

Page 270
1. Pax Romana
2. Aqueducts
3. Constantine
4. Byzantium/Constantinople
5. Byzantine Empire

Matching
1. C
2. A
3. B
4. D

Family Members
Father #1 Head of the family
Mother #6 Entertained guests at home and assisted in business
Girls #3 were schooled at home
Boys #5 between the ages of 12 and 18 attended school
Slaves #2 did the housework
#4 were sometimes teachers

Page 271
1. Zeus
2. Ares
3. Hera
4. Artemis/Apollo
5. Aphrodite
6. Athena
7. Poseidon/Hades
8. Demeter/Persephone
9. Hestia
10. Mount Olympus

Page 272
Jupiter—Zeus
Juno—Hera
Pluto—Hades
Venus—Aphrodite
Diana—Artemis
Mars—Ares
Neptune—Poseidon

Answer Key (cont.)

Page 273

Word Box	Matching	Word Box
1. Africa	1. B	1. Re
2. Mediterranean	2. A	2. Anubis
3. delta	3. D	3. Thoth
4. Menes	4. C	4. Horus
5. Memphis	5. E	5. Osiris
6. pharaoh		6. Isis

Page 274

1. Shabti
2. Inundation
3. Scribe
4. Rosetta
5. Polytheism
6. Great Pyramid of Giza
7. Amulet
8. Mummy
9. Papyrus
10. Sphinx
11. Vizier
12. Champollion
13. Scrolls

Page 275

1. Gregory I
2. north
3. east
4. Latin
5. missionaries
6. monks
7. monastery
8. nuns
9. convents
10. sick/poor
11. pope

Page 276

12. Charlemagne
13. Franks
14. empire
15. A.D. 800
16. Holy Roman Empire
17. education
18. trade
19. Louis the Pious
20. Muslims
21. Magyarz
22. Vikings
23. 1066
24. feudalism

Page 277

1. B
2. C
3. D
4. B
5. B
6. D
7. C
8. A
9. C

Page 278

1. crusade
2. guilds
3. apprentice
4. charters
5. justice
6. jury
7. Magna Carta
8. nationalism
9. castles

Page 279

10. page
11. squire, quintain
12. knight
13. accolade
14. duel
15. lute
16. moat/drawbridge
17. portcullis
18. dungeon (donjon)
19. armor/coat of arms
20. Joan of Arc
21. plague

Page 280

1. Leonardo da Vinci
2. Michelangelo
3. Dante
4. Geoffrey Chaucer
5. Miguel de Cervante
6. William Shakespeare
7. Johannes Gutenberg
8. Thomas More
9. Martin Luther

Page 281

10. John Calvin
11. Ignatius Loyola
12. Henry VIII
13. Parliament
14. Cromwell
15. Whigs/Tories
16. Marie Antoinette
17. Estates General
18. Napoleon Bonaparte
19. William and Mary
20. Guillotine

Page 282

1. E
2. L
3. F
4. I
5. C
6. J
7. B
8. D
9. G
10. A
11. H
12. K
13. factories
14. union
15. strike
16. assembly line
17. cholera